THE THEOLOGY OF JONATHAN EDWARDS

Conrad Cherry received his A.B. from McMurry College in Abilene, Texas, and his B.D. and Ph.D. from Drew University, Madison, New Jersey. He is currently Assistant Professor of Religious Studies at Pennsylvania State University.

THE THEOLOGY
OF
JONATHAN EDWARDS
A Reappraisal

CONRAD CHERRY

ANCHOR BOOKS
1966
DOUBLEDAY & COMPANY, INC.
GARDEN CITY, NEW YORK

The author is grateful to the following for permission to use copy-
righted material:

William Sloane Associates for selections from *Jonathan Edwards* by
Perry Miller, copyright 1949 by William Sloane Associates, Inc.;
published in a paperback edition by Meridian Books in 1959.

Princeton Theological Seminary, Speer Library, for quotations from
François Turrettini, *Institutio Theologiae Elencticae*, translated
by G. M. Giger, an unpublished, microfilmed manuscript.

Theology Today for material from "Jonathan Edwards and His Detractors" by Clyde A. Holbrook, which appeared in the October, 1953, issue.

The Viking Press, Inc., for verses from *Times Three* by Phyllis Mc-
Ginley. Copyright 1957 by Phyllis McGinley. Reprinted by permission of The Viking Press, Inc., and Martin Secker & War-
burg Limited, London.

Yale University Library for material from "Miscellanies, Nos. 77–
1017" by Jonathan Edwards.

Yale University Press for material from *Works of Jonathan Edwards*,
edited by Perry Miller.

The Anchor Books edition is the first publication of
THE THEOLOGY OF JONATHAN EDWARDS

Anchor Books edition: 1966

Library of Congress Catalog Card Number 66–24336
Copyright © 1966 by C. Conrad Cherry
Printed in the United States of America
All Rights Reserved

ACKNOWLEDGMENTS

It is my pleasure to acknowledge gratefully the assistance I received on this project from a number of persons and institutions. The Speer Library at Princeton Theological Seminary placed at my disposal its fine collection of Puritan works. The staff of the Beinecke Rare Book and Manuscript Library at Yale University extended to me every courtesy during my work on their collection of the Edwards manuscripts and saved me countless trips to New Haven by microfilming for me many of those manuscripts. I am indebted to Dr. Thomas Schafer of McCormick Theological Seminary, who permitted me to read his transcriptions of Edwards' "Miscellanies" which are deposited in the Beinecke Library; those who have tried to decipher Edwards' handwriting know the value of having a transcription of the original at hand. Professor Schafer's edition of the "Miscellanies," soon to be published in the Yale edition of Edwards' works, will doubtless prove a boon to all future Edwards studies.

The initial research was conducted for a doctoral dissertation submitted to the Graduate School of Drew University. Professor Will Herberg and the late Professor Carl Michalson of Drew offered encouragement and frank comments at an early stage of the study, and the final version has taken their criticisms into account. My greatest debt is to my friend and former teacher, Professor H. Gordon Harland. It was he who stimulated my interest in Edwards and American religious thought through courses and conversations; and he offered helpful criticisms at every stage of the present study.

The completion of this book is due in great part to help received from Pennsylvania State University. A grant from the Research Fund of the College of Liberal Arts financed secretarial assistance and trips to libraries. And the Department of Religious Studies, operating on the tried supposition that teaching and research are complementary, provided time for research and writing.

My wife and Mrs. Ira Masemore typed most of the various manuscripts; to them I am grateful for promptness and efficiency.

C. C.

University Park, Pennsylvania
Summer, 1966

CONTENTS

Acknowledgments | vii
List of Abbreviations | x
Introduction | 1

PART ONE: The Act of Faith
Chapter I: The Internal Dynamics of the Act: Cognition and Volition | 12
Chapter II: The Internal Possibility of the Act: The Spirit | 25
Chapter III: Word and Spirit | 44
Chapter IV: Conversion: Nature and Grace | 56
Chapter V: The Posture of Faith | 71

PART TWO: The Reality of Faith
Chapter VI: Justification by Faith | 90
Chapter VII: Covenant Relation | 107

PART THREE: The Life of Faith
Chapter VIII: Faith and Practice | 126
Chapter IX: Practice and Assurance of Faith | 143

PART FOUR: Controversy over Faith
Introduction | 160
Chapter X: Rationalism and Enthusiasm | 164
Chapter XI: Neonomianism and Antinomianism | 186

Conclusion | 216
Notes | 218
Works Cited or Referred to | 250
Index | 261

LIST OF ABBREVIATIONS

Misc., Townsend – Edwards' "Miscellanies" in *The Philosophy of Jonathan Edwards from his Private Notebooks*, ed. Harvey G. Townsend (Eugene, Ore.: University of Oregon Press, 1955).

Misc., Yale MSS – Edwards' "Miscellanies" Journal. Yale Collection (Yale Beinecke Rare Book and Manuscript Library).

WD – *Works of President Edwards*, ed. Sereno E. Dwight, 10 vols. (New York: S. Converse, 1829–1830).

WL – *Works of President Edwards*, 8 vols. (Leeds, England: Edward Baines, 1806–1811).

WW – *Works of President Edwards*, 4 vols., reprint of the Worcester Edition with additions (New York: Jonathan Leavitt & John F. Trow, 1843–1844).

WY – *Works of Jonathan Edwards*, 2 vols., ed. Perry Miller (New Haven: Yale University Press, 1957–). Vol. I, ed. Paul Ramsey, 1957; Vol. II, ed. John E. Smith, 1959.

INTRODUCTION

Toward the end of the last century Jonathan Edwards was examined psychologically and was judged a fanatic who expounded unpalatable Calvinist doctrines adopted in a "period of religious delirium."[1] The picture of Edwards as a curious, rather mad, eighteenth-century preacher preoccupied with hell-fire, a God of wrath, and the hatred of "all of Adam's children with a hatred bordering on the pathological"[2] is an image that is still with us. It is clearly embodied in Phyllis McGinley's little rendition of the God of Edwards:

> Abraham's God, the Wrathful One,
> Intolerant of error—
> Not God the Father or the Son
> But God the Holy Terror.[3]

Images have a way of fixing themselves in the American consciousness, and this image of Edwards is not easily shattered. But recent reappraisals of the life and thought of Jonathan Edwards have performed a significant measure of iconoclasm in the process of attaining a more accurate view of the man and his times. It is becoming apparent that the caricatures of Edwards as a hater of men, a hell-fire preacher, a worshiper of a wrathful God usually arise from a very limited acquaintance with Edwards' works or from a Procrustean attitude toward figures of the past. We have been wisely warned that too often Edwards' famous Enfield sermon, "Sinners in the Hands of an Angry God," has been taken as the model of Edwards' preaching without balancing it with his other sermons or, sometimes, without a very careful study of the symbols and the intention of that sermon itself. Even more productive of the Edwards caricatures has been the temptation to treat as so much nonsense—or at best, as comic quaintness—whatever cannot be adjusted to some nineteenth- or twentieth-century world view. Clyde Holbrook has directed us to the fact that the caricatures are as much a commentary

on the interpreters of Edwards as on Edwards himself. The
tendency has been to paint Edwards as a religious fanatic because his sense of man's tragedy and eternal destiny "before a
majestic and holy God whose purposes are not identifiable
with ours" is at odds with his detractors' theological assump-
tions that tame God "to the point where he can will or execute nothing which would offend a cultured Westerner."[4]

Certainly a part of the breakthrough to a fresh understanding of Edwards is owing to the renaissance in Puritan studies
in our century. Historical, literary, philosophical, and theological approaches to the Puritans of New England have been
setting aside old stereotypes in order to get an unbiased picture of early American life and letters. Not only has this
meant a greater appreciation of the historical context of Puritan New England, of the peculiar problems and challenges
facing seventeenth- and eighteenth-century Puritans; it has
also meant the recognition that contemporary American traits
are linked with New England Puritanism—traits other than
those associated with our historically misleading term "puri-
tanical." The mingling of the sense of national destiny with
religious zeal and purpose, for example, has a complicated
history in this country; but it certainly found an impetus in
the Puritan effort to set up in the New World a political-
religious "City upon a Hill" for all the world to behold. To
the degree that new approaches to Puritanism correct what
Edmund S. Morgan has rightly judged a common tendency—
attributing "whatever is wrong with the American mind . . .
to its Puritan ancestry" and smothering the remainder of Puritanism "under a homespun mantle of quaintness"[5]—the picture of Edwards, himself an heir and proponent of Puritanism, is also corrected.

Nevertheless, even when the stereotyped images are abandoned, interpreters of Edwards still feel uncomfortable with
Edwards' Calvinism. To alleviate the pain of embarrass-
ment, features of Edwards' thought are frequently searched
out which "transcend" his Calvinism or which prefigure the
post-Puritan era of American thought. Perhaps such a procedure would not be totally inappropriate if Edwards had
not so obviously addressed himself to problems current in his
eighteenth century or if he had not consciously chosen Puritan

Calvinism as the framework for so much of his thought. One therefore suspects a ghost of the perspective yielding the older caricatures in a recent study of Edwards, which proceeds on the assumption that it is at the points where Edwards departs from main-line Puritan theology "that the present-day student has most to learn from America's most neglected theologian."[6] And Perry Miller, to whom every contemporary student of Edwards and the Puritans is profoundly indebted, leads one to conclude that Edwards is to be appreciated primarily at points other than where traditional Calvinist tenets receive extensive treatment.[7] In his brilliant portrayal of Edwards as an American precursor of modern epistemology and physical theory, Miller frequently minimizes themes of Calvinist thought which were at the forefront of Edwards' reflective concerns.[8]

For good or for ill, Edwards was a Calvinist theologian; and, as a Calvinist theologian, he claimed the heritage of his New England forefathers. Edwards did request his readers not to refer to him as a "Calvinist" if they meant that he was dependent on every feature of Calvin's own thought or that he held certain doctrines because Calvin "believed and taught them," and there is evidence that his Puritan tradition drew as much, if not more, from the Rhineland reformers as from Calvin. Yet Edwards was willing "to be called a Calvinist, for distinction's sake,"[9] and his thought was pervaded by the same visions that had caught the imagination of both Calvin and the Puritans: the sovereignty and freedom of God; the drama of history as the story both of man's tragic fallenness and of God's renewed purpose to deliver; man's frailty and unworthiness in comparison with the justice and mercy of a majestic God; the personal and social value of a disciplined, "holy" life of "practice." And though Edwards would have resisted having his thought reduced to that of his Puritan predecessors, he would have also insisted that if one learned from him *only* at the points where he departed from their thought, then one would not really learn from him at all. It was no thoughtless appeal to tradition when, on the occasion of the death of his influential uncle, Col. John Stoddard, Edwards praised Stoddard as a "strong rod of the community" because he "was thoroughly established in those religious principles and doctrines of the first fathers of New England."[10]

To be sure, Edwards was no slave to his theological heritage. As we shall see, he was critical of many aspects of his Puritan tradition, and he held that it was a thinker's task in each generation to bring new light to bear upon perennial concerns. In the preface to a book by his friend and former student, Joseph Bellamy, Edwards discourages the theologian "in an obscure part of the world" from taking refuge in formulations of the past:

They . . . who bring any addition of light to this great subject, *The nature of true religion,* and its distinction from all counterfeits, should be accepted as doing the greatest possible service to the Church of God. And attempts to this end ought not to be despised and discouraged, under a notion that it is but vanity and arrogance in such as are lately sprung up in an obscure part of the world, to pretend to add anything on this subject, to the informations we have long since received from their fathers, who have lived in former times, in *New England,* and more noted countries. We cannot suppose that the Church of God is already possessed of all that light, in things of this nature, that ever God intends to give it; nor that all Satan's lurking-places have already been found out.[11]

Furthermore, Edwards' intellectual interests were broad for a man of frontier America. Although he complained that he was not "better informed what books there are, that are published on the other side of the Atlantic,"[12] he eagerly accepted what books friends could send him from abroad. His "Catalogue" of books[13] reveals a reading interest in philosophy, science, mathematics, and literature as well as theology; and he continued to borrow from the various disciplines in his reflections. It is now patent fact that he turned to his own design the insights of such thinkers as John Locke, Francis Hutcheson and the Cambridge Platonists. But the interests which occupied Edwards' chief attention were theological—interests which increasingly had their immediate occasions in the theological issues facing eighteenth-century New England. His philosophical and scientific interests were bent to a theological purpose.[14] Edwards chose to broaden, impregnate and sometimes alter his Calvinist theology, rather than transcend it. And Edwards' Puritan ancestors would themselves have delighted in Edwards' efforts to feed new life into theology with the broadest possible learning. Daniel Boorstin illustrates a difference between Quaker and Puritan attitudes toward "worldly knowledge" with the story of the Quaker who in the 1750s patronized the shop of a studious barber. The barber once displayed proudly a book in algebra which he had been studying. The Quaker records that his reply to the barber was: "I said it might be useful to some, but that I could take up grubbing, or follow the plough, without studying algebra; as he might also shave a man, etc. without it. Besides I found it a more profitable and delightful study, to be quietly employed in learning the law of the Lord written in mine own heart, so that I might walk before him acceptably." Boorstin comments that in contrast to the Quaker's sanctimonious remark, in the same situation "a Puritan might have admired the barber's industry, have expressed interest in his subject, and finally perhaps have noted that God himself was the greatest of all algebraists."[15] For Edwards, as for his forefathers, most any subject could be studied to the glory of God; and to the degree that such subjects could strengthen the appeal of the great themes of Calvinist theology, they were bent to that purpose.

There is, of course, no guarantee that Jonathan Edwards' century and conceptual framework will not be received as just so many "dead husks" by us in the twentieth century. History has a way of denying us such guarantees. There are, for example, historical factors which may well stop our ears to any real hearing of Edwards' Calvinism. In doing battle with its theological and philosophical foes (notably Deistic rationalism), Calvinist orthodoxy hardened its traditional doctrines into static, revealed truths, rational consent to which was made tantamount to religious faith even if that involved a *sacrificium intellectus*. This was a far cry from Edwards' own understanding of the doctrines as living symbols of a living faith, but those who are heirs of this petrifying process tend to hear Edwards through it. There are many such factors in American religious history which unpleasantly filter Edwards' words. Yet we are possessed of abilities and forces that may *at least* make us aware of the filters and *at best* free us for authentic understanding. For one thing, we are quite simply capable of bringing our past under examination—of inquiring into how our political, social and religious ideals and faiths have been shaped by our past; and which aspects of our history have been deleterious, and which beneficial, for our present and future self-understanding. A leap completely out of our own contemporary skins is both impossible and undesirable; but a degree of historical self-transcendence *is* possible and is able to deliver the meaning and relevance of Edwards' thought and century. Furthermore, we have witnessed a phenomenon on the twentieth-century intellectual scene which has shed new—or at least, neglected—light upon Calvinism. The leading doctrines of the Calvinist tradition have been reinterpreted as symbols laden with meaning relevant to the contemporary situation. Whatever quarrel one may have with specific features of the theologies of such thinkers as Karl Barth and Reinhold Niebuhr, they have, in diverse ways, reclaimed Augustinian and Calvinist categories in order to prick the contemporary conscience, wean man away from religious sentimentality, and throw him up against the hard reality of a God who judges as well as forgives. This has meant a calling into question: Western man's all-too-easy conscience; his sometimes hidden belief that he can, through the manipulation of his world and others, manipulate his ultimate destiny; his identification of his humanitarian feelings with righteousness, which amounts to a glorious façade for unrighteousness and injustice. And it has meant that the doctrine of original sin points once again to man's drive to deify himself and his own private systems, that the doctrine of free and "irresistible" grace represents man's inability to fulfill the demands of his essential being and his need of an unearned gift of freedom and meaning from beyond himself, that the once deplorable doctrine of predestination symbolizes man's precarious situation in the presence of a God whose will cannot be reduced to our purposes.

The following chapters consider the thought of Jonathan Edwards from the perspective of his theory of faith under the conviction that Edwards was first and last a Calvinist theologian and that his thought can still be meaningfully understood by one two centuries removed from it. The propriety of approaching Edwards from the point of his understanding of faith can emerge only in the consideration itself. But we do have certain immediate indications of the significance of this understanding for Edwards. It is noteworthy that a group of the sermons preached during the revival of the 1730s in Northampton were discourses on the doctrine of justification by faith alone, that Edwards kept a workbook on the subject of faith which spanned the greater part of his theological career, and that there are notes on the subject scattered throughout his major private notebook—the so-called "Miscellanies." But we would contend further that Edwards' understanding of the nature of faith is central to the whole of his intellectual endeavor and germane to his major works. We do not intend to engage in the enterprise commonly known as "motif research," which seeks to discover the fundamental factor "in virtue of which a particular outlook or system possesses its own peculiar character as distinct from all others."[16] In a theologian of Edwards' stature there are a number of fundamental and distinctive motifs operative, and his outlook cannot be reduced to any one of them. Nevertheless, any one of a number of motifs may serve as a window through which we may observe other aspects of his thought. Edwards' understanding of faith will serve as our window; some features of his thought inevitably will receive, at best, a quick glance, but we are persuaded that the doctrine of faith will open sufficiently on those units of Edwards' thought which were pivotal for his stance in the eighteenth-century religious situation.

Edwards' theoretical temper need not lead us to conclude that he chose to spin doctrines in thin air. He took up his reflective task within and in relation to a specific setting in the history of ideas and institutions. An early biographer does record that Edwards cultivated the habit of spending about thirteen hours a day in his study, "in the investigation of difficult subjects, in the origination and arrangement of thoughts, in the invention of arguments, and in the discovery of truths and principles."[17] To this extent, there is probably a great deal of truth in Ola Winslow's suggestion that Edwards found in his study a certain release from the taxing practical demands of pulpit and parish.[18] Nevertheless, his unpublished notebooks, his sermons, and his published treatises indicate that he withdrew to study and reflection in order to return to the concrete situation armed with thoughts and analyses appropriate to that situation. The environment which served to focus most of Edwards' mature reflective concerns was an American religious scene torn by conflicts between rationalism and emotionalism and between neonomianism and antinomianism. Opposition between these extremes, fostered in great part by the revivals of the Great Awakening, was increasingly to shape religion in America from the eighteenth century on. The last part of our study is an examination of the manner in which Edwards' elaborations on the nature of faith were attempts to heal these splits within American religious life and thought.

Our study is not biographical, but a brief sketch of Edwards' life will provide some details relevant to our discussion of his thought and, especially, to our consideration of his controversies.

Jonathan Edwards was born in East Windsor, Connecticut, on October 5, 1703. He was the fifth child, and only son, of Rev. and Mrs. Timothy Edwards' eleven children. Jonathan entered Yale College in 1716, graduated in 1720, and stayed on for advanced work in theology for another two years. Much later Edwards was to record that during the early part of his graduate study he experienced a "new sense of things," a new grasp and conviction of God's glory and excellency. He left Yale for a brief ministry in a Presbyterian church in New York, spent a summer in East Windsor continuing his studies, and returned to Yale to receive his Master of Arts degree in 1723. He was appointed tutor at Yale in 1724, his work at this post being interrupted by a severe illness which lasted several months. In 1726, he resigned his tutorship to accept a call as pastoral colleague to his aging maternal grandfather, Solomon Stoddard, at Northampton, Massachusetts. In July, 1727, Edwards married Sarah Pierrepont of New Haven. Sarah gave Jonathan eleven children, eight daughters and three sons. In February, 1729, Solomon Stoddard died, leaving the Northampton parish entirely in the hands of his grandson. Edwards' pen was busy during his Northampton ministry, turning out numerous notes, discourses and sermons. Above all, the Northampton period witnessed Edwards' examination and defense of the New England Awakening; his most substantial theological examination of revivalism was his *Treatise on Religious Affections.* Edwards' own preaching was an instrument of "surprising conversions" in Northampton in the 1730s; and in the early 1740s his town came under the full impact of the Great Awakening, receiving a visit from the English itinerant George Whitefield himself. But also in the 1740s Edwards' relations with Northampton became strained—a dispute over salary and Edwards' reprimand of certain children caught reading a "bad book" created much of the tension. The tension between pastor and congregation reached its height and a controversy ensued when Edwards offended the people by abandoning the policies of his revered grandfather in requiring profession of faith as the qualification for full church communion. Finally the matter went before a council of ministers and lay delegates which, on June 22, 1750, advised the separation between Edwards and his congregation. Ten days later Edwards preached his farewell sermon, but he remained in Northampton for almost a year. He received invitations from several churches but, upon advice from a council, decided to go to Stockbridge, Massachusetts, as pastor of the local church and as missionary to the Indians there. At Stockbridge, besides preaching to both settlers and Indians, working out an educational system for the Indian schools, and fighting off the shameless exploitation of public land and money by local grafters, Edwards found time to write his *Freedom of the Will,* his *Doctrine of Original Sin,* and two companion essays: *The Nature of True Virtue* and *The End for Which God Created the World.* In 1757 the College of New Jersey chose Edwards as its president; he accepted the invitation reluctantly, feeling that his temperament and his deficiency "in some parts of learning, particularly in Algebra, and the higher parts of Mathematics, and in the Greek Classics" should disqualify him. Edwards reached Princeton in February, 1758; he died of a smallpox inoculation at the age of fifty-four on March 22, 1758, only a few weeks after assuming his presidential office.

PART ONE:

THE ACT OF FAITH

CHAPTER I

THE INTERNAL DYNAMICS OF THE ACT: COGNITION AND VOLITION

Jonathan Edwards once proposed for himself a major treatise on the subject of "saving faith," which would follow the method of answering certain questions dealing with a variety of theological subjects. The first question would be of primary importance:

Whether justifying faith in its proper essence implies, besides the act of judgment, also an act of the inclination and will.[1]

Edwards never wrote the treatise, but this first inquiry continually occupied his attention in his published and unpublished writings. The question is almost as old as theology itself, but it became particularly pressing for Edwards as it was raised with renewed emphasis by eighteenth-century revivals of religion. During the Great Awakening the intellectual and volitional elements of religious faith were torn asunder for a host of New Englanders. The revivalist minister and the excitement of events frequently laid the ground for that unfortunately limited choice that has since plagued American Protestantism: either emotional, active participation in "things religious"; or an intellectual, dispassionate approach to religion. But the question of the roles of cognition and volition in faith had roots for Edwards which stretched beyond the immediate occasion facing him. It was a question that had troubled Puritan thinkers for some time, and standing directly, though critically, within the Puritan tradition, Edwards examined its struggle with the problem.

From its beginnings Calvinism had described religious faith as a kind of knowledge, but a knowledge which reaches into the very depths of man's being. Calvin himself had stressed that faith is a knowledge of God's revelation, of the Word of God; yet "the Word of God is not received by faith if it flits about in top of the brain, but when it takes root in the depth of the heart. . . ."[2] For the Puritans also faith was more than rational assent. It was an act of the "whole man"; it was rooted in the inclination and affections as well as in the intellect.[3] In the words of the English Puritan John Preston, the "subject of faith" is "the whole heart of man," "both the minde and the will."[4] Nevertheless, though the Puritan theologians intended to point to the whole man as the subject of faith, their intention was often markedly frustrated by a faculty psychology that proved inadequate for expressing the unity of the subject. As one student of Puritan thought has said, although the Puritan theologian sought to portray faith as the response of the whole man to God, when he delineated what was involved in the response he alternately emphasized the intellect and the will as the principal faculty in the act of faith.[5] And although this alternation could occur in the same theologian, it is usually possible to classify the Puritan theologians according to their predominating emphasis.[6] Thomas Shepard, a seventeenth-century New England Puritan whose writings were carefully read by Jonathan Edwards, represents the "intellect-emphasis." Shepard affirms that the "whole soul is drawn to Christ in the work of faith," but he subordinates will to intellect when he elaborates what this means.

Because, as the gospel first reveals Christ to the mind, and then offers him to the will, so faith, which runs parallel with the gospel, first sees Christ (there the mind, one part of the soul, goes out,) then receives Christ gladly, (there the other part, the will, goes out,) and so the whole soul comes to Christ.[7]

Buttressing this concept of the priority of the understanding in the act of faith is Shepard's general psychology (a psychology that was to be appealed to with great force by the eighteenth-century critics of revivalism), which views man's intellectual powers as a distinct faculty, the proper function of which is to sit as "coachman" over the unruly steeds of passion that otherwise overpower man.[8] William Ames, a proponent of the "volition-emphasis," conceives the movements in the faith-act in reverse order: "saving knowledge" "follows the act of the will, and depends upon it." Here the understanding, as intellectual assent, is subordinated to the embracing, choosing movement of the will.[9]

Edwards was thus handed by his theological forebears a clear *effort* to account for personal unity in the act of faith, but he was also handed a *way* of accounting for that unity which continually frustrated the effort. Obviously a great portion of the problem turned on the manner in which the faculty-psychology tended to conceive the human faculties as distinct entities with separate functions. When faith occurred, the will did something, the intellect performed another function, and so on. The questions would naturally arise: What faculty operates first? Is one faculty the controlling operation of the mind? With man so divided into distinct faculties, the temptation was to describe the nature of the faith-act in terms of their distinct operations rather than in terms of the unity of the human subject.

As we have seen, Edwards designed to inquire into this problem in his proposed treatise, and in his private notebook on faith he continually reminds himself that faith is not only "an exercise of the understanding" but also "a falling in of the inclination, the choice, the affection"—it is an "according of the whole soul" with God.[10] Yet Edwards intimates that he is not content with simply describing faith as an act of *both* the understanding *and* the inclination. For faith is a *sense of the heart*—an act which is a willing, affective, "loving knowledge" of God's truth.[11] It is a human act in which the human faculties are virtually blended. Although Edwards would continue to speak of the "faculties" of the human mind, he was aware that it was inappropriate to conceive them as distinct human entities and maintained that in religious faith the hard-and-fast distinctions between intellect, will, and affections break down. Edwards was encouraged in this insistence by a number of sources, but certainly a key source was the Scriptures. He writes himself a note in a private workbook: "How the Scriptures are ignorant of the Philosophic distinction of the Understanding, and the Will; and how the sense of the Heart is there called *Knowledge*, or *Understanding*."[12] "For with the heart man believeth unto righteousness" (Rom. 10:10). Edwards was also a serious student of the books of his grandfather and predecessor at Northampton, Solomon Stoddard. Stoddard had warned in his *Nature of Saving Conversion* that understanding and will "are not two things, but one and the same soul, diversely denominated according to *two* several *ways* of *working*, which are inseparably conjoined."[13] And certainly Edwards received a great deal of assistance on this question from the British philosopher John Locke.

The extent of Locke's influence on Edwards has been a subject of some debate among contemporary students of Edwards, especially since Perry Miller's suggestion in 1949 that Edwards thoroughly embraced Locke's empiricism.[14] Edwards was early exposed to the epistemology of John Locke; notes made during his college days indicate a critical wrestling with the philosopher's *Essay Concerning Human Understanding*, and he continued to appeal to Locke in his published writings.[15] Edwards' earliest biographer records that when Jonathan read Locke's *Essay* in undergraduate study at Yale, he was so delighted with the work that he read it with more pleasure "than the most greedy miser, when gathering up handfuls of silver and gold from some newly discovered treasure."[16] Yet as Leon Howard has recently observed, Edwards was a miser who critically appraised his treasure.[17] In "The Mind," in large part a penning of his reflections on his reading of Locke, Edwards explicitly rejected Locke's definition of identity and Locke's position that "uneasiness" determines the will.[18] Nevertheless, although Edwards was not totally persuaded by every feature of Locke's philosophy, he did find that the insights into the nature of the mental act in Locke's *Essay* provided an appropriate way of conceiving the character of "faithful knowledge." Above all, Locke's treatment of the human faculties and his theory of the "simple idea" became useful for Edwards in a description of the internal dynamics of the act of faith.

In his *Essay* Locke distinguishes between two basic *powers* of the human mind: (1) the power "to begin or forbear, continue or end several actions of our minds and motions of our bodies"; and (2) the power to perceive within the mind such things as ideas, the signification of signs and words, and the agreement or disagreement of ideas. Locke is willing to allow the traditional *designation* of these powers as the faculties of "will" and "understanding" so long as the traditional *error* is not committed of viewing them as "some real beings in the soul that performed . . . actions of understanding and volition." It is not the will that wills or understanding that understands; rather, man as possessed of the powers of volition and perception is the willing and knowing agent. In short, Locke is concerned to overcome that form of the faculty-psychology (often operative in Edwards' theological harbingers) which annuls the integrity of the willing and knowing human agent by conceiving the mental powers as separate, self-activating entities.[19]

Edwards was fully persuaded by this Lockean argument; as he says of the will in his major treatise on that subject: "the will itself is not an agent that has a will: the power of choosing, itself, has not a power of choosing. That which has the power of volition or choice is the man or the soul, and not the power of volition itself."[20] To be sure, distinctions between powers of the self are to be maintained. There are two basic powers: intellect, or the power of perception and speculation; and inclination or will, the power by which man chooses anything. Affections or emotions do not constitute a separate power or faculty; they are the lively, vigorous exercises of the will, man's choosing something at a high degree of liking or disliking.[21] With his distinction between human powers Edwards intends to connote what the older faculty-psychology at its best also intended: not separate entities in man, but the self in its various powers and various comportments toward objects and ideas. But as we have seen, frequently the Puritan proponents of the faculty-psychology ended with a description of the faculties as self-activating entities in a hierarchy of action. This quite naturally led to the subordination of one faculty to another in a definition of the faith-act. Edwards, through his use of Locke, was concerned to give the lie to this description of the human self and its consequences for an understanding of religious faith.

But Edwards does not rest his case there. He not only desires with Locke to abandon the description of the faculties' operations as operations of separate entities; he also argues that in the very essence of the faith-act even the clear distinctions between the *powers* of the self break down. The human act of faith per se does not consist of distinct movements of intellect and will. Thomas Manton, a seventeenth-

century English divine, had articulated a view growing quite
naturally from the faculty-psychology when he said that there
are three distinct acts of faith: (1) *assent*, or a believing rationally in God's truth; (2) *consent*, which is a "hearty accepting of Christ" and a "practical act of the new nature";
and (3) *affiance*, trust, dependence, or confidence—a "quiet
repose of heart in the mercy of God or fidelity of Christ,
that he will give me pardon and life. . . ."[22] Edwards' comment on Manton's observation is:

The distinction of the several constituent parts or acts of faith, into
assent, consent, and affiance, if strictly considered and examined, will
appear not to be proper and just, or strictly according to the truth
and nature of things; because the parts are not entirely distinct one
from another, and so are in some measure confounded one with another: for the last, viz., affiance, implies the other two, assent and
consent, with particular relation or application to himself [i.e., man]
and his own case, together with the effect of all in his own quietness
and comfort of mind, and boldness in venturing on this foundation,
in conduct and practice.[23]

The division of faith into distinct acts of assent, consent, and
affiance suggests a chronological sequence of movements dependent upon the several functions of the distinct faculties
(intellect, will, and affection). Edwards argues that the
movements of the self designated by the three words interpenetrate, or are confounded with, one another. A psychology
which describes the human powers as self-activating faculties
tends to destroy the unity of the human subject; and the
view of faith which isolates distinct movements of the self
that are products of the distinct faculties obscures the basic
unity of the act of faith. Faith may be compendiously termed
affiance or trust, but it also includes in its very nature judgment regarding the reality of its object, a consent to that object as "good, eligible or desirable," and a dependence on,
hope in, and venturing in practice on the foundation of, the
object.[24] In faith the powers of intellect and will tend to
merge into one; strictly speaking, the various movements of
the self in the act of faith are not distinct acts but are different modes of the same act.

Edwards, therefore, is faced with the task of further explicating the internal dynamics of the act of faith while affirming the harmonious interpenetration of human cognitive and volitional powers. The explication is grounded upon a definition of the knowledge involved in faith, and the definition is partially dependent upon John Locke's understanding of the "simple idea," modified and utilized according to Edwards' own interests and purposes.

Rejecting the doctrine of innate ideas, Locke had contended that the raw materials for all knowledge are derived from experience. That is to say, "Our observation employed either, about external sensible objects, or about the internal operations of our minds perceived and reflected on by ourselves, is that which supplies our understandings with all the *materials* of thinking." These two experiential fountains of our fundamental ideas are "sensation" and "reflection," and the fundamentals of knowledge springing from the fountains are "simple ideas" (e.g., ideas of yellow, cold, bitter, thinking, willing). "Complex ideas" (e.g., beauty, a man, the universe) are formed by the mind's repeating, comparing or uniting the simple ideas given through experience. It is important to see that for Locke the mental activities appropriate to each of the two kinds of ideas are not to be confused; for "it is not in the power of the most exalted wit, or enlarged understanding, by any quickness or variety of thought, to *invent* or *frame* one new simple idea in the mind, not taken in by the ways before mentioned" (i.e., by way of sensation or internal reflection).[25] And the reception and possession of a simple idea is a discrete experience, incapable of reproduction through language. "He that thinks otherwise, let him try if any words can give him the taste of a pine apple, and make him have the true idea of the relish of that celebrated delicious fruit."[26]

The "simple idea" is employed by Edwards in a description of the act of faith: the simple idea becomes the principle for explaining the harmonious interpenetration of the cognitive and volitional powers of the human agent. A statement in Edwards' notebook on faith summarizes the way in which the two powers harmoniously converge on the idea: "Faith is the entire acquiescence of the soul in the idea of Christ as my Saviour in a sense and conviction of his reality and goodness as a Saviour as the Gospel reveals him."[27] Edwards does not confuse the simple idea which is received with the operations of the mind with respect to the idea.[28] Nor does the mind give itself the simple idea in which it acquiesces—as we shall see in the next chapter, it is a gift of God's Spirit. Yet the idea involves itself so intimately in the unity of man's being that it is immediately saluted by the powers of intellect and will.[29] And the knowing that attends to the simple idea is a sense of the heart; it is affective knowledge, or knowledge that is thoroughly penetrated by the lively, vigorous exercises of the will. Edwards, therefore, exploits the Lockean notion of the simple idea in a description of knowledge in religious faith; but in his firm insistence that understanding and will harmoniously salute the religious idea he departs from Locke, who was highly suspicious of responses in religion which were *uncontrolled* by dispassionate reason.[30]

Though Locke proved helpful to Edwards for spelling out the type of knowledge involved in the act of faith, Edwards was by no means solely dependent in this enterprise upon Lockean insights and categories. In order to elaborate upon the same phenomenon, Edwards drew upon the terminology of the Augustinian tradition of "illumination," a tradition firmly embedded in his own Puritan heritage. The "idea" of faith is a "light" in the mind that calls forth a full mental response. Again, man can never give himself this "light" by the operation of his natural faculties. To that extent the mind is passive. Nevertheless, the reception of the light is an active receiving:

The natural faculties are the subject of this light; and they are the subject in such a manner, that they are not merely passive, but active in it; the acts and exercises of man's understanding are concerned and made use of in it. God, in letting in this light into the soul, deals with man according to his nature, or as a rational creature; and makes use of his human faculties. But yet this light is not the less immediately from God for that; though the faculties are made use of, it is as the subject and not as the cause; and that action of the faculties in it, is not the cause, but is either implied in the thing itself (in the light that is imparted) or is the consequence of it.[31]

Edwards alternately refers to the illuminating divine light of faith as both the source of the mental reality that elicits understanding and will, and the mental reality itself. Here it is sufficient to note that the simple idea, the divinely bestowed light in the mind, enlightens the man so that he has a "sense of the heart"—a kind of knowledge in which understanding and "will or disposition" co-operate and interpenetrate.[32] So this sense of the heart is not a new faculty; it is not a new human power supernaturally added to other human powers. The faculties or powers given "naturally" to man, or to man even apart from faith, are the powers operative in the knowledge of faith.

The essence of faithful knowledge is constituted, then, by the conjoined operation of understanding and will. Edwards never tired of urging that in the act of faith the common distinction between human powers breaks down. Nevertheless, the man of faith is by no means restricted to the mental posture characterized by the interpenetration of cognition and volition. He also thinks and wills in ways in which the two human powers are not so closely joined. On the basis of the volitional knowledge in the sense of the heart, the movement of man's mind may be a more speculative operation of reason—or one not held in strict affective attendance to the new simple idea—and still be a mental movement appropriate to the man of faith. The sense of the heart "sanctifies the reasoning faculty" and assists it in its discursive reasoning about religious objects. By having lovingly understood "the truth and reality of divine things" with a sense of the heart, a man may in all propriety engage in a less passionate, more speculative examination of those same things, but without the prejudice that his ratiocination is the only level of understanding religious truth. And having passionately engaged the divine truth with a lively sense of the heart, "even the speculative notions" may become "more lively."[33] Speculative theological understanding is not to be confused with the knowledge every faithful man may have, for the unlearned are as capable as the learned of the knowledge of the sense of the heart.[34] Nevertheless, the knowledge of faith, the sense of the heart, may properly lead to a faithful man's more discursive mental endeavors; in fact, Edwards exhorted his congregation at Northampton to increase their "speculative" as well as their "practical" knowledge of divine truth.[35] Similarly, one may speak of the sense of the heart as the stimulant and determinant of the volition that leads to definite, observable actions.[36] Here volition is not strictly identical with the willing involved in the sense of the heart. In short, intellect and will may have other legitimate operations for the man of faith than those immediately involved in the sense of the heart. Or, in accordance with Edwards' insistence that the faculties are not really entities that operate on their own, the faithful man's relation to God's truth in the knowledge of faith does not preclude his comporting himself toward that truth in other ways. Yet the sense of the heart, faithful knowledge per se, is such that no "clear distinction between the two faculties of understanding and will" can be made, for in this knowledge the two faculties do not act "distinctly and separately."[37]

Edwards was fond of drawing an analogy between the spiritual knowledge of faith and the sensation of "tasting." The sense of the heart is a "holy taste" or "disposition of heart."[38] It is a "spiritual taste and relish of what is excellent and divine."[39] The metaphor of tasting in spiritual knowledge was readily available to Edwards in his reading background: in the Scriptures, John Calvin, the seventeenth-century Puritans, and the Cambridge Platonists.[40] And for Edwards the tasting-sense peculiar to the knowledge of faith took on a Lockean twist. As we said, the perception of the simple idea, like the tasting of a pineapple, is an immediate, discrete, uncontrived experience for Locke. The Edwardean "tasting" in faith is an experience which one man cannot have for another —and which he cannot give another. And it is a kind of knowing which is radically different from a mere knowing *about*. Just as one cannot perceive the sweet taste of honey *for* another and give it to another, so knowledge in faith is a knowing which one man cannot attain for or give to another. Just as one really knows the sweet taste of honey only when he actually perceives it and not when he knows *about* it, so one really knows the simple idea of faith when he directly perceives it and not when he withdraws to contemplate it.[41] Such a description of faith is, in consequence, a rejection of anything resembling the Thomistic distinction between implicit and explicit faith, which allows "the simple minded" to "have faith implicit in the faith of the wiser . . . to the extent to which the wiser adhere to the divine teaching."[42]

More obviously the taste metaphor is a way of stressing that the knowledge of faith is, unlike mere ratiocination, rooted equally and harmoniously in both basic human powers. It underscores Edwards' proposal that the sense of the heart is that understanding "wherein the mind don't only speculate and behold, but relishes and feels."[43] The emphasis on human feeling implicit in the taste metaphor is to be viewed in accordance with Edwards' description of faith as the intimate joining of cognition with a lively, affectionate volitional operation; it is not to be construed as the substitution of a state of unconscious feeling for a state of knowledge. Ola Winslow pursues this unfortunate interpretation:

Taken out of its eighteenth century idiom, his idea is simply that feeling lies nearer than thought to the source of religious consciousness, and is the gateway to "religious experience" as distinguished from religious knowledge. The "sense of God" is an emotional, not an intellectual experience.[44]

Perry Miller says much the same: "By maintaining a sharp distinction between 'mere notional understanding' and the sense of the heart, Edwards fully intended to subordinate understanding to feeling."[45] This line of interpretation has even led one critic to conclude recently that Edwards emphasizes an "*anti-intellectual tradition.*"[46] This approach to Edwards' "tasting" in faith clearly amounts to a subordination of one human power to another in the faith-act—a subordination which, as we have seen, Edwards is always eager to avoid. It provides no framework for explaining Edwards' insistence that the sense of the heart involves in its very essence *a lively act of knowing*. To be sure, the sense of the heart, the "tasting" of divine reality, is not "reasoning" if reasoning is narrowly defined as "ratiocination, or the power of inferring by arguments."[47] For the sense of the heart is not in its essence a judgment regarding the truth *about* an object, wherein the judging subject is detached as an observer from his object in order to infer that object. One is intimately bound up with the object in an attitude of love and adoration. Nevertheless, there is definitely a type of judgment, or better "conviction," of the truth of the object in religious faith. As we have already seen, "conviction of the truth and reality of divine things" is indirectly involved in faith to the extent that faith "sanctifies the reasoning faculty" and assists it in its reasoning about the things of religion. But there is also a conviction *directly involved* in the sense of the heart. A sensing "of the divine excellency of the things of God's word doth . . . directly and immediately convince of the truth of them" by "a kind of intuitive and immediate evidence."[48] Here the conviction of divine truth is not achieved by distancing oneself from the truth in order to behold it and subject it to "rational proof." Rather, as the knowing and willing subject senses the divine truth in all of its superlative excellency, the mind is, as it were, overpowered by the divine reality. The sense of the heart is, in its very essence, an act of judgment, not an unconscious state of feeling. The reality of faith's object demonstrates its truth to the mind and, through such demonstration, evokes man's judgment as to its truth. The judgment is one of the fully responsive person: it is an affective, volitional judgment.

While engaged in reflection on the nature of faith in the privacy of his study, Jonathan Edwards occasionally confessed the difficulty of defining faith. He shared with John Locke the feeling that "it is a difficult thing to find words to exhibit our own ideas";[49] he sometimes despaired at the very penury of words adequate to express clearly all that is involved in faith. Nevertheless, Edwards believed that faith "may be more perfectly described than defined by a short definition . . . a great many words express it better than one or two."[50] Our examination of Edwards' understanding of the act of faith according to the powers of cognition and volition is but a partial and very formal description of what is involved in that act for Edwards. "A great many words" are still needed: words about faith's object, possibility, and general posture. Why does religious faith arise? What exactly is it that one knows when he has the "simple idea" of faith? What does it mean to say that this knowledge involves volition; i.e., what kind of action accompanies faith? These and a host of other questions must be answered before the chief dimensions of religious faith emerge. Yet as Edwards apparently presupposed in the outline for his proposed dissertation on religious faith, a proper starting point is a consideration of the place and relation of judgment and inclination in faith. Such a consideration is an effort to portray what is internally involved on the part of the human subject when faith occurs. It is an effort to conceive philosophically the scriptural representation of faithful knowledge as something springing from the heart. And such an effort was crucial for an Edwards who was persuaded of the validity of the attempt of his theological forefathers to address the problem but who was dissatisfied with their overall result; and it was crucial also, as we shall see in more detail later, because the question of intellect and will in faith was at the very center of the controversies growing out of the Great Awakening.

CHAPTER II

THE INTERNAL POSSIBILITY OF THE ACT: THE SPIRIT

The internal dynamics of the act of faith are not fully specified for Edwards when one has described the harmonious interpenetration of cognition and volition. For faith is not just *any* movement of the heart, not just any volitional judgment. Faith is an affective knowing that has a specific *possibility*. We saw in our preceding chapter how the two human faculties or powers are organized around the new "simple idea" of divine truth. One way of getting at Edwards' understanding of the possibility of faith is to ask: What is the source of that idea? And what enables the human powers to entertain the idea? Edwards assigns the internal possibility of faith to God operative as Spirit.

Edwards spelled out his view of God in some detail according to Christian trinitarian principles. The intricacies of Edwards' doctrine of the Trinity need not detain us; in brief, the doctrine is modeled after his psychology of the faith-act. God the Father eternally generates his own idea (the Son or Logos) out of himself and is both a source and object of his loving inclination (the Holy Spirit); the "whole divine Essence" subsists in all three persons.[1] This theory of the Trinity is not without parallels in Augustine's view, which finds the analogy for the Trinity in the human mind's knowing and loving itself.[2] For our purposes, Edwards' trinitarian formulations are important because they stress that God is the beginning and end of man's salvation; the possibility of justifying or saving faith rests entirely with God in his three-fold operation.

The F. appoints & Provides the Redeemer, & himself accepts the Price and grants the thing purchased; the Son is the Redeemer by offering himself & is the Price; & the H. Gh. Immediately communicates to us the thing Purchased by communicating himself & he is the thing Purchased. . . . So that Tis G. of whom our good is purchased & tis G. that Purchases it & tis G. also that is the thing Purchased.[3]

The doctrine of the Trinity underscores for Edwards that at every crucial point man's redemption is dependent upon the eternal purposes of God, from the Father's providing a Redeemer, to the Redeemer's paying the price for man's salvation, to God's Spirit communicating the reality of redemption. Yet two tendencies are inherent in this trinitarian explication of redemption, tendencies emerging especially from this way of explaining the Spirit: the tendency either to confine the redemptive process to the Godhead; or the tendency to deify man so that he may be redeemed. If God is the alpha and omega of redemption by being not only the source and purchaser but—by virtue of his Spirit—*the thing purchased* as well, in what way is *man's* salvation purchased in redemption? Does not Edwards' trinitarian description, as it stands, suggest that redemption is an affair that occurs simply between the persons of the Trinity? And if the human sinner *is* intimately involved in the affair of redemption, *how* is he involved? Does he in some way *become* the Holy Spirit which is "purchased"? Edwards addresses these problems in the course of describing the manner and nature of the Holy Spirit's communicating the possibility of faith.

Paul Ramsey, in his introduction to Edwards' *Treatise on the Will*, remarks that Edwards sometimes expresses the saving relation between man and God in terms of the infusion of the Holy Spirit, sometimes "in terms of Platonic, Johannine, and Augustinian illuminism," and sometimes through a description of Locke's "simple idea" as a new and holy principle in the life of man.[4] This is indeed the case. And as Ramsey adds, these three descriptions demonstrate "how wrong it is to reduce Jonathan Edwards' system to that of John Locke, while ignoring the traditional doctrine of infusion and not giving equal weight to his Augustinian doctrine of illumination."[5] We would only add that the categories of infusion and illumination usually provide the framework for Edwards' use of Locke's simple idea. The rise of the new simple idea or holy principle is explained as either an infusion or an illumination. Infusion and illumination are *two different descriptions* of the same reality, *not two distinct operations*. For Edwards, the "ordinary," "saving" operation of the Holy Spirit is one in kind[6] whether it be described as illumination or infusion. But the two descriptions are Edwards' two attempts to explain the nature of the operation of God's Spirit in providing the possibility of faith.

Illumination

Toward the end of his 1733 sermon on divine illumination, Edwards summarizes the way in which the Holy Spirit, as Divine Light, is related to faith as the "saving close with Christ":

This light, and this only, will bring the soul to a saving close with Christ. It conforms the heart to the gospel, mortifies its enmity and opposition against the scheme of salvation therein revealed: it causes the heart to embrace the joyful tidings, and entirely to adhere to, and acquiesce in the revelation of Christ as our Saviour: it causes the whole soul to accord and symphonize with it, admitting it with entire credit and respect, cleaving to it with full inclination and affection; and it effectually disposes the soul to give up itself entirely to Christ.[7]

God's illuminating Spirit creates the possibility of the human agent's acting as fully responsive man in faith. Illumination of the mind by no means affects merely the human capacities of knowing exclusive of the power of the will. Rather, the Light's affect is upon the willing-knowing, the affective understanding within the essential act of faith. The whole "heart" is conformed to the gospel: one is moved by the Light to judge of the truth of God's revelation in Christ, and to make that judgment while cleaving to the truth "with full inclination and affection." As we shall see later, this means that Edwards does not need to posit two distinct operations of the Spirit: one upon the understanding (illumination), and another upon the will (infusion).

One is still left with the rather thorny problem, however, of how the *Divine* Light is related to the *human* seeing. This is the core of the question we raised at the outset. How is man involved in the affair of redemption when the Holy Spirit is communicated to him? When God's Spirit abides as Light in the human mind, how does it abide there and what is its relation to the human faculties?

Edwards sometimes applies "spiritual light" to the human seeing or tasting in the faith-act, and at other times he applies it to the Divine Light which is *shed upon* the mind. In the sermon on illumination cited above, the Divine Light often refers to what was discussed in our preceding chapter as the sense of the heart: "This spiritual light primarily consists in . . . a real sense and apprehension of the excellency of things revealed in the word of God."[8] In the *Treatise on Religious Affections* the other signification prevails: "The Light of the Sun of Righteousness don't only shine upon them [the saints], but is so communicated to them that they shine also, and become little images of that Sun which shines upon them."[9] This distinction borne in mind, the question of the relation between the two "lights," divine and human, remains.

On the one hand, Edwards is eager to portray the Divine Light which creates faith as an abiding, vital, rather constant reality that is intimately joined with the natural human faculties; on the other, he desires to avoid depicting the illuminating Spirit as so involving itself in the human mind that either the Light is collapsed into human being or human nature is mystically absorbed in the Spirit. To insist on the former position without falling into the latter hazards Edwards finds a difficult task indeed. But it is for him a worthy task, since in his view the constancy of the Spirit distinguishes the saved from the unsaved man; yet if the hazards are not avoided, the distinction between God and man, between God's Spirit and man's nature as man, is blurred.

The Holy Spirit in his saving operation or in his creation of saving faith does not move simply "upon" or "toward" the human faculties of intellect and will; he is united with them as their new principle of operation. Here lies the difference between "natural man" and the recipient of grace:

The Spirit of God is given to the true saints to dwell in them, as his proper lasting abode: and to influence their hearts, as a principle of new nature, or as a divine supernatural spring of life and action. The Scriptures represent the Holy Spirit, not only as moving, and occasionally influencing the saints, but as dwelling in them as his temple. . . . And he is represented as being there so united to the

aculties of the soul, that he becomes there a principle or spring of
new nature and life.[10]

Thus in terms of illumination, the Divine Light does not
only shine *upon* the mind of the saint; it is *communicated to
the mind* as an indwelling principle on the basis of which the
mental faculties operate.[11] To put it another way, the simple
idea of faith is not only given to the mind of man by the
Spirit; the Spirit also is the possibility of "understanding" the
idea—he is the new foundation on the basis of which intellect
and will harmoniously interpenetrate each other. The same
Spirit who supplies the divine truth to be known simultaneously provides the possibility for knowing it. There is, therefore, this constancy and indwelling characteristic of the saving
operation of God's Spirit. The Divine Light may act upon the
natural man as an occasional and largely extramental agent—
"A body that continues black, may be said not to have light,
though the light shines upon it";[12] but it acts within the
mind of the man of faith as a vital and abiding principle
which is actively united with the human faculties.

Nevertheless, though there is this abiding quality of the
Spirit in the saints and though there is a *union* between the
saint's mental powers and the Light, the distinction between
saint and Spirit persists and the Spirit's abiding in the person
is not manageable by the person. *The Divine Light is not
identical with the human faculties; it is not collapsed into
human being. The Light or Spirit is rather a new foundation
laid in the human being in which man participates and from
which the human powers operate.* Edwards insists that the
saint is not "Godded with God" or "Christed with Christ"
through the Spirit's becoming in some way identical with the
human agent.[13] Rather, the Holy Spirit as Divine Light is
the saints' foundation in which they participate or of whose
fullness they "partake"; "to use the Scripture phrase, they
are made partakers of God's fullness (Eph. 3:17–19; John
1:16), that is, of God's spiritual beauty and happiness, according to the measure and capacity of a creature. . . . And
the influences of the Spirit of God in this, . . . make the
creature partaker of the divine nature."[14] *Participation* is an
ontological concept that has been surrounded by numerous

vagaries in Western thought from Plato to Tillich, and Ed
wards hardly clarifies the concept to the extent that we may
wish. But the gist of what Edwards intends to connote with
the notion is that the Holy Spirit becomes the new principle
for a new kind of exercise of the human faculties, without
assuming an identity with human being as such. Hence new
faculties are not given in illumination, but a new basis is
given to the mind from which the natural faculties operate
in a new way. The new operation of the faculties is none
other than the affective knowledge characteristic of the "sense
of the heart."[15]

Furthermore, the Spirit in illumination never becomes a
human "possession" that is manageable by human mental
powers. The Holy Spirit is his *own* possibility, and the Light
which is shed upon the mind is under his own "control." To
be sure, in genuine illumination the Spirit adopts human
nature as his "lasting abode" and "communicates himself
there in his own proper nature";[16] yet the Divine Light is
"immediately" from God—that is, it is a gift of grace, it is
owing "exclusively to the arbitrary operation and gift of
God."[17] The Spirit or Light abides as a permanent principle
in the soul of the saint, but it abides by its own power and
guarantee. There is an interesting parallel here with a reflec
tion on the nature of memory in Edwards' notebook "The
Mind." Edwards departs somewhat from John Locke's con
ception of the mnemonic powers of the mind. For Locke it
is possible sometimes by a sheer act of the will to recall
ideas stored in the memory.[18] But for Edwards the mind
appears more passive in the remembering process: the ideas
may really abide in the mind without actually being per
ceived and may arise only as the laws of nature establish the
conditions necessary for their being remembered.[19] For the
issue under discussion this means that the human powers of
the mind, even in their disposal toward the simple idea in a
"new sense," do not call up or control the simple idea of the
Spirit at will. The Divine Light is both its own possibility of
abiding in the mind and the possibility for the rise of the
new sense.

Within his doctrine of illumination, then, Edwards has ad
dressed the problem we saw arising out of his trinitarian un

derstanding of redemption. In his trinitarian operations God is the beginning and end of man's redemption; redemption is communicated by the Spirit's indwelling the human soul and becomes efficacious through faith as man participates in, or partakes of, the illuminating Spirit. Although the saint or "illumined man" participates in God's Spirit by having the Spirit vitally attached to the basis of his human powers, he partakes of and does not become identified with the Spirit. Although the Divine Light itself abides in the mind as a new and permanent principle of human act, it remains a "supernatural" principle and is never absorbed into human being per se; and it is not possessed by or at the disposal of the human agent. No new faculties are given, but the natural human powers are given new exercises from a new foundation. The Holy Spirit as the illuminating principle is the internal creative possibility and foundation for the act of faith.

The nature of "spiritual illumination" demanded much of Edwards' attention during the revivals of religion in the Great Awakening. We will later deal with this historical context and the role Edwards' ideas on illumination played in it. Here it is important to note what was at the center of Edwards' attempt to speak within the controversies over the Awakening. The question, of course, that Edwards and his contemporaries were forced to answer was: Are the revivals which are sweeping the colonies authentic works of the Spirit of God? But before this issue could be decided, the normative question had to be answered: What is the authentic work of the Spirit of God, and how does it differ from what may pose as the work of God's Spirit? Underlying Edwards' discerning of the concrete signs and manifestations of the true operation of God's Spirit are his distinctions between the "supernatural" and the "natural" operations of the Spirit, and between "divine" and "imaginative" illuminations.

The distinction between the natural and the supernatural operations of God's Spirit hinges on Edwards' thesis that the Divine Light may assist natural man occasionally and externally, but not as a continuous, internal, vital principle that is united to his faculties. Consequently, natural man has no new exercises (the exercises of faith), for he has no new principle for the exercises. For example, the Spirit may enlighten and enliven a man's conscience, thereby bringing him to a consciousness of his guilt and enabling him to discern right from wrong. But then the conscience, a principle of nature, is only *assisted* by the Spirit to accomplish what is its natural capacity to do on its own. "The Spirit of God, in those convictions which unregenerate men sometimes have, assists conscience to do this work in a further degree than it would do if they were left to themselves. He helps it against those things that tend to stupefy it, and obstruct its exercise." In the Spirit's supernatural or saving influence, on the other hand, nature is not simply assisted. Man is now given a basis from beyond himself, yet internally related to himself through participation, from which he acts. This kind of acting is not something man has as a natural capacity or as his own possibility; it is supernaturally given as a possibility by God who indwells the human mind as divine and supernatural light.[20] Although the human faculties in the act of faith are the same faculties given to all men, they are exercised not by virtue of their natural capacities to act but solely by virtue of the Holy Spirit at their foundation.[21] And because of this "supernatural" foundation, the faculties perform new exercises (those performed in spiritual knowledge). Only through the supernatural or saving operation of the Spirit does man dwell in God and God in him (I John 4:12, 15–16), does man partake of God's holiness (Heb. 12:10), does he live by Christ's life (Gal. 2:20), thereby "seeing light in God's light, and being made to drink of the river of God's pleasures" (Ps. 36:8–9).[22]

At the height of the New England revivals, Edwards was made increasingly aware that one's imagination is easily stirred by the excitement and emotion of surrounding events. It was necessary, therefore, to distinguish the work of the Spirit of God from the imaginative illuminations of the mind that arise out of revivalistic excitement and that tend to pose as divine illuminations:

Natural men may have lively impressions on their imaginations; and we cannot determine but the devil, who transforms himself into an angel of light, may cause imaginations of an outward beauty, or visible glory, and of sounds and speeches, and other things; but these are things of a vastly inferior nature to spiritual light.[23]

Edwards defines the imagination as the mental power with which one "can have a conception, or idea of things of an external or outward nature (that is, of such sort of things as are objects of the outward senses), when those things are not present, and be not perceived by the senses."[24] In the midst of the Awakening, many confused illumination by the Spirit with "sensational" visions—for example, with visions of the bodily form of the Christ in all its splendor or crucified gore, given through the imaginative powers. Edwards was not beyond admitting that such external visions might well occur during a truly saving work of the Spirit of God since the Spirit is capable of stirring up a weak mortal's imagination.[25] But he refused to admit that such imaginative visions were genuine marks of spiritual illumination. Not only is the unbeliever as capable as the believer of having lively imaginations of divine things; the devil himself can create such "illumination." What neither the unbeliever nor the demonic powers can give the mind, however, is that spiritual illumination which opens up the act of faith, which gives the "simple idea" in which a man's whole being acquiesces in spiritual knowledge.

Edwards' interpretation of the Holy Spirit's inward illumination of the mind is meant to be read in conjunction with his interpretation of the "Word"—otherwise we wrongly interpret him as a spirit-mystic. Yet this much is presently apparent: in his description of the possibility of faith being opened by the Divine Light, Edwards is concerned to point to the leap into faith as a leap not available to man on the basis of his manhood; it is a leap founded on God's grace, on the gift of the Spirit alone. Although faith is not a leap out of manhood into absorption into the divine life, it is a leap into new manhood provided by the Holy Spirit who gives old human powers new or faithful exercises. Edwards accounts for the same miracle of faith by describing grace as the infusion of a divine habit.

Infusion

Peter van Mastricht, a Dutch theologian whose system of divinity Jonathan Edwards highly recommended to his friend Joseph Bellamy,[26] expressly called for an interpretation of grace in terms of both illumination and infusion. This meant for van Mastricht, as well as for most of Edwards' Reformed theological precursors, that the human agent is so constituted that grace must be twofold in its internal function: it must influence both the mind and the will. For "if we should make the absurd supposition of the understanding's being most clearly enlightened, and yet the will not renewed," said van Mastricht, "the will would not follow the practical judgment, because in that case the understanding would not dictate agreeably to its propensity."[27] For faith to occur, the understanding must not only be illumined by a luminous principle; the will must also be bent by the infusion of a divine habit. In accordance with the traditional separation of the human faculties into distinct domains, this view of grace divided the work of the Spirit into two separate operations. For the English Puritan John Preston, "God puts a new light into the understanding, he raiseth it up to see and beleeve"; but the seeing and believing are not completed until "there is another act which God also workes on the will. . . ."[28] Even while attempting to express the unity of God's saving operation, the Puritan preacher Richard Sibbes had implied that God must operate savingly in two ways: "God hath so joined these together, as that whensoever he doth savingly shine upon the understanding, he giveth a soft and pliable heart."[29] Edwards' grandfather, Solomon Stoddard, attempted to overcome the division of God's saving grace into two distinct acts by assigning a volitional influence to the Holy Spirit's illumination of the mind:

Conversion is wrought by Light: God is the Author of Conversion. . . . And the way wherein he doth it, is by *letting spiritual light into the Soul*; by irradiating the mind . . . by inlightening the mind he changes the heart.[30]

Although, as we have seen, Stoddard anticipated his grandson by suggesting that understanding and will be conceived not as "two things, but one and the same soul, diversely denominated according to *two* several *ways of working*, which are inseparably conjoined,"[31] the consequence of his theory of illumination is nevertheless the division of the faculties and the subordination of volition to understanding. God's saving operation on the understanding is immediate, while His operation on the will is only mediate (i.e., mediated through the illumined understanding).[32]

In conformity with his notion that the act of knowing and the act of willing are not to be torn apart in the immediacy of the act of faith, Edwards intends, in denominating the Spirit's operation as infusion, neither to suggest an operation distinct from illumination nor to assign a separate domain (the will) for infusion. Edwards does frequently speak of infusion of grace with specific reference to the will,[33] but he does this in the context of the controversy over whether the will is self-determining without proposing that the will is the special domain for the infused *habitus*. It is manifest in the *Treatise on Religious Affections*, for example, that Edwards refers to the same reality when he speaks of illumination and infusion, for it is in the context of kinds of "illuminations" that he discusses the seed of grace implanted in the soul.[34] In his "Treatise on Grace," infused grace is by no means confined to the will; infusion is there discussed with reference to both faculties.[35] The infusion of grace is nothing other than the illumination of the mind by the Divine Light: the divine habit given to the soul is the same reality which opens the possibility of faith through spiritual illumination.

Since illumination and infusion are the same reality for Edwards, it would be superfluous to rehearse in detail here the nature of the Spirit's operation in infusion. But what we must attempt to decide is why Edwards discusses the doctrine of the Holy Spirit under the rubric of infusion as well as illumination when, in fact, he has the same phenomenon in mind. Further, we must ask whether the language of infusion has any peculiar theological consequences.

In his doctrine of infused grace Edwards was obviously falling back upon categories long employed by Protestant scholasticism. Though the Reformed scholastics frequently

were concerned to set their ideas of grace and faith in distinct
opposition to "enemy Rome," in fact their categories of infusion were those of medieval Scholasticism which presented
a portrait of grace not often clearly distinguishable from the
Roman Catholic portrait, with the exception that infusion
was not tied up with sacramentalism. François Turrettini,
another seventeenth-century theologian highly spoken of by
Edwards,[36] represented the attitude of Protestant scholasticism when he complained of the implications of the doctrine
of infusion yet insisted on its necessity. Turrettini admits
that the Thomist notion of a physical determination of the
human will by an infused *habitus* is really an inadequate way
of conceiving grace. It is inadequate because, in Turrettini's
language, it tends to confuse natural acts of providence with
supernatural acts of grace. That is, to call grace a habit in the
human soul is to suggest that faith occurs "habitually" or
"naturally" when man is moved "physically" by the habit.
Nevertheless, Turrettini opts for the Thomist view of grace
rather than the Jesuit position that God's grace simply evokes
the action of the human will through "moral suasion." If
properly understood, the physicalistic notion of grace places
our salvation squarely in God's hands, whereas the suasive
view throws the burden of salvation on the strength of sinful
man's will.[37] There were for Turrettini only two major options: either man's will is moved to faith by a physical cause,
that is, by the Holy Spirit as a habit in the soul; or man is
simply attracted or persuaded by the Spirit to make his own
choice out of absolute freedom. Edwards' reflections follow
much the same line. He believes, on the one hand, that

if there be any immediate influence or action of the Spirit of God at
all on any created beings, in any part of the universe, since the days
of the apostles, it is physical. If it be in exciting ideas of motives, or
in any respect assisting or promoting any effect, still it is physical;
and every whit as much so, as if we suppose the temper and nature
of the heart is immediately changed.[38]

Even the Holy Spirit in illumination, therefore, influences
man physically—that is, the Spirit moves the human powers
as their immediate, efficient cause, just as things in the natural world are moved by efficient physical causes. As we shall

observe later, Edwards does distinguish between natural and moral necessity in causation. But faith is directly caused, determined, by the influence of the Spiritual habit. The only alternative, as far as Edwards can see, is the acting of the human powers as their own immediate cause in regeneration—which is tantamount to sinful man's saving himself. Hence "those that deny infusion of grace by the Holy Spirit, must, of necessity, deny the Holy Spirit to do any thing at all";[39] the Spirit operates as an infused power in the soul, directly moving human powers to action.

On the other hand, Edwards recognizes with Turrettini that speaking "physically" of grace as an infused habit inclines toward a naturalizing of the supernatural. Therefore, when one describes grace as a habit in the soul of the saint, he must be careful not to turn the habit into "a natural disposition to act grace, as begotten in the soul by the first communication of Divine Light, and as the natural and necessary consequence of the first light. . . ."[40] Edwards is here arguing the same point he made in his doctrine of illumination: grace as a habit, even though it is vitally attached to the human faculties, cannot be collapsed into human being. It does not become man's own "natural" principle. It is the foundation that the human soul has from beyond itself though internally related to itself through participation. And the habit of grace remains grace: it is not given over to human control. It must be admitted, however, that Edwards sometimes speaks of the grace infused by God as a "quality" of the human soul without invoking this distinction between nature and grace, thereby failing to heed his own plea for caution in the matter.[41]

But when the distinction between grace and human nature is sufficiently made, the doctrine of infused grace stresses, in a way not always explicit in talk of illumination, that the internal gift of grace is abiding and dependable. We have seen that the new principle of the Holy Spirit is not bound by the exercises of the human faculties it founds; its presence is not ensured by human powers. Nevertheless, the new principle dependably abides in the heart of the true saint. It is this abiding infused habit or principle of grace, rather than

the liveliness of the human powers, which finally determine
whether or not a man's life is authentically religious:

. . . the degree of religion is rather to be judged of by the fixednes
and strength of the habit that is exercised in affection, whereby hol
affection is habitual, than by the degree of the present exercise: an
the strength of that habit is not always in proportion to outwar
effects and manifestations, or inward effects. . . .[42]

The change wrought in the person at conversion is an abid
ing change, even though "conversion don't entirely root ou
the natural temper."[43] The abiding quality of the Christian'
life is due not to the lively exercises of his own powers bu
to the stability of the Holy Spirit infused into the soul. Whe
the saint breathes forth St. Paul's words that "it is no longe
I who live, but Christ who lives in me" (Gal. 2:20), h
confesses from the depth of his soul, says Edwards, what i
intended in the doctrine of infused grace.[44] The infuse
Spirit of the trinitarian God is none other than God's Spiri
of Love in Christ indwelling the saint's heart. The new in
fused principle that the saint has in faith he has from beyon
himself; yet the principle is closer to him than his breathing
And man may be comforted by the truth that God not onl
implants this abiding habit "against great opposition of th
heart, and from Satan and the world," but that he wi
maintain it as well.[45]

One is at first astounded to find that Edwards praises th
piety of David Brainerd (an eighteenth-century missionary t
colonial Indians, who was betrothed to Edwards' daughte
Jerusha) because his "religion did not consist in unaccount
able *flights* and *vehement* pangs" but was more "like th
steady lights of heaven, constant principles of light, thoug
sometimes hid with clouds."[46] Brainerd's memoirs, collecte
and edited for publication by Edwards, reveal a frame c
mind particularly given to "flights" and "pangs"! No soul eve
rose to higher spiritual peaks of delight only to descend
into the lowest valleys of melancholia, than did Brainerd's
But Edwards' eye is upon the "principle," the "light," th
"habit," which is not to be confused with psychological state
of the saints. His vision is directed toward that abiding habi
which persisted in, through, and behind the risings and fal

ngs of Brainerd's spirits, toward that "great change" and "abiding change" wrought in conversion which abides as the saint's foundation but not as his controllable possession.[47] And the saint's own basis of confidence is never to be his own subjective states but always the divine principle which upholds him. "Where God infuses grace, He will give it predominance by His upholding it. . . . This is not owing to our strength, but to the strength of God who won't forsake the work of His hands. . . ."[48]

Faith and Love:
The Act and Its Principle

The preceding discussion of the Holy Spirit as the internal possibility of the act of faith provides an avenue for approaching an issue which has been forcefully raised recently by Thomas A. Schafer.[49] Schafer points out that according to Edwards faith arises from the principle of love. He suggests this means that in faith the act of belief is subordinated to the affective, volitional aspect of faith and that sanctified acts of obedience are the main thing in faith. This is testified to, Schafer feels, in Edwards' views that holy love as an infused habit is the foundation of faith and that the "essential self" is identical with volition or inclination. Schafer quotes in support a number of miscellaneous observations in which Edwards does in fact say that faith "arises from a principle of love," that "love is the main thing in saving faith." Yet passages can be adduced from Edwards which appear directly to contradict those adduced by Schafer. In his *Qualifications for Communion*, for example, Edwards asserts that the "exercise of love" is a "fruit of faith";[50] and in an unpublished note he maintains that there can be no love to God "without seeing something of the divine glory."[51] It is apparent here that there is no priority of love to faith insofar as both are considered as human acts, and that faith as seeing and judging is not subordinated to the affective, volitional aspect of faith. Either Edwards is contradictory in his understanding of the relation between faith and love or else some way other than Schafer's must be found for accounting for the relation.

It is our contention that there prove to be for Edward[s] three different ways in which faith and love are related; th[e] differences depend on whether love is conceived as a huma[n] "act" or a divine "principle." Faith arises from love when lov[e] is conceived as the Divine Love that dwells in the heart o[f] man as the principle of his acts. Love either arises from or i[s] *exercised* in faith, on the other hand, when man acts on th[e] basis of the divine principle. The human act of love is eithe[r] that affective, volitional adherence to God or to the truth o[f] the gospel intimately joined with judgment, exercised in th[e] very essence of the "sense of the heart"; or it is the "workin[g] love" or "practice" directed primarily toward the neighbor which arises from but is potentially included in every authen[-] tic act of faith.[52] If these distinctions are borne in mind Edwards' seemingly contradictory statements about the prior ity of faith to love, or love to faith, are resolved. The key to the distinctions is Edwards' view of the Holy Spirit: *the love which is the foundation of faith, that from which faith arises, is neither the exercise of a human faculty nor a human work but is the Holy Spirit himself*. This demands some elabora tion.

"The love of God is shed abroad in our hearts by the Holy Ghost, which is given unto us" (Rom. 5:5). With this pas sage before him, Edwards remarks that "the Scripture seems in many places to speak of love in Christians as if it were the same with the Spirit of God in them, or at least as the prime and most natural breathing and acting of the Spirit in the soul."[53] The Divine Love is God as Holy Spirit:

So that as the Son of God is spoken of as wisdom, understanding and *Logos* of God . . . and is, as Divines express things, the personal Wisdom of God; so the Holy Spirit is spoken of as the Love of God, and may with equal foundation and propriety be called the personal Love of God.[54]

When God dwells in the heart of the saint as a luminous or habitual principle, He dwells as Holy Spirit or as Personal Love. All Christian *acts* of love, whether they are directed toward God or man, arise from this *principle*, which dwells and breathes in the heart of the saint.[55] The chief end of creation, in fact, is the emanation and re-emanation of God's loving glory: God communicates his Love of himself to the creatures, and this Love is reflected back to Him through the creatures' love to God.[56] But the creature's act of knowledge of God is not separated from or subordinated to his act of loving Him. Both human actions are equally founded on the communication of God in his Spirit, as the human agent partakes of the divine fullness in that Spirit.[57] The act of faith, therefore, is founded not on one of its interpenetrative powers (will or affective inclination) but on the principle or the habit of the faith-act, which is the Divine Love or the Holy Spirit. And, as we have seen, Edwards consciously guards against identifying this principle with human being or collapsing it into the human faculties. Love is, indeed, the principle from which faith arises for Edwards. But this principle of love is the Holy Spirit himself, on the basis of which, in the act of faith, cognition and volition are exercised in a new way. "Gods Sp. or his love doth but, as it were, come and dwell in our hearts and act there as a vital Principle."[58]

Continuing his observation about the relation between faith and love in Edwards, Schafer comments that Edwards makes faith dependent upon a prior sanctification.[59] He cites a passage from one of Edwards' "Miscellanies" which contains an argument *against* the position that santification cannot be "one moment before the exercise of faith." The upshot of the argument appears to be an abandonment of the traditional Calvinist position that sanctification is a progressive struggle for holiness that *grows out of* faith, and the adoption of a view repugnant to the thrust of Reformation Protestantism, the view that faith is dependent upon man's first becoming sanctified or holy-in-himself. Schafer's conclusion is that Edwards makes inherent holy states of man the conditions of faith and justification.[60] It is indeed true that Edwards makes faith and justification by faith dependent on a type of sanctification, but this sanctification is not really a "holy human state." The sanctification upon which the act of faith (through which one is justified) is dependent, is the gift of God's Spirit which resides within man as the principle of his act. (And as we shall see in the next chapter, this operation of the Spirit does not occur apart from the Word.) In the "Miscellany" selected by Schafer, Edwards says:

What is held by some, that none can be in a state of salvation before they have particularly acted a reception of the Lord Jesus Christ for a Saviour, and that there cannot be sanctification one moment before the exercise of faith, as they have described it, cannot be true as they explain this reception of Christ. There must be the principle before there can be the action in all cases. There must be an alteration made in the heart of the sinner before there can be action consequent upon this alteration. Yea there must be a principle of holiness before holiness is in exercise. Yea an alteration must not only be before this act of faith in nature as the cause before the effect, but also in time, if this embracing of Christ as a saviour be a successive action, that is, an action when one thought and act of the mind in any wise follows another, as it certainly is. For first there must be an idea of Jesus Christ in the mind, that is an agreeable and truly lovely idea of him. But this cannot be before the soul is sanctified.[61]

The "alteration of the heart," the "principle of holiness," the ideational act in the mind prior to the active reception of Christ in faith is what Edwards elsewhere denotes the presence of the Holy Spirit. It is the Divine Light, the new simple idea, the spiritual habit which elicits, causes, founds the volitional knowledge of the act of faith. It is the new principle of faith. And though Edwards is not beyond referring to the divine principle as a "disposition" of the human soul, he refuses, as we have seen, to settle the divine principle in human states or powers. The "sanctification" that precedes faith is the Divine Light given as the foundation of human states and powers. Holiness is the foundation of faith, but it is God's own holiness communicated to and participated in by man. A holy act is the basis of the act of faith, but it is a holy act by the Holy Spirit who founds the human act.

It is perhaps best to call this action of the Holy Spirit which is the foundation of faith a *kind* of sanctification. Traditionally Reformed theologians held to a "progressive" sanctification: it was the activity of God's Spirit in man's inward parts whereby regeneration, initiated by vocation, was continued and gradually completed as man struggled in the race of life and as the Spirit more and more cleansed man of his sin.[62] Sometimes the term "regeneration" was virtually identical with "sanctification," embracing the whole work of the Spirit in man.[63] At other times "regeneration" designated the new birth of man in conversion which does not admit of degrees, while "sanctification" referred to the progressive cleansing by the Holy Spirit.[64] Although Edwards applies "sanctification" to the gift of the principle which awakens the act of faith, and although he is not careful at all times to distinguish sanctification from regeneration and calling, he by no means falls away from his Reformed tradition in meaning. He points out that due to the sin remaining even in the hearts of the saints who are given the spiritual principle, life continues to be a "race or a battle" for them, and the Holy Spirit must continue to do his cleansing work.[65] The original "sanctification" does not absolutely "perfect" man or make him holy-in-himself. Yet faith, the beginning of the struggle in holiness, is a gift of the Holy Spirit: it has its rise from a Holy Principle. And in this also Edwards is in touch with the depths of his heritage; Calvin himself had said, "Faith itself has no other source than the Spirit."[66]

Love is for Edwards the principle, the habit, the foundation from which faith arises. This Love is God himself vitally present to the powers of man. A type of sanctification precedes the human act of faith only because the possibility of that act is a gift of the *Holy* Spirit who abides in man as Love.

CHAPTER III

WORD AND SPIRIT

Protestant thought has frequently expressed its disapproval of the "subjectivism" that attaches to some views of the Spirit. The demur is usually couched in terms of the polarity of "Word and Spirit": if one emphasizes the "internal" work of the Spirit in effecting religious faith without due emphasis on the "outer" work of the Word, one's account of faith is too subjectivistic—it concentrates on what happens within the human subject without proper regard to what God does outside the subject. This undue concentration on spiritual inwardness leads to religious fanaticism without the check of objective standards, the abandonment of outward means of grace, and a harping on one's feelings and inner experiences. Under this conviction, Luther directed a number of attacks against those sixteenth-century "enthusiasts" and "heavenly prophets" who were inclined to reduce religious experience to the inward workings of the Spirit.[1] And the Puritans of early New England, under similar convictions, dealt harshly with Quakers and antinomians.[2]

The desire to avoid spiritualist subjectivism has led, in the history of Christian thought, to the opposite extreme: a concentration on the "objective" Word largely to the exclusion of vital, individual experience. If the tendency of Quakerism was toward subjectivism, the tendency of Puritanism was toward legalism and authoritarianism.[3] Edwards, like his English contemporary John Wesley, sought to combine the objective and subjective principles of religion by maintaining a harmonious balance of Word and Spirit.[4] Edwards may sometimes give the impression that he is dispensing with the "outer" aspect of grace when he speaks of the "immediacy" of the Spirit. But Edwards does not attach such a meaning to the "immediate" operation of the Spirit. He holds that Word and Spirit function together in opening the act of faith. Just as the internal movement of the act of faith remains unspecified apart from reference to faith's internal possibility, so the internal possibility is unspecified apart from reference to faith's orientation to its immediate object, the Word of God. John Calvin had said, "God works in his elect in two ways: within, through his Spirit; without, through his Word."[5] And Edward A. Dowey's interpretation of Calvin's statement is equally applicable to Edwards: "These two elements are not to be separated from one another. They are functionally one term."[6] For Edwards also, Word and Spirit, the objective and the subjective aspects of religious faith, function as "one term." The Spirit, the inward divine possibility of faith, is the Worded Spirit; and the Word, the outward divine point of orientation of faith, is the Spirited Word.

Within Edwards' trinitarian scheme, the Word of God is primordially the Idea, the *Logos*, the Son, eternally generated out of the Father, and is the price paid, the Redeemer, in man's salvation. The Holy Spirit is the eternal love communicated back and forth between Father and Son; as the thing purchased in redemption, He is the eternal love communicated to the elected sinner. When man partakes of the Spirit, he partakes of the Word's benefits—he is redeemed. "All the blessedness of the Redeemed consists in their Partaking of X's fullness, which consists in Partaking of that Spirit which is given not by measure unto him."[7] Yet the role of the Spirit in communicating redemption by no means usurps the role of the *Logos* as mediator. It is part of God's "Wisdom Displayed in Salvation" that both the Holy Spirit, as the principle of the act of faith, and the act of faith itself are active by a mediator:

The saints, in all their spiritual transactions with God, act by the Spirit: or rather, it is the spirit of God, that acts in them. . . . But in these their spiritual transactions with God, they act by a *mediator*. These spiritual and holy exercises cannot be acceptable, or avail any thing with God, as from a fallen creature, but by a mediator. Therefore Christ in being mediator between the Father and the saints, may be said to be mediator between the Father and the Holy Spirit, that acts in the saints. And therefore it was meet, that the mediator should not be either the Father or the Spirit, but a middle person between them both.[8]

This mediator, in conjunction with whom the Spirit always savingly works, is none other than the eternal *Logos* of God, who is also the immediate object of the act of faith opened by the Spirit.[9]

In one sense the whole cosmic order is the Word of God and the object of faith, for the natural world and its beauties reveal the divine truth to which the act of faith is directed. Nevertheless, "the beauties of nature are really emanations or shadows of the excellencies of the Son of God."[10] All the works of God in nature and history are "a kind of voice or language of God";[11] yet the divine words and images of nature are incomprehensible apart from the Master Image, the Divine *Logos* incarnate in Jesus the Christ. Jesus as the Word is "the grand medium of the knowledge of all others [i.e., all other men]. They know [God] no otherwise than by the exhibitions held forth in and by him, as the Scripture is express" (Matt. 11: 27).[12] Edwards devoted some rather imaginative reflection to an illustration of the manner in which the visible, material things of the world are "images," "shadows," "imitations" of invisible, spiritual things.[13] Yet there is no ground for following Perry Miller's interpretation of this Platonic scheme of shadow and reality as an exaltation of natural over Christological revelation or as a culmination of spiritual knowledge in a perception of the divine in nature.[14] The Word of God sounds most clearly, for Edwards, in Christological revelation; the Christ is the Master Image given in history which clarifies the natural images of God. Only through and on the basis of this Image does the mind of man attend to the natural images as shadows of divine truth. Therefore perception of the divine revelation in nature is fulfilled only in a confrontation with the revelation of God held forth in the scriptural testimonies to Christ: nature in itself, apart from Scripture and the divine Word which shines through it, has only led the world into "the grossest theological errors."[15]

The Word is given to each believer, then, not primarily in the images of nature but historically; that is, through the Scriptures and through the Church's proclamation. Edwards, in fact, refers to both Scripture and preaching as the Word of God—the former being the more common reference. Nevertheless, neither the words of Scripture nor the words of the preacher are by their own power the Word of God. There is no correlation between the human bearers of the divine content and the content itself, generated from the side of the bearers. The Scriptures and the language of the preacher become the Word of God only through the power of God's Spirit. It is in this context that we must understand Edwards' reference to the operation of the Spirit as "immediate."

François Turrettini had summarized the Reformed thesis that in its saving work the Spirit of God is immediate: "*Although the Spirit in effectual calling does not act without the Word, still he does not act only mediately through the Word, but he also acts immediately with the Word on the soul, so that the calling necessarily produces its effect.*"[16] The intention here is not to sever the Spirit from the Word but to ascribe effectual calling to God alone. The Spirit acts *with* the Word, but *immediately with* the Word on the heart of man. To make faith the result of a strictly mediate operation of the Spirit meant to Turrettini to make conversion dependent on what lies naturally in the power of the Word as a human means of grace. The power of God's grace cannot be reduced to its vehicles; the words of the scriptural authors and the words of the preacher are not of themselves, as human agents, capable of divine operation. Hence, Turrettini continues,

although the opening of the heart is objectively ascribed to the Word also in its own manner . . . because it usually takes place not without the Word, but at its presence; and is ascribed to the ministers of the Word instrumentally, because they are the instruments employed by God in this work; still it cannot be brought about simply by the Word, or by the Word presented by men of God, unless to the Word approaches the internal power of the Spirit distinct from the Word, by whose intervention the Word presented from without to the mind may be received by it with faith.[17]

Edwards is more emphatic than Turrettini about the close connection between Word and Spirit: when the heart is opened to faith by the Spirit, this event is not just *usually* but *always* an occurrence in the presence of the Word. "Indeed a person cannot have spiritual light without the word."[18] But the indispensability of the Word does not mean that the light or the inward operation of the Spirit is *caused* by the Word *as a human vehicle*. Rather, the Spirit is given *immediately* by God. Yet immediacy does not signify an operation of the Spirit apart from the Word or really even, in one sense, an operation unmediated by God's Word:

> When it is said that this light is given immediately by God, and not obtained by natural means, hereby is intended, that it is given by God without making use of any means that operate by their own power, or a natural force. God makes use of means; but it is not as mediate causes to produce this effect. . . . The word of God is no proper cause of this effect: it does not operate by any natural force in it.[19]

The immediate operation of the Spirit, therefore, stands for an act of God that is not generated by the Word *as a natural cause*. As A. V. G. Allen remarked in the last century, "Edwards assumes, as a first principle, that when God speaks to man His word must be very different from man's word."[20] God's Word is really *God's* Word when it is accompanied by the Spirit dwelling in the human heart; when unaccompanied by the Spirit it is simply another natural, human word. The "immediate" operation of the Spirit is the operation of God's Word *as God's Word*: the Spirit's immediacy is the character of the operation of God's Word which distinguishes it from simply another human word. This is a way of stressing that when the human words of Scripture and preaching become God's Word, they become this not by their own power but by the power of God alone; they effect faith not as natural or human causes but through a divine cause operative in them. Edwards says this has been true since the beginning of the propagation of the gospel: when the gospel was "preached only by a few fishermen, who were without power and worldly interest to support them," the gospel prevailed "from no other cause than the power and agency of God."[21] The gospel is truly the good news as God's Word to man when God's Spirit is at work. The external call of the gospel is savingly efficacious when it becomes simultaneously the internal possibility of faith by virtue of the Holy Spirit; but the possibility of faith is internally opened by the Spirit only in the presence of the external call.

Though Edwards insists on this conjunction of Word and Spirit, he nevertheless acknowledges that Scripture and preaching may be of value for a man's faith before they are actually joined by the internal work of God's Spirit or before they become the Word of God proper. They may serve as means of grace outside the immediacy of the act of faith. For example, a thorough knowledge of the things of Scripture, apart from the illumination of the mind by the Spirit and hence apart from the interpenetrative movements of cognition and volition in the act of faith, is of use to the Spirit when he finally does work faith. Here the Bible is valuable as a "book of instructions."[22] The knowledge acquired from the Bible as a book of instructions is not yet the knowledge of faith, but it is "mental matter" upon which the Spirit may work in awakening faith. The ideas derived from this "natural" knowledge of the truths of Scripture may become the "matter for grace to act upon when God shall be pleased to infuse it. . . ."[23] The ideas so furnished by and derived from Scripture are by no means the new simple idea of faith, nor is the new simple idea reducible to them. For "grace is from God as immediately and directly as light is from the sun, and that notwithstanding the means that are improved. . . ."[24] Yet since the light or new idea of grace has its seat in the mind of man, and since that mind is not empty but is full of ideas derived from experience, grace operates in the context of the experientially derived ideas. Although the knowledge of faith is not reducible to the mechanics of natural sense experience, yet the mind that "knows" in the knowledge of faith is not a *tabula rasa* upon which the simple idea is imprinted; it is a mind formed by sense experience and reflection. "The matter which the principle of grace acts upon is those notions or ideas that the mind is furnished with of the things of religion or of God, Christ, the future world," etc. "If there could be a principle of grace in the heart without these notions or ideas there, yet it could not act, because it could have no matter to act upon."[25] Hence Edwards believes it profitable for a man to supply his mind with those ideas that Scripture holds forth to all men, even to men outside faith. "God hath told us about what things we should chiefly employ our understandings, having given us a book full of divine instructions, holding forth many glorious objects about which *all* rational creatures should chiefly employ their understandings."[26] Scripture thus rationally understood is not yet the Spirited Word of God that produces faith, but it is that potentially since it supplies mental matter upon which the Spirit may work.

Proclamation of the Word of God may also be a means of grace prior to the actual gift of grace. Although the preacher of himself and by the strength of his own words can never supply the simple idea of faith, preaching can and should convey knowledge to the mind, a knowledge upon which the Spirit may work. Even rational, deductive arguments—a device frequently employed by Edwards in the pulpit—about the truths of Scripture may supply the minds of the congregation with knowledge or ideas yet to receive illumination. "How often have we an account in the Acts of the Apostles of reasoning and disputing with men to bring them to believing and of many brought to believe through that means."[27] Only God through his Spirit, never the force of rational argument, can bring men to a saving understanding of the Word; yet the arguments can provide knowledge about the Word which becomes the matter upon which God's Spirit may work. In short, the delivery of the preacher can be a *means* of grace only as it conveys knowledge, and this definitely refers to "speculative" as well as "practical" knowledge. Edwards preached to an age not yet totally lethargic about the finer, more discursive features of theological reasoning; at this stage of American religion, interest in the practical "how" of faith and practice had not yet completely replaced interest in the doctrinal "what." Those sermons of Edwards which elicited strong emotions from the members of the congregation and had them crying to God for deliverance were carefully reasoned, doctrinally exacting pieces of work. It was as unforgivable for the congregation as it was for the minister to allow a thorough doctrinal knowledge of Scripture to degenerate into an unknowing emotional utterance of and response to Scripture. The sermon, therefore, was to instruct the mind, and as instruction it could become a means of grace.

No speech can be any means of grace, but by conveying knowledge. Otherwise the speech is as much lost as if there had been no man there, and he that spoke, had spoken only into the air. . . . He that doth not understand, can receive no faith, nor any other grace; for God deals with man as with a rational creature; and when faith is in exercise, it is not about something he knows not what.[28]

Doctrinal understanding of scriptural truth could never become for Edwards a valid substitute for a "sense of the heart"; but the preacher would abandon an important and necessary feature of his task if he allowed this fact to obscure the need to instruct his congregation in the theological ramifications of scriptural truth.

The words of Scripture and the words of proclamation cease to be *simply* means of grace and become truly the Word of God when they are joined with God's Spirit in the creation of faith. Here the human subject is not simply "instructed"; he is lovingly inclined toward the truth of the Word as his saving object. Now one has a "new sense and taste" of Scripture: he attends to it in the affective cognition of faith. And although this knowledge of faith occurs within the setting of ideas achieved through natural experience, those ideas are not the source of the knowledge; it is strictly a new simple idea given by God. This new knowledge of faith is a "spiritual application" of the Scripture as the Word of God. It is an application of scriptural truth "to the heart, in spiritually enlightening, sanctifying influences."

A spiritual application of an invitation or offer of the gospel consists in giving the soul a spiritual sense or relish of the holy and divine blessings offered, and also the sweet and wonderful grace of the offerer, in making so gracious an offer, and of his holy excellency and faithfulness to fulfill what he offers, and his glorious sufficiency for it; so leading and drawing forth the heart to embrace the offer; and thus giving the man evidence of his title to the thing offered. And so a spiritual application of the promises of Scripture, for the comfort of the saints, consists in enlightening their minds to see the holy excellency and sweetness of the blessings promised, and also the holy excellency of the promiser, and his faithfulness and sufficiency; thus drawing forth their hearts to embrace the promiser, and the thing promised; and by this means, giving the sensible actings of grace, enabling them to see their grace, and so their title to the promise.[29]

When Word and Spirit are joined, when Scripture is spiritually opened as God's Word, the knowledge of faith is "drawn forth." The blessings and promises of Scripture are so applied that man heartily embraces the God in Christ who offers the gifts, as well as the scriptural blessings and promises themselves.

In view of the excesses of the New England revivals, Edwards was careful to distinguish this spiritual application of Scripture from the receipt of spiritual truths through enthusiastic flashes and private revelations. "An application not consisting in this divine sense and enlightening of the mind, but consisting only in the words being borne into the thoughts, as if immediately then spoken . . . is a blind application. . . ."[30] The revelation of secret facts of divine things or the immediate suggestion of scriptural words or ideas, which some experienced during the Awakening, are not the gracious work of the Spirit. Unsaved men are capable of such revelations "as is manifest in Balaam, and others spoken of in the Scripture";[31] and secret voices are not beyond the power of demonic forces.[32] The gracious, saving operation of the Spirit is not one severed from or added to scriptural truth; rather, Scripture is "improved" by the Spirit in the sense that man's heart is opened by the Spirit to the divine truth of Scripture. The saving Spirit does not give men "*new statutes* and *new precepts*. He graciously gives them eyes to see, and ears to hear, and hearts to understand" in faith the statutes, precepts, and promises already contained in Scripture.[33] Again, Edwards would not divorce the "objective" from the "subjective" aspect of faithful knowledge; the testimony of the Word in Scripture and the testimony of the Spirit in the human heart are "functionally one term."

Like the words of Scripture, the words of the preacher may cease to be simply means of grace and become truly the Word of God when joined with God's Spirit. The event which occurs in such proclamation is typified for Edwards in the sounding of the trumpets at Jericho: "That sound typified the sound of the gospel by the preaching of gospel ministers, the walls of the accursed city Jericho signifying the walls of Satan's kingdom."[34] When the Spirit does his work in the heart, the proclaimed gospel is received as divine truth, Satan's kingdom falls before the faith elicited, and the Word of God is sensed, tasted, relished, heard as man's saving object. Here the preacher does not simply inform the understandings of his congregation—though that task is never abandoned. His words become the instruments for holding forth the Word of God and eliciting the hearty cognition of the act of faith. It is the business of the minister to saturate himself with Holy Scripture so that he may hold forth its beams of light to enkindle the hearts of his hearers.[35]

The holding forth of beams of Scripture to the congregation never meant for Edwards the stringing together of uninterpreted scriptural phrases. Though faith can never be aroused merely by the mechanics of the sermon or the preacher's rhetoric, the Spirit may work in and through such conscious efforts to win the hearts of the hearers. In his farewell sermon to the people of Northampton in 1750, Edwards briefly described what he conceived to be his task in proclamation:

I have used my utmost endeavors to win you: I have sought out acceptable words, that if possible I might prevail upon you to forsake sin, and turn to God, and accept of Christ as your Saviour and Lord. I have spent my strength very much in these things.[36]

In his search for "acceptable words," Edwards felt it incumbent upon him to discover and employ language which would not simply store the mind but which would, as well, appeal to the whole man, to man as both a knowing and a willing agent, in the hope that through the power of the Holy Spirit his words would become the Word of God and call forth the act of faith. For "our people do not so much need to have their heads stored, as to have their hearts touched; and they stand in the greatest need of that sort of preaching, which has the greatest tendency to do this."[37] Men may abound in the "light" of understanding and yet not have the "heat" of affections which must accompany the act of faith. Hence Edwards intends to "raise the affections of my hearers as high as possibly I can, provided they are affected with nothing but truth. . . ."[38] This raising of the affections may be accomplished not only by affective words but also by an affective manner of speaking.

I think an exceeding affectionate way of preaching about the great things of religion, has in itself no tendency to beget false impressions of them; but on the contrary, a much greater tendency to beget true apprehensions of them, than a moderate, dull, indifferent way of speaking of them.[39]

Edwards was fully aware that affective delivery could be, and in fact often was, highly emotional at the cost of sound— and sometimes sane—content. The antics of the extreme enthusiasts, like James Davenport, soon became proof of that. But this was no argument for him against the fact that sound content and warm affection could accompany each other in the sermon and that the subject matter proclaimed and the faith-response sought were such that airy, heartless speculation from the pulpit was inappropriate.[40]

Yet finally neither affective words nor affective manner of address can of themselves work faith. It is not by the power of human speech but by the grace of God alone that words can become the Word. The most affective and sensational preaching cannot of itself instill the new simple idea of faith into the mind of man. This must be a gift of God operating as Holy Spirit. Perry Miller correctly points out that "this did not mean for Edwards—any more than for Kierkegaard —that the rhetorician simply builds up a wall of words around the listener, and then reclines, to let the Spirit of God work or not work." For the Spirit works in and through the understanding gained through rhetoric. And "it is a strength, not a weakness, of language that no matter how sensational it becomes, it has to depend upon something happening to the recipient outside and above its own mechanical impact"; for "if it produced in the listener or reader an emotion that contained no more than what the rhetoric imparted, 'then is the affection, however elevated, worthless and vain.' "[41] The "plus" element attained in saving knowledge is the act of grace, the work of God's Spirit. The idea of God in Christ which the man of faith heartily embraces is the same idea presented to him by the Holy Spirit as the foundation of his act. The words of Scripture and of preaching become the Word of God when they are "idealized" by God's Spirit— when they become man's saving objects by being made vitally present to him as "new ideas" through the Spirit's operation. Word and Spirit are functionally one term.

CHAPTER IV

CONVERSION: NATURE AND GRACE

Jonathan Edwards' depiction of faith supposes at every point that faith is a gift of God; it is a possibility only as God gives it through Word and Spirit. In fact, the keystone of Edwards' Calvinist theology is the unremitting insistence that God is sovereign in man's salvation. Man is absolutely dependent upon the sovereign will of God for everything belonging to his salvation, "from the foundation to the top stone."[1] Edwards was, indeed, a revivalist who called men to conversion; but he was of what William McLoughlin has called "the old revival tradition." Edwards could not have dreamed of saying with Charles Grandison Finney, the father of modern American revivalism, that conversion to saving faith "is not a miracle, or dependent on a miracle in any sense" but "is a purely philosophical result of the right use of the constituted means."[2] Edwards spoke of the "surprising work of God" when he referred to the conversions elicited by his preaching in Northampton—they were miracles of grace, not results "worked up" by revivalist methods.[3]

In accordance with his Calvinist view of the sovereignty of God in conversion to faith, Edwards appeals to a doctrine of predestination. His doctrine is supralapsarian with respect to election and sublapsarian with respect to reprobation: God decreed from eternity to save certain men, apart from any consideration of the state of their lives; but he decreed the rejection of others only on the basis of their sin.[4] In certain periods of the history of Calvinism the theory of predestination assumed primarily speculative, nonexistential value. It was used as the fundamental doctrine on which to erect an elaborate scheme for the explanation of the mind of God and the soteriological status of every man in the universe.[5] This was at some remove from the use predestinarians like Augustine, Luther, and Calvin had made of the doctrine. As Dillenberger and Welch have said, for Luther "predestination is a confession about the trustworthy character of

God . . ."; and "Calvin moved from faith to an elaboration of predestination as a way of showing that God is wholly the author of our faith and that every notion of work or merit must be rejected."[6] For Edwards also predestination is an existential affirmation that what a man is in faith, he is by the sovereign will of a trustworthy God. It is a way of affirming that faith is not a product of human nature, that it is not achieved through man's obedience to the law. Saving faith is predestined: it is by grace alone; a free, undeserved gift of God.

Regenerative conversion by grace, therefore, in which man is turned to a life of faith, is "immediate." We have seen how Edwards applies the term "immediate" to the work of God's Spirit to stress that He is unmediated by the natural power of His means. To emphasize much the same thing, "immediate" can take on the meaning of "instantaneous." As in the creation scene in Genesis, in the new birth "something is brought out of nothing in an instant. God speaks and it is done."[7] Regeneration by Word and Spirit is instantaneous in that it is a leap from an old way of being into a new way of being which is irreducible to the potentialities of the old way. There is a moment "when" the transition is made from old to new creaturehood. "God speaks and it is done." Conversion as an instantaneous transition does not mean, however, what it so often came to mean for revivalists: that the whole of regeneration is collapsed into one irrecoverable moment of time; or that the Christian should search out a moment of religious conversion-experience for his own assurance. Though instantaneous conversion is of the essence of regeneration, it does not exhaust the meaning of the new birth. There is in regeneration the progressive sanctification in which God continues throughout life to cleanse the elect of sin and assist them in the "race of life." In one sense, says Edwards, "grace is growing: from its first infusion, till it is perfected in glory, the kingdom of Christ is building up in the soul."[8] Although Edwards does select out of his surroundings certain instances of conversion as examples of the surprising work of God and does not deny that one may be able to state when his new birth occurred,[9] still the time of a person's reception of grace is not always obvious to him since the manner of the Spirit's operation is often "unsearchable and untraceable." And above all, one is to avoid a confidence in his religious experience since it breeds religious pride and a confidence in oneself rather than in God.[10] Within these circumscriptions Edwards affirms that regeneration is done at once and not gradually: it begins from the gift of grace and not from any gradual improvement of human nature prior to grace. When the elect are effectually called into faith by Word and Spirit, "there is something immediately put into their hearts, at that call, that is new, that there was nothing of there before, which makes them so immediately act in a manner altogether new, and so alien from what they were before."[11] In one respect the new birth is as gradual as the growth of the fetus in the womb; yet like the beginning of the fetus its actual beginning is all at once. "In the new birth there is certainly a very great change made in the soul" just as in the natural birth "when the rational soul is first infused, the foetus immediately upon it becomes a living creature and a man, that before had no life."[12]

Edwards' conception of instantaneous conversion, then, is grounded in the conviction that an immense chasm exists between nature and grace, a chasm that can be bridged only from the side of grace. Human nature's gradual improvement of itself can never produce the movement into saving faith. Like Augustine and Luther, Edwards rejects any Pelagian (for Edwards, "Arminian") scheme that allows men to take chief credit for their salvation by attributing the dawn of faith to natural human powers.[13] The new life in faith is given from beyond the capacities of human nature, no matter how those capacities are gradually improved.

A. B. Crabtree, in his interpretation of Edwards' theological anthropology, has claimed that Edwards "steps over the threshold of Catholic anthropology, and approaches the very center" of it when, in his doctrine of the Fall, he argues that man's natural abilities are retained but his spiritual principles lost through Adam. Edwards even contends, Crabtree continues, "that human nature is complete as human nature without the supernatural principles"; yet "instead of traversing from this point the road of semipelagianism as Catholic theology had so often done, he identifies human nature with radical and unmitigated evil and reaches a position scarcely to be distinguished from that of Flacius."[14] This claim is certainly correct to the extent that Edwards does employ the scholastic distinction between natural and supernatural principles in his description of the results of the Fall. But the distinction results in neither Pelagianism nor a devaluation of human nature as such. Edwards' explanation of the consequences of the Fall is:

The case with man was plainly this: when God made man at first he implanted in him two kinds of principles. There was the *inferior* kind, which may be called NATURAL, being the principles of mere human nature; such as self-love, with those natural appetites and passions, which belong to the *nature of man*, in which his love to his own liberty, honour, and pleasure, were exercised. . . . Besides these, there were *superior* principles, that were spiritual, holy, and divine, summarily comprehended in divine love; wherein consisted the spiritual image of God, and man's righteousness and true holiness. . . . Which though withdrawn, and man's nature forsaken of these principles, human nature would be human nature still. . . . When man sinned and broke God's covenant, and fell under his curse, these spiritual principles left his heart. . . .[15]

On the one hand, the corruption of the *imago dei* through the withdrawal of the spiritual principles means that man and his natural powers avail nothing before God for salvation; on the other, however, it means that man still remains man after the Fall—*on one level at least*—on the level of natural human concerns. Edwards does not attempt, through the notion of the retained natural principles, to preserve the Semi-Pelagian "natural inclination to virtue" after the Fall.[16] Edwards' language is unambiguous: man is "naturally blind in the things of religion";[17] "all that a natural man doth is sin."[18] "The inside of the body of man is full of filthiness, contains his bowels that are full of dung, which represents the corruption and filthiness that the heart of man is naturally full of."[19] Because of this filth and corruption, fallen man is hardly "inclined naturally to virtue"; on the contrary, he is inclined away from love of God and his glory, i.e., away from true virtue.[20]

The corruption of the *imago*, however, does not spell the destruction of the goodness of human nature. It will become clear in the next chapter that the "natural principle of self-love" retained by sinful man is not, in and of itself, an evil. Above all, the human faculties are not destroyed in their natural operations by the removal of the supernatural principles. Natural man is still capable, for example, of the reasoning power which sets him apart from inferior animals.[21] To be sure, the supernatural operations of the faculties are lost. When fallen man sets himself to worship God through the employment of his natural faculties, he worships not the true God but idols. Natural man is so constituted that his faculties are hindered *about the things of religion*.[22] Edwards has in mind much the same notion championed by Luther and Calvin: fallen, unenlightened reason is of use and value in the Kingdom of Earth or in the realm of man's political, domestic, and natural affairs; but in the Kingdom of Heaven, or *coram deo*, it is of itself a servant of sin and avails nothing for righteousness.[23] Every man's loss of supernatural principles through Adam's fall does not signify that men thereby become something less than men by becoming absolute instances of evil. Rather, the evil arises when man turns to "things religious"; then the natural human principles are not kept in their proper place.

These inferior principles are like *fire* in a house; which we say is a good servant, but a bad master; very useful while kept in its place, but if left to take possession of the whole house, soon brings all to destruction. Man's love to his own honour, separate interests, and private pleasure, which before was *wholly subordinate* unto love to God and regard to his authority and glory, now disposes and impels him to pursue those objects, without regard to God's honour, or law. . . .[24]

The result is idolatry. On the basis of his natural principles, man sets up his "separate interests" and "private pleasure" in the room of the Creator; in this the "apostasy of man does summarily consist."[25]

Edwards' view of the fallenness of man and of the sovereignty of God's grace in saving faith is the basis for his approach to a question made momentous by the Reformed stress on the "immediacy" of the Spirit. What is the role of the "means of grace," of the vehicles of grace in history? The subject of the means of grace became all the more problematic as some groups growing out of the Puritan tradition queried: If God's Spirit is not efficacious by power inhering in the means, why not dispense with those means altogether? We discussed in the preceding chapter how Scripture and preaching may be understood as means of grace. There are for Edwards other means of grace as well: the Christian Sabbath, prayer, the instruction of Christian parents, and the Church in its worship and practice.[26] Baptism and the Lord's Supper are means of grace only in a very restricted sense: they are instituted as seals of faith for professors of faith (in the case of infant baptism, for children of professors) rather than, like preaching, as converting ordinances for those outside faith as well.[27] At this point Edwards set himself against the position of his grandfather Stoddard, involving himself in a controversy that resulted in his dismissal from the Northampton pulpit in 1750—a controversy that will occupy us in our concluding part. "Seeking," or the attendance on the means of grace to the end of finally receiving faith, is itself also a means of grace. Seeking salvation is a means when it brings man to an awareness of his own helplessness and to a despair in his own strength. Finding is not guaranteed by the seeking; God converts in his own good time. Intense seeking after faith—say through prayer—does not guarantee faith; nevertheless seeking can be a valid means of grace.

It is therefore quite a wrong notion that some entertain, that the more they do, the more they shall depend upon it. Whereas the reverse is true: the more they do, or the more thorough they are in seeking, the less will they be likely to rest in their doings, and the sooner will they see the vanity of all that they do. . . . You must undertake the business of seeking salvation upon these terms, and with no other expectations than this, that if ever God bestows mercy it will be in his own time; and not only so, but also that when you have done all, God will not hold himself obliged to show you mercy at last.[28]

Douglas J. Elwood has suggested that Edwards joined that line of Puritan theologians who inclined away from outward means of grace by emphasizing the internals of grace in the immediate operation of the Holy Spirit.[29] But Edwards makes it quite clear that the internal, immediate operation of the Holy Spirit replaces neither the outward means of grace nor the human seeking through the means. He joins a host of other Puritans in holding that God operates within man immediately but always in conjunction with the external means of grace. External means, particularly church forms and ceremonies, prevent grace from "disordering" the personal and social aspects of human life: regeneration by the Holy Spirit is ordered by being given in conjunction with the ordinances and means of grace established historically in the Church.[30] And the human seeking of salvation within the means of grace provides the framework within which God chooses to work by his Holy Spirit when converting man.[31] Nevertheless—and this is Edwards' principal point on this subject—*God has sovereign disposal over the means and the striving attached to them.* It is the power of God alone which decides the efficacy of the means. In fact, "God may sometimes make use of very unlikely means, and bestow salvation on men, who are under very great disadvantages; but he does not bestow grace wholly without any means."[32] At all times "it is of God that we have these means of grace, and it is God that makes them effectual. . . . It is of God that we have ordinances, and their efficacy depends on the immediate influence of the Spirit of God."[33] Hence means are not unnecessary, but it is the height of pride and "vain self-flattery" for a man to believe that seeking salvation in the means will itself give him the salvation:

Some hope by their strivings to obtain salvation of *themselves.* They have a secret imagination, that they shall by degrees, work in themselves sorrow and repentance of sin, and love towards God and Jesus Christ. Their striving is not so much an earnest seeking to God, as a striving to do themselves that which is the work of God.[34]

There is in Edwards' thought, therefore, no devaluation of the outward means of grace or of attendance on them but, rather, a typically Calvinist confession that only by the power of the grace of God do they become means of evoking faith and repentance.

Puritan theology had frequently articulated the relation between nature and grace, and between striving for faith and the actual receipt of faith, in terms of a doctrine of "preparation for salvation." This doctrine became the focus of some important controversies within the Puritan fold, and it caused Jonathan Edwards no little concern in his attempt to formulate his theory of conversion. The doctrine of preparation was part of what E. S. Morgan has called a Puritan "morphology of conversion," a formal structure in which each stage in the conversion of a sinner could be located and distinguished from the next stage; "so that a man could check his eternal condition by a set of temporal and recognizable signs."[35] The morphology was made up of a stage of preparation, divided into various steps, which preceded the stage of saving faith. For Richard Sibbes and Thomas Shepard, the steps in preparation were conviction of sin, compunction for sin and humiliation or self-abasement before God.[36] For William Perkins they were man's living under the outward means of grace, man's consideration of the law in relation to his own practice, his recognition of his particular sins and his fear of punishment in view of that recognition.[37] Whatever individual steps were enumerated, Puritan theologians were usually agreed that God first prepares man for the reception of faith through the law. As William Ames said, "that man be prepared to receive the promises, the application of the Law doth ordinarily goe before to the discovery of sin, and inexcusableness and humiliation of the sinner. . . ."[38]

In a diary entry of August 12, 1723, Edwards indicates that his acquaintance with the Puritan morphology of conversion was anything but passing or insignificant for his life and thought:

The chief thing, that now makes me in any measure to question my good estate, is my not having experienced conversion in those particular steps, wherein the people of New England, and anciently the Dissenters of Old England, used to experience it. Wherefore, now resolved, never to leave searching, till I have satisfyingly found out the very bottom and foundation, the real reason, why they used to be converted in those steps.[39]

Edwards did witness the steps, to a degree, in his own religious experience and in the "surprising conversions" which occurred in his parish in the 1730s. Prior to his receiving the "new sense" of faith, Edwards suffered legal convictions and "violent inward struggles" over his sinful state;[40] and in his account of conversions in Northampton, he refers to "distressing apprehensions of the anger of God," terrors and fears which grew out of conviction of sin and which preceded the sense of God's grace and mercy.[41] Theologically also Edwards must have discovered, at least partially, the "bottom and foundation" of the steps in conversion, for he definitely incorporated three steps of preparation in his scheme of salvation. God's usual manner of bringing man to faith is to convict him of his sin, give him displeasure against that sin, and make him humble through an awareness of his unworthiness of salvation.[42] In short, Edwards contended, in agreement with his forefathers, that man is prepared by the law for the reception of grace and that usually this preparation involves legal conviction, compunction, and humiliation.

Yet the matter could not rest there for Edwards. The "bottom and foundation" of the problem lies not simply in *whether* there is a legal preparation for faith but more pertinently in the *manner* and *nature* of the preparation. Two consequences could, and sometimes did, follow from the Puritan notion of preparation, consequences which must have continued to plague Edwards as he sought to apply the steps to his "own estate": (1) so structuring conversion that the scheme of salvation becomes frozen into a *fixed* and *necessary order* of steps; and (2) confusing law with gospel by forcing the beginnings of saving faith back into legal preparation itself. Both became results in some of the seventeenth-century American Puritans' elaborate defense of the preparation scheme over against the antinomianism of Anne Hutchinson and her associates, who inclined away from any legal preparation and toward an unprepared gift of grace in conversion.[43] Edwards sought to avoid both consequences while embracing a doctrine of legal preparation for salvation.

Admitting that man is normally convicted and humbled by the divine law written into nature and Scripture before he receives grace, Edwards refuses to grant that this process can be so universalized that it must of necessity apply to every man, or to different men in the same way. In the first place, the work of the Holy Spirit cannot be so schematized that its *modus operandi* is fixed to a definite, rigid, and clearly discernible pattern:

. . . nothing proves it to be necessary, that all those things which are implied or presupposed in an act of faith in Christ must be plainly and distinctly wrought in the soul, in so many successive and separate works of the Spirit that shall be, each one, plain and manifest, in all who are truly converted. . . . What we have principally to do with, in our inquiries into our own state, or directions we give to others, is the nature of the effect that God has brought to pass in the soul. As to the steps which the Spirit of God took to bring that effect to pass, we may leave them to him.[44]

The great terrors of conscience, which normally arise out of being struck by God's demands prior to the gift of converting grace, *may* come *after* conversion.[45] Though it may be properly argued that one will never really receive Christ in faith until he is humbled to the extent of depending no longer on his own righteousness, "yet this won't prove that pride must first be mortified and humility infused in a distinct work before conversion."[46] Furthermore, against the attempt to stretch *all* legal preparation over a long period of trial and struggle, Edwards points out that in many accounts of conversion in the Scriptures the whole of conversion is wrought "in a few hours" without any lengthy period of conviction and humiliation,[47] and that some genuine conversions in Northampton had not been preceded by lengthy preparations.[48] Edwards' argument on this point is a considered rejection of the view of Solomon Stoddard, who, in his concern to embrace in the visible church not only professing believers but also those long struggling in preparation, had insisted that "ordinarily we find that much time is consumed in the work of preparation."[49] Therefore, while recognizing that preparation for salvation *usually* involves certain steps, Edwards will neither fix the work of the Spirit to an inflexible series of stages nor confine human experience to a universal pattern of conversion.

Those Puritan theologians who were prone to see the beginnings of faith in legal preparation usually claimed that there was a chasm separating preparation and justifying faith; but the chasm was bridged—perhaps unintentionally—from the side of preparation in the attempt to stress the necessity of the law in conversion. Thomas Shepard, for example, remarked that a gulf separated the last step of preparation (humiliation) from faith, but the gap was filled when he said, "Faith . . . is to be expected, not only as begotten in us, but as it is in the begetting of it in the conviction and humiliation of every sinner."[50] Edwards holds with the English Puritan John Owen that although the sinner convicted by the law may be capable of justifying faith, he does not yet have that faith through the conviction.[51] Edwards will turn neither to the antinomian extreme of eliminating legal preparation as the normal antecedent of faith, nor to the legalistic extreme which posits the beginning of faith in legal conviction. The work of the law on natural man in preparing him for faith through conviction, compunction, and humiliation still leaves him as natural man. He is not yet a recipient of "special grace"; he receives only "common grace" or the common operation of the Spirit. The Spirit simply assists the natural human principles "against the prejudicing, blinding tendency of sin" so that one is aware of his sin, guilt, and impending eternal misery.[52] The faculties do not have in legal preparation that new spiritual basis which founds the act of faith; they are assisted to do what they do naturally or from themselves.

That conviction of guilt which a natural man may have from the Spirit of God is only by the Spirit's assisting natural conscience the better and more fully to do its office. Therein common grace differs from special. Common grace is only the assistance of natural principles; special is the infusing and exciting supernatural principles; or, if these words are too abstruse, common grace only assists the faculties of the soul to do that more fully which they do by nature. . . . But special grace causes the faculties to do that that they do not by nature. . . .[53]

The *source* or *origin* of conviction, humiliation, and faith is therefore of determinative significance for Edwards.[54] With regard to the New England revivals this meant that the terrors of conscience, experienced at the hands of the revivalist who proclaimed the threats of the law and God's judgment, were not marks of conversion to faith. When one is prepared for faith by the law or by the Spirit's "common" operation through the law, this preparation is not yet what is prepared for, viz., the faith given through the saving work of the Spirit.

Put another way, one is not truly or *savingly* convicted and humbled in legal preparation. One's heart is not "wean'd" by the law from sin and self-righteousness.

No sound divine will assert that sin is mortified in order of time before grace is infused. The truth is that the case is the same with regard to the objects of his lusts and a man's own righteousness. There is a legal work commonly preparing the way for a man's being weaned from each. A legal conviction to beat and force him from his own righteousness and a legal repentance to beat him off from the objects of his lust. But the heart is not truly wean'd from either till grace is infused.[55]

It follows that there is need for not only a legal but also an "evangelical" conviction, humiliation, and repentance. In the latter only is the soul really weaned from sin. Only in conjunction with faith does the law complete its work. Conviction of and compunction for sin, to the extent not only of recognizing one's sin but of sensing it in all of its depth as an affront to God, is a companion of the sensing of the gospel-comforts in faith. Similarly, evangelical humiliation and joyful faith "keep company together." "So that at the same time that God lifts up the soul with comfort, and joy, and inward sweetness, he casts it down with abasement."[56] Repentance can be taken in two ways for Edwards: to connote a sense of and sorrow for our sinfulness; and to refer to the actual turning to the mercy of God for the remission of sin. When the latter, and for Edwards the more proper, sense is intended, "faith is in it."[57] Evangelical repentance is, in fact, part of the whole movement of faith. One must still distinguish between faith and repentance since their immediate objects are different: repentance has reference primarily to the evil to be delivered from (sin), while faith has reference to both "evil to be delivered from and good to be obtained" (salvation).[58] "It is true, repentance, in its more general, abstracted nature, is only a sorrow for sin and forsaking of it, which is a duty of natural religion"; but evangelical repentance is a movement of faith; that is, "a dependence of soul on the Mediator for deliverance from sin, is of the essence of it."[59] Edwards' distinction between the legal and the evangelical relation to sin is not an attempt to undercut the need for the terrorizing and convicting work of the law: much

of Edwards' preaching indicates the belief that legal preparation is God's usual way of dealing with sinful man. But law
finds its end and fulfillment only in gospel; conviction, humiliation, repentance, and faith become "like strings in concert:
if one is struck, others sound with it,"[60] when experienced
through faith in the good news of the Christ.

Edwards' position on "preparation" provides the context
in which he is to be appraised regarding the role for which
he has so often been remembered: a proclaimer of the terrors of the law and the wrath of God. Leonard Trinterud
points out that the object of eighteenth-century preaching of
the terrors of the law, which was indigenous to Puritan
theology, was "not to frighten men into heaven, but that
they might be 'slain by the Law'" or "be compelled to
abandon, in the face of the law's requirements, any pretense
of not needing salvation through grace."[61] Edwards was
fully in sympathy with such preparatory preaching, and there
is no denying that in many of his sermons God's wrath and
the sinner's jeopardy and condemnation before the law are
depicted in vivid images. It is really inaccurate to subsume
all these homilies under the category "hell-fire sermons." Even
the famous Enfield sermon, "Sinners in the Hands of an
Angry God," does not have hell-fire as its predominating
image. As E. H. Cady has discerned in his study "The Artistry
of Jonathan Edwards," "by almost any count, fire-imagery
amounts to little more than a quarter of the total figures" in
the Enfield sermon. "Hell is in [the] picture, but only at
the periphery. The focus is on the predicament of the sinner, how dreadfully he dangles *just before* he plunges to
eternal agony, and while he has time to repent and be saved."
Edwards employs the metaphors of the spider dangling over
a fire by a thin thread and of man's walking on slippery
places where a quick fall is always a live possibility, when
speaking of the sinner's predicament—rather than dwelling on
"color words" or "objective heat words."[62] But Edwards did
intend to represent in this and other imprecatory sermons
man's condemnation by the unfulfilled demands of God's
law, and the wrath of God that burned toward the sinner.
He intended to represent, in H. Richard Niebuhr's words,
"the precariousness of life's poise . . . the utter insecurity of

men and of mankind which are at every moment . . . ready
to plunge into the abyss of disintegration. . . ."[63] By being
so brought to an awareness of the life of sin, natural man
may be legally prepared for the reception of grace and mercy.
The wonder and joy of God's grace in Christ are more readily
sensed when sinners are "brought to reflect upon the sins of
their lives, and to see the wickedness of their hearts."[64]

Edwards sometimes preached sermons which tended to
dwell on God's wrath without much reference to God's
mercy, sermons explicitly preparatory and legal rather than
evangelical.[65] On the basis of such sermons one might argue
with some justification that, in these sermons themselves at
least, the fulfillment of law in gospel, the *telos* of legal preparation in faith, is not always apparent. But Edwards conceived the task of the preacher to be not simply the awakening of terrors in the conscience of the sinner through such
exposition of the law. In his own words, ministers "are set in
the church of God . . . to be the instruments of leading
souls to the God of all consolation . . . they are sent as
Christ was, and as coworkers with him, to preach good tidings
to the meek, to bind up the broken hearted. . . ."[66] And
running through many of those sermons which on the surface
are concerned exclusively with God's wrath, is a proclamation
of the merciful God whose wrath yet burns toward sin. There
is in "Sinners in the Hands of an Angry God," the sermon so
often taken as representative of Edwards' pathological preoccupation with a God of wrath, a stream of hope and mercy
running through the exposition of the wrath of God. *If* God
should withdraw his hand, the sinner would fall into destruction. *If* God should let sinful man go, he would swiftly "descend and plunge into the bottomless gulf."[67] This is a "big
if": it points to the angry God who is yet merciful even in his
wrath. As W. L. Anderson has said, "God's hand is the sole
power that prevents the fall into perdition. It is indeed the
hand of 'an angry God,' yet its grasp is so controlled by mercy
that the sinner 'has not dropped into hell.' "[68] Certainly, the
sinner is not to ignore his precariousness by assuring himself
that God is merciful—at any moment God could let him drop.
God's mercy does not cancel His wrath. But the God whose
ire is thoroughly provoked by sin is the same God who grants

"pardon for the greatest sinner."[69] Edwards never loses sight of this promise. And for him the end of being awakened by the law to the wrath of God is not that awakening itself but the reception of grace in the gospel.[70] The fulfillment of legal preparation lies in evangelical conviction, humiliation, and repentance; only in this fulfillment is the soul really "wean'd" from sin.

Edwards does not confine the use of the law to its preparatory work in conversion. The law is not only the "schoolmaster" which leads men to Christ by flailing them into a conviction of their helplessness and need for a Saviour; it is also "a rule of life," a "directory" according to which the people of God are to walk.[71] Edwards has in mind what were for John Calvin the "first" and "third" functions of the law: the function of condemning man of his unrighteousness; and that of teaching believers God's will and arousing them to obedience.[72] But Edwards will not identify faith with a living under the law according to either of the law's functions. The terrors of conscience which spring from the first function are only *preparation* for saving faith; and, though the man of faith has in the law a guide for his life as a Christian, the good moral life lived according to the law is not itself justifying faith and is not productive of the salvation received in faith. Man is not saved by any goodness or righteousness arising from his obedience to the law, "let it be an obedience to the ceremonial law, or a gospel obedience, or what it will. . . ."[73]

CHAPTER V

THE POSTURE OF FAITH

Edwards' portrait of the act of faith culminates in his view of the posture of the man of faith. In sum, the posture is this: one who receives religious faith is inclined away from himself and his own religious experiences toward the God who is the object and possibility of his faithful existence. God through his Spirit abides within the human heart; yet He does not rest man in his inward experiences but directs him in love and trust toward the truth of the Word. This "ecstatic" or projective posture of faithful existence became the foundation on which Edwards would address himself to those eighteenth-century enthusiasts who had no hesitancy in claiming their own religious experiences and spiritual gifts as the essence and authority of the religious life. Edwards would reply that one who is in faith does not turn for his confidence to his own experience—religious or otherwise—but stands out toward God and his promises in "disinterested love" and in trust and humility. Rather than human selfhood being lost or abandoned in this faithful projection (in some kind of mystical absorption), authentic creaturely identity is gained in the presence of the Divine.

Love to God

We remarked earlier that Edwards includes the human act of love in saving faith in two ways: either as the working love directed primarily to the neighbor, which is at least potentially included in every act of faith; or as the propensity of heart directed to God, involved in the very essence of faith itself. The latter, love to God, characterizes the stance of the man of faith. Faith is loving the God who reveals himself in the Word:

That saving faith implies in its nature divine love, is manifest by 1 John v. i, "Whosoever believeth that Jesus is the Christ, is born of God; and every one that loveth him that begat, loveth him also that is begotten of him." The apostle's design in this verse seems to be, to show the connection there is between a true and sincere respect to God, and a respect to and union with Christ; so that he who is united to the Son, is so to the Father, and *vice versa.*[1]

But the inclusion of love, as a uniting propensity of heart, in saving faith is demanded not only by the nature of the act of faith; above all, it is demanded by the nature of the *object* of the act. God revealed in the Christ and encountered by faith in all his holiness and excellency demands the response of love.[2] Faith is *constituted* as a loving encounter with divine truth not simply by reference to its being a human act of love but by reference to the human act and its object in conjunction. For it is the object of the act joined with the act, and not human cognition and volition *in abstracto*, which qualifies or specifies the act of faith in a certain way. The love in faith is qualified as a particular kind of love—viz., as *holy love*—by its *holy object*: "A holy love has a holy object: the holiness of love consists especially in this that it is the love of that which is holy, as holy, or for its holiness; so that 'tis the holiness of the object, which is the quality whereon it fixes and terminates."[3]

H. Richard Niebuhr, who was apparently influenced by the thought of Edwards in his theory of values, pinpoints what Edwards is after in his notion of the love to God included in faith: "To have faith in something as able to give value to our lives is to love it. Without such love there is no faith." The revelation toward which faith lovingly inclines is less "the disclosure of the essence of objective being to minds than the demonstration to selves of faithful, truthful being."[4] The object of faith presents itself principally not as an object for dispassionate reflection but as the ultimate value that gives value to the deciding, acting human self and that evokes a loving response to it from the self. In Edwards' terms, the object of faith is the holy and excellent God in Christ who "nearly concerns ourselves,"[5] the Truth which gives value to our lives or qualifies and specifies the self in a particular way. God is, for Edwards, always the "objective ground" of faith, but He is the objective ground which qualifies the human self. He is not a remote object, but one concerned "for us." Since it is this God with whom faith is concerned, love is included in the very essence of faith. The God revealed in Christ is not a truth properly attended to principally as an abstraction; He is the Truth and Good in One who calls forth "an entire yielding of the mind and heart . . . with the belief, and with the inclination and affection."[6]

It may seem strangely inconsistent with this consideration of God as the qualifying object of the human self to find Edwards maintaining that the love to God in faith is "disinterested." Faithful love to God is a love directed to God himself, a love which transcends consideration of the private interests of the human self. This view of love certainly accords with Edwards' position that genuine religion does not allow one to rest content with human states and experiences, but it would appear to contradict the proposal that God revealed in Christ "concerns ourselves" and is loved as such. One critic of Edwards suggests, in fact, that Edwards allows soteriology to drop into the background by understanding love to God apart from Christ's saving benefits.[7] That is to say, soteriology or the doctrine of salvation is concerned with what God has done *for man* in Christ; and one must apparently let the importance of this doctrine go unnoticed if he insists one is to love God in Christ disinterestedly, or apart from consideration of what is at stake for him the lover. Edwards' son, Jonathan Edwards, Jr., correctly discerned, however, that disinterested love to God did not mean for his father that the human self has no interest at stake in its love to God; rather it meant that regard for God "is *direct* and benevolent *not selfish*, nor arising from selfish motives."[8] The disinterested love to God is not a love apart from consideration of Christ's offer of salvation and what this means for man, but it is a love founded on something other than a consideration of Christ's offer from a selfish perspective. The distinction is perhaps a subtle one, but it is a distinction fundamental to Edwards' notion of faith and to his ethics. Faith is ecstatic in the sense that faithful man stands out ahead of himself in the inclining love to God. The love of God for himself is the projection of faith beyond man's selfish interests, and this projection is the foundation for man's loving other men authentically.

The nature of disinterested love to God is explicated in

the second and third genuine signs of gracious affections, developed in Edwards' *Treatise on Religious Affections*. (1) "The first objective ground of gracious affections," which essentially consist in holy love, "is the transcendently excellent and amiable nature of divine things, as they are in themselves; and not any conceived relation they bear to self, or self-interest."[9] (2) "Those affections that are truly holy, are primarily founded on the loveliness of the moral excellency of divine things. Or . . . a love to divine things for the beauty and sweetness of their moral excellency, is the first beginning and spring of all holy affections."[10]

In his attention to these two signs, Edwards attempts to assign what is primary to religious love rather than exclude what is secondary or appendant. The excellent and amiable nature of Christ, Scripture, and God ("divine things") calls forth the loving propensity of heart *not completely apart from* self-interest *in every respect* but apart from it as far as the *foundation* of love is concerned. As the founding object of the love in faith, God is loved without ambition. When love is grounded in self-love, it is not the love included in faith but the love that the most corrupted man can display. "Christ plainly speaks of this kind of love, as what is nothing beyond the love of wicked men, Luke 6:32: 'If ye love them that love you, what thank have ye? For sinners also love those that love them.'"[11] Unregenerate man loves God on the basis of his own narrow interests in and desires for the good of his self. The man of faith is first projected upon God on the basis of, and for the sake of, God's excellence and truth, and then he sees "God's love; and great favor" to him.[12] So self-interest is not precluded in faithful love, but it is included secondarily. "The saint's affections begin with God; and self-love has a hand in these affections consequentially, and secondarily only."[13] He first loves God for his revealed beauty and holiness, and consequentially loves Him out of consideration of what good God can bring him.

In one respect, self-love is included in the love to God from the beginning—so long as the self-love meant is simply "the general capacity of loving" or the loving of what is pleasing to oneself. But this is really too broad a definition of self-love.

Self-love may be taken for the same as his loving whatsoever is grateful or pleasing to him . . . it is undoubtedly true, that whatever a man loves, his love may be resolved into his loving what he loves—if that be proper speaking. If by self-love is meant nothing else but a man's loving what is grateful or pleasing to him, and being averse to what is disagreeable, this is calling *that* self-love, which is only a general capacity of loving, or hating; or a capacity of being either pleased or displeased; which is the same thing as a man's having a faculty of will. For if nothing could be either pleasing or displeasing, agreeable or disagreeable to a man, then he could incline to nothing, and will nothing.[14]

If self-love means the self in its inclining capacities to love what is pleasing, self-love is involved in faithful love from the start and not simply secondarily. When man is inclined toward God in holy love, he is qualified and specified as a willing, loving self and is not dispossessed of his selfhood through the loss of human powers. But in its more restricted and, for Edwards, more proper meaning, self-love is not a primary element in holy love. For here self-love means "a man's regard to his confined *private self*, or love to himself with respect to his *private interest*."[15] When such love becomes the basis of love to God, the love may not really be a love to God at all. It may be simply a gratitude directed toward a God conceived after a man's own imagination, toward a vision of God distorted by sinful man's myopia. For example, the man of unfaith may pretend to love God because he is grateful that God is merciful and good and yet overlook the truth that this same God is a God of justice whose wrath burns toward human sin.[16] Here God is filtered through man's "confined private interest" in salvation and is not loved as the God of both mercy and justice.

Expressed in terms of Edwards' third sign of gracious affections, the love in the new sense of faith inclines toward the *moral* as well as toward the *natural* perfections of God. The moral attributes of God are those "which God exercises as a moral agent, or whereby the heart and will of God are good, right, and infinitely becoming, and lovely; such as his righteousness, truth, faithfulness, and goodness; or, in one word, his holiness." The natural perfections are those that define God's "greatness; such as his power, his knowledge whereby he knows all things, and his being eternal, from ever-lasting to everlasting, his omnipresence, and his awful and terrible majesty."[17] Man without faith may sense God's om-nipotence, omniscience, eternity, or majesty—and love God on account of those attributes. But this is not the sense of faith which "tastes" God's holiness or moral attributes—a tasting which includes in its nature a love for God's holiness on account of the beauty of that holiness itself. One may sense the awful majesty of God's judgment on sin and grasp at God out of fear. But then the will is not really gained, the enmity of heart against God is not really destroyed, as when the man of faith has a "glimpse of the moral and spiritual glory of God."[18] Only to the new sense of faith does the beauty of holiness become "sweet to the taste."

We may now return to the crucial question about "disin-terested love." Is the love to God for himself, or for the sake of his own holiness, a love to God apart from his revelation in the Son? It would seem that if the believer loves God pri-marily without regard to the benefits he receives for himself through Christ, he loves God without regard to the divine manifestation of grace in the Christ. Edwards' answer is that one must distinguish between two ways in which God's Word of grace may appear attractive to man in Christological reve-lation:

either as *bonum utile*, a profitable good to me, that which greatly serves my interest, and so suits my self-love; or as *bonum formosum*, a beautiful good in itself, and part of the moral and spiritual ex-cellency of the divine nature. In this latter respect it is that the true saints have their hearts affected, and love captivated by the free grace of God *in the first place*.[19] [Italics mine in last phrase]

This distinction is illustrated in the difference between a man's willingness not to be damned and his willingness to receive Christ as Saviour. In the former case, one's inclination of will "goes no further than self, it never reaches Christ. You are willing not to be miserable; that is, you love yourself, and there your will and choice terminate."[20] The willingness to receive Christ, however, fixes and terminates on the holy God revealed. It neither arises from nor ends in self-interest but is founded on, qualified by, and projected upon God himself.

God is not lovingly known in faith apart from Christ and his benefits for man, but he is not primarily lovingly known on the basis of a *calculation of Christ's benefits according to one's own private interests*, which would transform the glory and wonder of God in Christ into a mere human utility. God revealed in Christ as "a profitable good to me" is not excluded in the affection of love in faith, but such a consideration is not the ground of the affection. Grace as "a beautiful good in itself" is the ground of the affection and of the self-interest in the affection. The question for Edwards is not whether God draws forth the volitional cognition of faith *either* as God in himself in Christ, transcendent of human interest, *or* as God for man and for human interest in salvation. The question is rather which is the foundation of the other. Edwards opts for the former as the basis since otherwise God is only "utilized" in love for the sake of man's self-interests. God is the Holy One who elicits from the saints a love for his own holiness. Faithful man's interests in salvation are consciously at stake in his love to God, but they have their basis in man's projective love in which God is loved for his own holiness and in which narrow human self-interest is transcended.

Joseph G. Haroutunian is probably correct in his judgment that Jonathan Edwards was first and last a "theologian of the Great Commandment."[21] Love to God finds an emphasis in Edwards' Protestant thought unparalleled by the earliest Protestant Reformers. Although both Luther and Calvin joined love to God with faith,[22] love was subordinate to faith both in emphasis and in order. This subordination was necessary because both Luther and Calvin viewed human love as primarily what Edwards calls "working love," a work which man performs from faith. Hence for the Reformers love to God was a good work flowing from and adorned by justifying faith[23]—the alternative was to involve works in justification and thereby contradict the whole Reformation argument against meritorious works in salvation. Edwards includes love in faith as that propensity of heart characteristic of the knowledge in the act of faith; and this love is stressed as of the very essence of, not merely the fruit of, faith. Here Edwards stands in much more affinity with his own century than he does with the sixteenth.[24] The question is whether Edwards' difference from the earliest Reformers in approach and emphasis spells, as well, a difference in substance. The answer to that question hinges on the way in which Edwards distinguishes meritorious *works* of love from the *act* of love in faith, a problem which will occupy us in our next chapter. At this point it is important to see that love to God is for Edwards of the very essence of the faith-act: it is faithful man's inclination toward God, his stance toward the God who reveals himself in all his holiness in the Word.

Trust and Humility

The posture of faith is characterized not only by the inclining love in its essence but also by the trust and humility integral to it. Trust and humility are partners of faith because of the tension involved in faithful existence. Rather than being possessed of sinless perfection, the man of faith lives in the tension between grace and the sin remaining in his heart. "A remaining depravity of heart in the greatest saints may be argued from the sins of most of those who are set forth in scripture as the most eminent instances and examples of virtue and piety."[25] Old man and new man "subsist together in the same person"—this forms the dialectic characteristic of true saints, in whom "grace dwells with so much corruption."[26] In fact, it is during the periods of "brightest illumination" by grace that the soul discovers how loathsome and polluted it is, "appearing like rottenness and corruption in that pure and holy light of God's glory."[27] Edwards adds that when one receives an authentic illumination by the Spirit, he is not of the opinion that he is "now perfectly free from sin, (according to the notion of the Wesleys and their followers, and some other high pretenders to spirituality in these days,). . . ."[28] Despite the somewhat exaggerated statement of Wesley's position on sin and perfection, Edwards is here adhering to a principle vital to Calvinist thought: sanctifying grace does not create sinless perfection in the saint, for as Calvin said following Augustine "there remains in a regenerate man a smoldering cinder of evil."[29] Ironically this sin remaining in the saints can be both a reason for rejoicing in the power of God and a source of further sin. On the one hand, God's work with the sinful saint is glorified in its continuing victory over its opposition: "It is a more glorious work of power to uphold a soul in a state of grace and holiness, and to carry it on till it is brought to glory, when there is so much sin remaining in the heart resisting . . . than it would have been to have kept man from falling at first, when Satan had nothing in man."[30] Yet the corruption remaining in the saints may also be the source of turning the work of God's Spirit into an occasion for further sin. For example, the saint may, by being weakened through his corruption, become so enraptured with the work of the Spirit in his life that he becomes proud of his own state of salvation, religious pride being the most abominable of sins.[31] At any rate, the tension between new and old man, between grace and sin remaining in the saints, is a mark of sainthood this side of the grave. It is corrective of the popular understanding of "puritan" to observe that Edwards and his Puritan forefathers could never enjoin that "do-good-ism" based on a simple confidence in man's moral perfectibility. The tension between the light of grace and the dark clouds of sin could build to such a pitch in the Puritan's experience that the result was what Richard Sibbes called a "holy despair" of himself and his own strength. Such despair was not a self-destructive attitude without hope: "A holy despair in ourselves is the ground of true hope. . . . In God the fatherless find mercy."[32] The Puritan used the diary to express this holy despair. As William Haller has put it, the diary "became the Puritan substitute for the confessional."[33] In its pages the Puritan "could fling upon his God the fear and weakness he found in his heart but would not betray to the world."[34] In his diary, kept with regularity only for a short period in the early 1720s, Edwards manifests the holy despair in his own strength as he flings his heart upon God:

Alas! how soon do I decay! O how weak, how infirm, how unable to do any thing of myself! What a poor inconsistent being! What a miserable wretch, without the assistance of the Spirit of God! While I stand, I am ready to think that I stand by my own strength, and upon my own legs; and I am ready to triumph over my spiritual enemies, as if it were I myself, that caused them to flee:—when ala I am but a poor infant, upheld by Jesus Christ. . . .[35]

The tension between sin and grace in the saint and th resultant despair in his own strength call for the projection c faith beyond the self's own self-contained "experience" c "estate" of salvation. In his "Personal Narrative" Edwards r marks on the truth of this for his own life:

The sweetest joys and delights I have experienced, have not bee those that have arisen from a hope of my own good estate; but in . direct view of the glorious things of the gospel. When I enjoy thi sweetness, it seems to carry me above the thoughts of my own es tate; it seems, at such times, a loss that I cannot bear, to take o my eye from the glorious, pleasant object I behold without me, t turn my eye in upon myself, and my own good estate.[36]

The eye of faith is fixed upon its object rather than upon it self. And though the object is not one isolated from the self it nevertheless is an object which itself constitutes man a faithful without being reduced to man's own estate. In fact it may appear to the believer that sin is more predominant ir his experience than grace; yet it does not follow that sin rules his heart. For the predominance of the love to God in faith derives "from the nature of the object loved, and the nature of the principle of true love" more than from "the *degree* of the principle."[37] That is to say, the supreme loveliness of the God loved, when joined with the principle of love granted by the Spirit, gives love predominance in the lover's heart and not the *degree* of the *exercise* of affection in the subject's act. Hence when the man of faith ceases to attend to his object and merely attends to himself in his own act— when he loses his holy despair of his own strength and trusts in his own "good estate"—he loses the moorings of faith.

Trust or hope (Edwards frequently uses the terms interchangeably) and brokenheartedness or humility are therefore concomitants of faith—both are marks of man's projection upon God. Trusting or hoping in the sufficiency of Christ revealed in the promises of the gospel is not the "first act" of faith, though it springs immediately from faith or is *implied* in the essence of faith. The "first act" or concern is simply inclining toward and embracing Christ with a sense of his mercy; "hope in the promises may immediately follow in a moment," but it does follow and is founded on that first act.[38] And when the hope does occur, it remains hope; it does not become complacent self-satisfaction. Thus "there is hope, that I *may* obtain justification by Christ, though there is not contained in its [faith's] essence a hope that I have obtained it."[39] As we shall have occasion to see later, this hope does not cancel a *present* enjoyment or assurance of salvation through faith—a present enjoyment and assurance that yet never become human possessions. Here Edwards is stressing that the man of faith does not hope in what he possesses or has obtained but in what is given from beyond him in what *God promises*. Trusting in God's promises in Christ is the opposite of a complacent satisfaction with what one already has. Faith involves a hoping beyond one's present spiritual possessions to what God will yet do:

The greatest eminency and perfection, that the saints arrive to in this world, has no tendency to satiety, or to abate their desires after more; but on the contrary, makes 'em more eager to press forwards; as is evident by the Apostle's words, "Forgetting the things which are behind, and reaching forth unto those things which are before, I press toward the mark." . . .[40]

Because authentic faith does not allow one to rest content with himself, humility is a mark of religious faith. Edwards is well aware that pride may pose as humility: one may be extremely proud of his own lowliness and say in his heart, " 'This is a great act of humiliation: it is certainly a sign of great humility in me, that I should feel thus, and do so'; his meaning is, 'This is great humility for me, for such a one as I, that am so considerable and worthy.' "[41] This is a confidence in human experience and is the opposite of true Christian humility. Genuine humility refuses to acknowledge as righteous *any* human experience, including humility itself.[42] Humility is not a self-contained possession; it is not something one "has" to which he can point. It is a relation. When one stands in relation with God, he is humbled: he is struck by the truth that he can claim no worthiness for his own part. There exists no humility "unless the creature feels his distance from God, not only with respect to his greatness, but also his loveliness."[43] In the presence of God one stands shorn of all merit and worth. "It is God's pleasure to manifest the weakness and unworthiness of the subject, at the same time that he displays the excellency of his power and the riches of his grace."[44] The man of faith is thus humbled regarding all his possessions: his hope lies beyond him, yet near him, in the just and merciful God revealed in Christ.

The Continuity of Faithful Selfhood

Inasmuch as in Edwards' vision grace is not continuous with human states and possessions, and inasmuch as the saint is simultaneously old man and new, the question arises as to whether there is any continuity to faithful selfhood. The man of faith cannot point to his own experiences and states of body and mind as self-constituting elements since self-contained human states do not preserve the miracle of faith. Does man then lose continuous selfhood in faith? Edwards' answer is that it is God himself who constitutes the subject as continuously faithful from moment to moment. He elaborates upon this idea under the rubrics of the Augustinian doctrine of "perseverance" and a philosophical theory of "identity."

The feature of stability in a godly man's life is God. Whatever changes he passes through in this tension-ridden life, the saint has as "his chosen portion" the God "who is unchangeable."[45] This means that though the saints are continually caught in the war between sin and grace, God will see to it not only that grace will be the dominant principle in the heart but also that grace will continue as such. The saints persevere in faith not by their own strength or goodness but by the power of God alone. "Seeing therefore that God manifests his all-conquering power in giving grace a place in the heart in spite of . . . enemies, he will doubtless maintain it there against their united efforts to root it out."[46] Grace as *inherent* in man does not fully explain the perseverance of grace against the opposition of sin. Adam is proof of that. "The principle of holiness in the hearts of our first parents, where it had no corruption to contend with, was overthrown." The recipient of grace is "kept from falling, not by the inherent power of grace itself, but as the Apostle Peter tells us (1 Pet. i. 5), 'by the power of God through faith.'"[47] The difference between a man persevering by inherent grace and his persevering by grace through faith is the difference between a man continuing a saved man by his own strength on the basis of grace already received and his continuing solely by the renewed efforts of God. It is a difference discernible in the contrast between the "covenant of works" made with Adam and the "covenant of grace" made with Christ. Adam was called upon by God to persevere by his own strength and merits on the basis of the divine gifts to him, but the man of faith has a mediator for his perseverance. "Thus the second Adam has persevered, not only for himself, but for us; and has been sealed to confirmed and persevering and eternal life as our head; so that all those that are his, and that are his spiritual posterity, are sealed in him to persevering life."[48] Man continues in faith by the power of God alone, and he is availed of that power through the mediatorial office of Jesus Christ to whom he is united in faith. Hence, it is all "one act of faith to commit the soul to Christ's keeping in this sense, viz., to keep it from falling."[49]

Edwards provides a philosophical principle to account for the continuity of the faithful self in his theory of personal identity. John Locke had suggested human consciousness as the principle of personal identity, his premise being that since man is basically a rational animal man's personal identity consists in the identical consciousness which accompanies thinking-being. "As far as this consciousness can be extended backwards to any past action or thought, so far reaches the identity of that person."[50] Edwards early disavowed Locke's position, arguing in the following manner: "Can any one deny, that it is possible, after my annihilation, to create two beings in the Universe, both of them having my ideas communicated to them, with such a notion of their having had them before, after the manner of memory, and yet be ignorant one of another; and, in such case, will any one say, that both these are one and the same person, as they must be, if they are both the same person with me."[51] In his lengthy treatise on original sin, Edwards develops a metaphysical principle to account for the identity of guilt between Adam and his posterity; the principle also accounts for the identity of all created entities. Created substance, he says, exists from moment to moment as continuous substance by "the *arbitrary* constitution of the Creator." What exists at each moment is an entirely *new* effect (i.e., not a new form of a preceding effect) of God's causation. For example, the

brightness of the *moon*, as we look steadfastly upon it, seems to be a *permanent* thing, as though it were perfectly the same brightness continued. But indeed it is an effect produced every moment. It ceases, and is renewed, in each successive point of time; and so becomes altogether a *new* effect at each instant; and no one thing that belongs to it is numerically the same that existed in the preceding moment.[52]

Created existence would be a throng of unconnected and discontinuous moments apart from the continuously unitive power of God. This, believes Edwards, is the proper philosophical interpretation for "In him we live, and move, and have our being."[53] Applied to the doctrine of original sin, the interpretation means that there is a continuity between the sin and guilt of the past and the sin and guilt of the present on the basis of the "divine establishment."[54] But the principle applies not to "bad habits and acts" alone; it applies to "good" ones as well. "It is this that must account for the continuance of any such thing, anywhere, as *consciousness* of acts that are past; and for the continuance of all *habits*, either good or bad: and on this depends everything that can belong to *personal identity*."[55] The man of faith exists as a man of faith from moment to moment not on the basis of his being a man of faith, but solely by the power and establishment of God. Both the origin and the continuance of faith are a result of the direct power of God; what a man of faith has in each moment does not guarantee him what he will have in the next. Apart from the divine continuance, man's faith would be an unconnected series of moments—his personal identity in faith would be lost.

Edwards' "Mysticism"

Edwards has occasionally been made by his interpreters to wear the mantle of "mysticism." Christian mysticism has had a long and influential history, and the popular assumption that it was a monolithic movement marked by an overbearing penchant for ghostly, extrasocial flights into the "other world" simply will not stand the historical test. In all probability, a case could be made that Edwards—especially in his views of the Holy Spirit and spiritual knowledge—shared attitudes with some of the great Western mystics. But this is not our concern here, for those who have dressed Edwards up as a "mystic" have nothing so historically refined in mind. It is important to deal with these mystical interpretations of Edwards because if Edwards is a mystic in their sense, much of what we have found Edwards saying about the posture of faith is seriously contradicted.

Those interpreters in the earlier part of this century who found a mysticism in Edwards have already provoked some sound rebuttals. Lately, however, the mantle has again been placed on Edwards from a slightly different approach. The earlier interpreters proposed that Edwards inwardly rebelled against the rigid objectivism of Calvinism (though he was forced by his time outwardly to embrace many of its forms) by dwelling on the internal communication of God to the soul. And he held to an idea of the mystical absorption of the individual in the absolute, an idea existentially testified to in Edwards' record of his own religious experience.[56] Clyde Holbrook has correctly replied to this: (1) Edwards stressed a warm conviction of God's presence, but he remained strongly committed to the "objectivism" of Calvinism in that his new sense of God was "of God's reality and beauty standing over and beyond man and the natural world." We have noticed in some detail this refusal of Edwards to blur the distinction between the object of faith and the human subject. (2) Edwards' description of his conversion experience is pervaded by the idea that God lies outside man and is one on whom the converted is *dependent*, not one in whom he becomes absorbed in mystical identity.[57] Thomas Schafer has added on this point that in Edwards' account of his personal experience of the Divine, "the infinite Being with which he seeks union always retains the element of personality; and Edwards, in his most abandoned raptures, never loses the sense of individual finite personality." Edwards' creaturely sense of sin "counteracts all tendencies toward complete identification with the divine."[58] Edwards does record in his "Personal Narrative" that upon thought of the excellency of the Supreme Being after reading I Timothy 1:17, it occurred to him "how happy I should be, if I might enjoy that God, and be rapt up to him in heaven, and be as it were swallowed up in him forever!" And he later experienced "a kind of vision" (not unlike St. Paul's being "caught up to the third heaven") when he was "sweetly conversing with Christ, and wrapt and swallowed up in God." It is significant, however, that this reaction was initially prompted by a scriptural passage stressing God's eternity, invisibility, and immortality, and that the following part of Edwards' narrative reveals that the vision of God did not mean absorption or loss of creaturely identity, for Edwards continued to have creaturely "longings" after God even at the height of his new sense of the Divine.[59] In all fairness to the early mystical-interpreters, it may be noted that a Neoplatonic metaphysic sometimes employed by Edwards suggests at points a monism in which the distinction between uncreated and created being is not always clear.[60] Yet the intention of the metaphysic is to stress the manifestation of the glory of God in all creation, and this overriding intention supersedes the spelling out in any detail the relation between the identity of the Creator and the identity of the creature. Furthermore, when Edwards speaks soteriologically rather than cosmologically, the traditional Calvinist gulf between Creator and creature is clearly maintained. A typical statement is one we have already quoted in part: "The glory of divine power and grace is set off with the greater lustre, by what appears at the same time of the weakness of the earthen vessel. It is God's pleasure to manifest the weakness and unworthiness of the subject, at the same time that he displays the excellency of his power and the riches of his grace."[61] Edwards apparently either did not see the possible contradiction between his Neoplatonist metaphysic and his Calvinism, or else he was willing to live with the contradiction.[62] At any rate, there is in Edwards' thought and own life no manifest attempt to absorb man into the divine in "mystical" identity.

Douglas J. Elwood has more recently renewed the mystical interpretation of Edwards, but with a slightly different approach. He contends that Edwards' mysticism is a Spirit-mysticism that has deep roots in the Puritan tradition. Although Edwards attempts to guard against an absolute identity between God and the creature, "Edwards' mysticism reaches its height in his identification of Christian grace with the actual presence of God in the human heart."[63] Elwood believes that there is for Edwards an internal and mystical union of God with the soul; here Edwards stresses along with certain other Puritans a personally and inwardly experienced grace rather than a grace experienced through outward means. We have already demonstrated that Edwards' view of the inward operation of grace never replaces an emphasis on the necessity of grace working in and through outward means. For that reason Edwards is not an heir of the Spirit-mysticism which appeared in segments of Puritan thought. As Jerald Brauer has shown, the radical Spirit-mystics of left-wing Puritanism not only shifted "from the orthodox Puritan stress on the personal operation of the Holy Spirit in salvation to the view that the Holy Spirit, in effecting man's salvation, dwells personally and substantially in a man's heart"; they also either "viewed all externals and even sacraments as things indifferent . . ." or else "repudiated all visible aspects of the Church. . . ."[64] Edwards certainly holds that the Spirit dwells "personally" and even "substantially" in the saint's heart, but this position never leads him to a slighting of the visible means of grace. But within Elwood's rendering is a remnant of the older mystical-interpreters of Edwards. He thinks that since for Edwards *God himself* is communicated to the saint by the Spirit, there is a "union, if not in some sense identity" between God and the human soul.[65] As we saw in our second chapter, *union* between the Spirit and the soul there is; but *identity* there is not. God in his Spirit communicates himself to the saint, but He joins the saint as the saint's new principle or foundation and not as human-absorbing divinity. "Union" means for Edwards "participation." The saint participates in, but is not absorbed in, the Holy Spirit. On the basis of the new holy principle, the saint inclines in love away from self-contained experiences toward God; he does not lose his creaturely selfhood, but gains it anew in that inclination. The ecstasy of faith is not a mystical rapture in which man is cut away from the historical dimensions of his being. Rather man is constituted a faithful historical being in his standing out toward his object in love (affection) and from Love (the Spirit).

One had best leave the mantle of "mysticism" for another wearer than Edwards, for it fits him loosely at best. Even when the term "mystic" is defined broadly as "one who claims to know God through a form of spiritual inwardness,"[66] it is not strictly applicable; for in Edwards "spiritual inwardness" never replaces but complements the visible means of grace and the outward orientation of faith.

PART TWO:

THE REALITY OF FAITH

CHAPTER VI

JUSTIFICATION BY FAITH

"For we hold that a man is justified by faith apart from works of law. . . . And to one who does not work but trusts him who justifies the ungodly, his faith is reckoned as righteousness" (Rom. 3:28, 4:5). The human sinner is justified before God by faith alone, apart from the contribution of human merit or obedience to God's law. This Pauline confession, which became the theological rallying point of the Protestant Reformation, became as well, in the history of the Protestant churches, a scriptural verity on which the heartiest reflection continued to be exerted. What has applied in theological history to other theological axioms applied equally to this one: the religious thinker in each generation was called upon to interpret a fundamental confession for his own time and place. The sixteenth-century Reformers had proposed certain standards for an interpretation of "justification by faith" and had, perhaps, sufficiently addressed themselves to the doctrine for their setting; but they had hardly closed the door on future interpretation. Each Protestant epoch found itself having to come to terms with a host of questions surrounding the doctrine. In what way is human act involved in salvation? And how does that involvement differ from a work that "achieves" or "merits" salvation? An enunciation of the claim that the proper Pauline meaning is that one is saved by the free grace of God through faith, and not by anything that man does—including his acting in faith—does not resolve the problems but pitches them into more complexities. Granting that justification is a free gift of God, how is the human subject taken up into the gift? In what way and why is a man's faith "reckoned for righteousness" and not his works of love? What sets faith apart as deserving of the all-important copula *by* when linking the sinner with his salvation? It is here, at the point of the linkage between faith and its reality, that Edwards interprets the substance of the doctrine of justification and delineates the meaning of salvation by faith.

A dilemma has usually presented itself to the heir of the Protestant Reformation in his attempt to relate the human element in faith to salvation by grace. On the one hand, he is tempted to break the link between faith and its reality in a "forensic" understanding of justification: salvation is a divine declaration that occurs over man's head, as it were. Here the theologian does, in one respect, preserve the freedom of God's grace and the gift-character of salvation: justification is God's pronouncement through Christ of the sinner's right- eousness apart from the contribution of anything from the sinner. But he would, in another respect, risk destroying the gift character of salvation by ignoring the act of the human recipient. For what is a gift without the reception of a re- ceiver? On the other hand, if one makes the divine gift of salvation conditional, even partially conditional, on the hu- man act of faith or on anything man himself does, salvation is not owing to a divine, sovereignly free gift but to human effort. And as Luther replied to Erasmus, even if one makes salvation dependent on "just a little" human contribution, this only cheapens one's Pelagianism—better, or at least bolder, to have a Pelagianism which would wrest most of sal- vation out of God's hands than a sly one that attempts to make the grand design of salvation dependent on a little hu- man effort. At any rate, Luther and Calvin, in their efforts to overcome the latter tendency in late medieval theology, were not unaware of the danger of the former tendency. Both theologians held strictly to the theory of the imputation of righteousness in order to preserve the freedom of God and exclude human merit in salvation. God reckons the sinner in all his sin as righteous; He does not first demand an act of righteousness from man or pour righteousness into the soul on the basis of which He then reckons man as righteous.[1] Nevertheless, justification is *by* faith—faith is man's indis- pensable link with the righteousness imputed. As Luther put it, faith is the acceptance of the shelter of righteousness un- der Christ's wings, and, as such, is the "mean" between Christ's own righteousness and its imputation to us.[2] Calvin said that man "grasps the righteousness of Christ through faith, and, clothed in it, appears in God's sight not as a sinner but as a righteous man."[3] More specifically, according to Calvin faith is the "empty vessel" which receives but does not of itself contribute to salvation; it is the human "instrument" which God sovereignly uses for man's reception of imputed righteousness.[4]

Edwards' Reformed heritage leaned heavily on Calvin's understanding of the "instrumental" character of faith. "Faith . . . receiving and resting on Christ and his righteousness, is the alone instrument of justification," stated the Puritan-Presbyterian Westminster Confession of Faith.[5] Justification is a divine forensic act; this divine forensic act is apprehended and received by faith. It follows, said Turrettini, that "what is only the instrument for receiving righteousness cannot be our righteousness itself formally."[6] Couched in the theological terminology of Protestant scholasticism, faith becomes the "instrumental cause" of salvation. "The meritorious cause is Christ's righteousness, and the instrumental cause of applying this is our faith; so that we are justified by faith."[7]

Jonathan Edwards intends to adhere unequivocally to the doctrine of imputation; yet he is not fully satisfied with the manner in which his Reformed tradition has attempted to involve the human act of faith in justification. He would reassert against the Arminianism which was lapping at American shores, and which he believed was becoming fashionable among "modern divines,"[8] the full intention of the doctrine of imputation: salvation is not dependent upon human effort, but upon divine initiative. Yet for Edwards this doctrine lacks substance apart from an adequate portrayal of the role of faith in justification—a role not properly represented by the "instrument" metaphor.

It is fully evident, says Edwards, that in the fourth chapter of Romans Paul speaks of the justification of the *ungodly*; hence "God, in justification, has no regard to any godliness of ours."[9] The ungodly man, man as sinner, is the one counted as righteous. And the righteousness that is counted as the righteousness of the ungodly is none other than the righteousness of Christ:

. . . by that righteousness being imputed to us, is meant no other than this, that that righteousness of Christ is accepted for us, and admitted instead of that perfect inherent righteousness that ought to be in ourselves: Christ's perfect obedience shall be reckoned to our

account, so that we shall have the benefit of it, as though we had
performed it ourselves. . . .[10]

The ungodly man who is reckoned as righteous has no righteousness in himself, no righteousness poured into his being,
on the basis of which he is then justified. Rather the righteousness which Christ earns and possesses inherently is imputed to the sinner in the place of that righteousness which
he should have inherently.

A delineation of the manifold features of Edwards' doctrine of atonement would lead us too far afield.[11] For our
purposes what is significant in his theory of the "at-one-ment"
accomplished between God and man is the way in which the
notion of imputation of righteousness is developed according
to Christ's two major functions in relation to divine justice.
Christ by his righteousness both satisfies the punitive demands of the law for sin and positively fulfills the law in
order to achieve the atonement. The former he accomplishes
through his sufferings, the latter through his perfect obedience unto death.

The sufferings of Christ answer the demands of the law, with respect
to the sins of those who believe in him; and justice is truly satisfied
thereby. And the law is fulfilled and answered by the obedience of
Christ, so that his righteousness should properly be our righteousness. Though not performed by us, yet it is properly and reasonably
accepted for us, as much as if we had performed it ourselves.[12]

When the righteousness of Christ is imputed to the sinner,
that elect sinner is availed of the advantages of both Christ's
sufferings and his obedience. There is for man both the remission of sin or the nonimputation of guilt and the positive
imputation of Christ's righteousness as man's own righteousness.[13]

Edwards' understanding of atonement and forensic imputation is definitely set within a *Weltanschauung* which conceives the universe, and the divine and human roles within
that universe, after the manner of a capacious court of law.
God, as both the judge and the offended, witnesses a heinous
crime against him in the fall of man. And following the view
developed by Anselm, Edwards attempts to point to the grav-
ity of man's fallenness by referring to sin as an "infinite

crime" which deserves an "infinite punishment."[14] Nothing the offender can do will rectify the situation: he, as finite man, can only give finite satisfaction. Hence Christ enters the court as man's divinely appointed intercessor, who as a divine person of infinite worth is able through his suffering and obedience to satisfy the demands of the divine law, adequately bear the wrath of God for man's sin, and restore order to a universe disordered by sin.[15] God reckons Christ's suffering and obedience as man's own freedom from guilt and as his own positive righteousness.

The shortcoming of this picture of the universal law-court inheres not necessarily in its mythological character per se but in its failure to express sufficiently how the sinner is involved in the drama that transpires between God and man's mediator. Man tends to be a mere bystander in the whole affair. Edwards turns to an analogy of friendship to account for the human involvement that must occur. If a person greatly dependent on me and loved by me should offend me and break our relationship, says Edwards, and in spite of all I say to him is unable to obtain my forgiveness because of the depth of his offense, a dearer friend of mine who is the offender's relative might intercede for him and out of love undergo extreme pains and difficulties to procure his forgiveness from me. But "the person that had offended should, with a changed mind, fly to this mediator, and should seek favour in his name, with a sense in his own mind how much this mediator had done and suffered for him. . . ."[16] Only then—upon the offender's "sense" of the mediator—will I "be satisfied, and feel myself inclined, without any difficulty, to receive him into my entire friendship again. . . ."[17] Man is reconciled to God through Christ only as man has the "sense" in faith of Christ's excellency and sufficiency in procuring salvation. Man shares in justification, therefore, only through his act of faith. Faith is a qualification for justification.

Needless to say, this explanation of the sinner's involvement in justification poses, from the Reformation perspective, as many questions as it answers. What we have labeled the second danger clearly appears in it; viz., that of involving a human act in justification as a determining condition of salvation. Indeed, if justification is not efficacious *until* a human act is performed, the Calvinist refusal to allow any human contribution to be determinative of salvation is disavowed, and the Arminian doctrine that belief in Christ is the condition of salvation is invited in. We have already seen that Edwards' doctrine of imputation is directed against this Arminianism. How, then, can he in any sense understand the act of faith as a human qualification for justification? There are in Edwards' reflections on faith actually two ways in which this problem is addressed, the second being by far the more representative of the total range of his thought: (1) Faith as a human condition of justification is itself a gift of God; hence God provides his own condition for justifying man. (2) There is a "natural fitness" of faith between the soul and justification; here "condition-language" is replaced or greatly modified.

The former solution to the problem points from the start to the Calvinist scheme of election. The atonement is "limited": Christ's purchase of salvation is limited in its efficacy to those eternally and freely elected by divine decree. The elect are "qualified" for the benefits of the atonement by their faith; and this faith is a gift decreed by God and unearned by man.

We must *believe* in the Lord Jesus Christ, and accept of him as offered in the gospel for a Saviour. But, as we cannot do this of ourselves, Christ has purchased this, also, for all the elect. He has purchased, that they shall have faith given them; whereby they shall be [actively] united to Christ, and have a [pleadable] title to his benefits.[18]

A continuation of this same idea is Edwards' thesis that the elect have both their "objective good" and their "inherent good" from God in Christ alone. "Christ has purchased all, both objective and inherent good: not only a portion to be enjoyed by us, but all those inherent qualifications necessary to our enjoyment of it."[19] Both the salvation of the saints (their objective good) and their title to salvation (faith as an inherent good) are gifts freely given by God in Christ.

Within the scope of this first answer, Edwards has involved the human act of faith in salvation while endeavoring to preserve the intention of the doctrine of imputation. The faith which qualifies man for the imputation of Christ's righteousness is an inherent good which itself is a gift of God and a purchase of Christ. Hence man does not of himself produce his qualification for salvation, and grace remains free. Nevertheless, this answer risks obscuring one important aspect of imputation we have seen Edwards defending; viz., that it is *ungodly* man who is imputed as righteous. When faith is described as the God-given, *inherent human good* which qualifies for justification, it is only a short step to the ascription of a godliness, a holiness, to faith itself outside of and prior to actual justification. This would make a sanctified human act a prior qualification of justification (something of which Edwards has been accused).[20] Then it is no longer ungodly man, but inherently godly and holy man, who is imputed as righteous. And indeed Edwards at times comes close to taking this step in his understanding of faith as a God-given human qualification for salvation. As he puts it in one place, "it is not inconsistent with free grace to suppose that one holy act of ours, viz., faith by which we receive Christ and his salvation, is the condition of our salvation. . . ."[21] It *is* significant that he immediately tempers this statement by adding that faith is a condition of salvation only when it is viewed as "putting the soul into a natural fitness" with salvation; it is not a condition that is rewarded for its own holiness or "excellency."[22] With this he anticipates what we have singled out as his second solution. Furthermore, there are ample grounds, discovered in our second and third chapters, for interpreting Edwards' "holy act of faith" as "holy" by virtue of its foundation, God's Spirit, and not by virtue of the human subject's own being and act. But the choice of words and the manner of framing the answer are still unfortunate. To refer to faith as man's own "holy act," as the "inherent good" which is the condition for his enjoyment of the "objective good," is to enfeeble the proposal that it is *ungodly* man who is justified. Regardless of the qualifications added, the language strongly suggests that faith is a holy, human prius to justification. The consequence is one contrary to the thrust of Edwards' thought: it tends to tear apart Word and Spirit, make the subjective aspect of religious faith the foundation of the objective, and obscure the statement that it is ungodly man who is justified.

In his other approach to the problem of how faith is involved in justification, Edwards transcends the limitations of the first approach. The predestinarian understanding of faith is retained, but now faith is not referred to as man's own "holy act"; it is rather a "fit" act, an act of fit relation between the soul and Christ. It is not a holy human act outside of and prior to justification; it is sinful man's standing in relation with Christ and his righteousness—a relation through which man receives righteousness and holiness. Justification by Christ and the act of faith are now two inseparable aspects of the same gift of grace.

The crux of this proposal is Edwards' distinction between "natural" and "moral" fitness. Faith is a "naturally" fit, not a "morally" fit, relation. A person is morally fit or suitable for something when his own moral goodness, holiness, or excellence commends him to it. So, if one were morally fit for salvation or justification, the holiness or excellence of his act of faith would commend him to salvation. Then God would reward man with salvation because God respected the "moral excellency, or value, or amiableness of any of his qualifications or acts." On the other hand, one is naturally fit for something by virtue of the "natural concord or agreeableness" that exists between the human qualification or act and the reality that is attached to the act. Here man is naturally fit for *salvation by faith* because the two things belong together. God does not reward man with salvation because of the holiness of man's own act; rather, He looks on it as fitting that two things that belong inseparably together, are together; and out of His love for order He sees to it that Christ's righteousness flows to man through the union that man has with Christ through faith.[23] For Edwards, then, faith is a naturally fit relation with Christ and salvation, not a morally fit relation. The former points to two things that belong inseparably together: Christ and faith; the latter points to a kind of works-righteousness in which man's own holy act of faith earns salvation through Christ. Whence arises faith? Again Edwards must fall back upon his Augustinian-Calvinist tradition: it is a gift of God. But in this context, it is not a

gift bestowed outside a relation with Christ and his forgiveness that *deserves* the relation; it is rather the gift of the relation itself. Accordingly, Edwards explicitly disavows the Scholastic *meritum de congruo* as an explanation of the relation
between the human act of faith and salvation. Medieval
Schoolmen had in various forms distinguished between two
degrees of merit, *meritum de condigno* and *meritum de congruo;* and two degrees of grace, saving and general. Condign
merit was the merit to which God owed a reward in strict
justice and was achieved only by the help of saving grace,
while the merit of congruity proceeded from general grace or
from man's free will and was rewarded by God because his
mercy goes beyond strict justice. Edwards states that although
God looks upon it as fit and congruous that man is united to
Christ in faith, man does not thereby *merit* salvation con-
gruously.[24] Faith is not in any sense man's *earning* or meriting of salvation—even through power given him in Christ.
Rather, faith is the natural—i.e., the devoid-of-moral-worth—
vinculum between man and the righteousness of Christ.[25]

Perry Miller has proposed that Edwards drew upon his
study of Newton in this theory of the relation between faith
and salvation. Supposedly Isaac Newton helped Edwards
transcend the old cause-effect understanding of faith and salvation; one could now talk of faith as the antecedent of salvation without saying that faith "determined" salvation. Edwards, says Miller, "found in the new science (few besides
Newton himself understood that this was the hidden meaning of the *Principia*) the concept of an antecedent to a subsequent, in which the subsequent, when it does come to pass,
proves to be whatever it is by itself and in itself, without
determination by the precedent."[26] This new concept meant,
then, that faith "is not an instrument which works an effect,
but is part of a sequence within a system of coherence."[27] To
be sure, Edwards was a student of Newton's works;[28] and
Miller's reading Newton between the lines of Edwards' discussion of justification by faith is highly suggestive. Yet it is
also somewhat strained. We can hardly deny Miller the privi-
lege of finding Newton where he is not explicitly called
upon by Edwards; but we can and must question the clarifi-
cation that this Newtonian approach casts upon Edwards'

theory of the relation between the act of faith and salvation through Christ. For, in fact, Edwards does not focus upon faith as a nondetermining antecedent within a system of coherence. This whole scheme is transcended by focusing upon faith as the *actual relation or union* with Christ and salvation. As Edwards puts it, "there is a wide difference between its being suitable that Christ's satisfaction and merits should be theirs who believe, because an interest in that satisfaction and merit is a fit *reward* of faith—or a suitable testimony of God's respect to the amiableness and excellency of that grace—and its being suitable that Christ's satisfaction and merits should be theirs, because *Christ and they are so united, that in the eyes of the Judge they may be looked upon and taken as one*."[29] The contrast is not so much between two schemes of antecedent and consequence, as between all such schemes and actual union between the human qualification and the reality co-ordinate with the qualification. Edwards is here more evidently reclaiming a view central to earliest Calvinism than he is calling upon Newtonian insights. As François Wendel remarks, for Calvin "imputation is made possible only by our union with the Christ and because we become *at that moment* members of his body, although the union with Christ cannot be regarded as the cause of the imputation of righteousness. Imputation and union with Christ are, rather, *two inseparable aspects of one and the same divine grace*: the one is not possible without the other."[30] For Edwards also faith is the relation to Christ in and through which the righteousness of Christ is imputed to man as man's own righteousness. It is the tie, the bond, the union with Christ through which Christ's saving benefits are communicated on the basis of God's love of the "order" between two things that belong inseparably together: faith and its saving reality. God declares man just not out of respect "to the grace of faith itself," but out of respect to man joined with his saving object in faith. And when and if one must speak of priorities or antecedents, the determining antecedent is always the God who takes the initiative in man's salvation: man in faith is "wholly God's workmanship."[31]

The notion of the "natural fitness of faith" enables Edwards to come to terms with three major problems attending the question of faith: (1) how faith may be an indispensable qualification for righteousness and yet not be a "condition," properly so called; (2) why justification is *by faith* and not *by works*; i.e., what it is about faith that deserves such prominence in justification; and (3) whether faith as human act precedes justification, or justification precedes faith.

(1) Edwards states that the term "condition" is not properly applicable to justifying faith, first of all, because of the ambiguity of the word, deriving from its varied and often unspecified usage in theological as well as nontheological circles. Edwards does admit that we are often "forced" to use the word to denote the indispensability of faith in salvation;[32] and Edwards himself continues to use the word in his reflections on the nature of faith,[33] especially in the context of the Puritan doctrine of the "covenant." Yet faith's indispensability in salvation is not in itself a sufficient reason for calling faith a condition. Faith is not the only thing indispensable in salvation; other things are necessarily involved as well: for example, all those things "that accompany and flow from faith," such as the good works of loving and forgiving our fellow men.[34] Hence one cannot call faith a condition of justification if he simply means that faith necessarily accompanies God's imputation of righteousness. "There is a difference between being justified by a thing, and that thing universally, and necessarily, and inseparably attending or going with justification; for so do a great many things that we are not said to be justified by."[35] Faith has some particular bearing on justification which the good works implied in and flowing from faith do not have. This distinction between the nature of faith and the nature of works is the subject of our following section; it is sufficient to note here that faith's role in the scheme of salvation is not specified by the term "condition" if by condition be meant an "inseparable connection."[36] For works are also inseparably connected with justification.

Above all, faith is not the condition of justification as that which stands outside justification to be rewarded with justification. For that reason faith is not really an "instrument," even a God-given instrument, of salvation. Faith is the *bond* between the soul and Christ and Christ's righteousness and *is the actual reception* of Christ's righteousness. It is not something apart from justification which is *used for* the reception of justification. Edwards says that "there must certainly be some impropriety in calling" faith "an instrument, wherewith we receive or accept justification; for the very persons that thus explain the matter, speak of faith as being the reception or acceptance itself; and if so, how can it be the instrument of reception or acceptance?"[37] The act of faith which is the tie between the soul and Christ is the actual receiving of justification; hence it cannot be the instrument used for the receiving of it. The former idea suggests faith as the being-justified by Christ's righteousness, the natural fitness between soul and Redeemer; the latter suggests faith as something occurring outside justification which God uses to apply salvation. Obviously for Edwards the latter idea leans too closely to the Arminian notion that faith is a holy human act performed outside justification.

Since faith is not a condition preceding the reality of justification, it is not an "obedience" which God rewards with righteousness. Faith is no "new kind of obedience," and its object is no new kind of law. Edwards is here striking out against the Arminianism that was growing in popularity in England and America. It was, in Edwards' judgment, turning faith into obedience, into a human work—which was destructive of the meaning of the gospel and of faith. They who represent this legalistic understanding of faith "hold, that the old law given to Adam, which requires perfect obedience, is entirely repealed, and that instead of it we are put under a new law, which requires no more than imperfect, sincere obedience, in compliance with our poor, infirm, impotent circumstances since the fall. . . ."[38] First of all, this view is inconsistent with the Biblical meaning of the atonement: the Christ dies to satisfy for man's imperfection, for his sins of falling short of full obedience to the law; and since even men of faith never reach absolute perfection but are still condemned under the law, they still need to be covered by Christ's satisfaction. "They say it would not be just in God to exact of us perfect obedience, because it would not be just in God to require more of us than we can perform in our present state, and to punish us for failing of it, and therefore, by their own scheme, the imperfections of our obedience do not deserve to be punished. What need therefore of Christ's dying to satisfy for them?"[39] If faith is an imperfect obedience, it is a sin and is condemned from the start under the law. If imperfect obedience is not really imperfect—if it subsists under a new law which does not condemn it—what need then do we have of salvation by God? If our own imperfect works suffice for salvation, "Christ has died in vain." In other words, the Arminian divines contend that Christ purchases heaven for us by satisfying for our imperfect obedience and by then releasing us to a new and softer law. "But that is not purchasing heaven, merely to set us at liberty again, that we may go and get heaven by what we do ourselves."[40] Christ is not the agent who releases us for obedience deserving of righteousness; he himself is the source of the righteousness given through the bond of faith.

To understand faith as an obedience deserving of justification is finally to remove faith from Christ its object and set it outside Christ as a human act meriting salvation. This is to move faith from a context of natural fitness to one of moral fitness. It is to posit a moral human act outside the immediate context of salvation as the determinant of salvation. And "to suppose that we are justified by our own sincere obedience, or any of our own virtue or goodness, derogates from gospel grace."[41] Whatever glorifies the *freedom* of God's grace exalts that grace; and it is manifest that the freedom of grace appears in its being given to man who is *undeserving* of it: "it doth show a more abundant benevolence in the giver when he shows kindness without goodness or excellency in the object, to move him to it, and . . . it enhances the obligation to gratitude in the receiver."[42] Yet since faith is, like obedience, a human act, how does faith differ in its nature from a work of obedience to the law?

(2) The human act of faith differs from the human work in this: faith is an *act of receiving* while the work is either something done *in order to receive* (works-righteousness) or something done *on the basis of* and *under the coverage of* the receiving of faith (good works of faith). Faith is the active uniting with Christ, the active relation with God in Christ which is in its very acting a receiving. "In efficacious

grace we are not merely passive, nor yet does God do some, and we do the rest. But God does all, and we do all. God produces all, and we act all. . . . God is the only proper author and fountain; we are only the proper actors."[43] The human work which would attempt to merit salvation poses as a *part* which we do in order that God will do the rest. And although good works are potentially involved in faith-as-receiving since faith is a "working faith," good works are *expressions* of faith and are *good* solely by the righteousness of Christ received through the bond of faith. The human act of faith is the active reception of what God does in Christ. Hence neither faith nor any human virtue *prepares* man for the reception of Christ; the choosing of Christ in faith *is* the receiving of Christ and his benefits. The act of faith is in its very nature an active surrendering of all merit to Christ; it is a taking shelter under the wings of Christ for salvation,[44] not an act which presents itself to God in order to be rewarded with such shelter. Hence faith, unlike the meritorious work, gives credit for salvation to its Author, not to the human actor.

Because Edwards understands the act of faith as the receiving bond between Christ and the soul, he views the *imputation* of righteousness as, in a sense, a *making* man righteous. The interpreter of Edwards must proceed with caution here, since Edwards does not desire to claim that man is made holy-in-himself through imputation. Man is not given a self-contained righteousness on the basis of which he is then counted righteous. But man is made righteous in the sense that at the same time that Christ's righteousness is declared to be man's righteousness, it may become a living reality in that man's life. *God's forensically reckoning man righteous does not leave his concrete life untouched but invades it as a vitally present reality.* This is all part of the natural fitness between human life and the righteousness achieved by Christ: the natural fitness of faith. The man of faith, through the union, enjoys a communion with Christ and the benefits of salvation. To be sure, the element of hope is retained, for faith is the act of receiving Christ which continues to remain dependent upon God to make the imputed righteousness vitally present to the soul. But faith is the human bond between the righteousness earned by Christ

on the far side of man's being and man's concrete life in the
world. The existential enjoyment of being counted righteous
is to have overcome in faith that alienation between the soul
and God created by man's rebellion in sin. Faith "is that
by which the soul that before was separate and alienated
from Christ, unites itself to him, or ceases to be any longer in
that state of alienation, and comes into . . . union or relation
to him."[45] In faith one stands directly within the dynamics
of salvation. Therefore faith, and not the doing of works
either in order to receive salvation or to express faith, is deserving of the word *by* to express man's connection with justification. For faith is the only "qualification" for justification which actively receives Christ's righteousness while re-
lating away from itself to the Christ in whom man is righteous.

(3) Since justification is imputed in and through the act
of faith, it is really improper to speak either of faith preceding justification or of justification preceding faith. They are
inseparably connected.[46] There is a certain ontological order
in the decrees of God respecting justification, and there is a
certain temporal order in man's coming to Christ and receiving his benefits. But the order of decrees is dependent
upon the eternal intellect and will of God and not upon temporal sequence, and the temporal order of faith is not a movement of man *from* an act of faith *to* Christ and his benefits
but is a movement of faith itself within the context of salvation. God establishes it as his order of procedure, says Edwards, to decree the work of Christ and the salvation of an
elect soul by grounding that decree on another; viz., "on the
decree of giving faith as God's decree of bestowing happiness on the elect in this particular way, as a fallen creature, and by the righteousness of Christ made his own, by
being heartily received and closed with. . . ."[47] But as we
noted earlier, Edwards is a supralapsarian in his doctrine of
election: God decrees the election of man without view of a
future human condition, either good or bad. Hence although
God determines to ground the decree of salvation in the decree of faith, his decree to save creates its object: "The decree of God's communicating his goodness to such a subject,
does not so much as presuppose the being of the subject, be-

cause it gives being."[48] When God decides to ground salvation in the gift of faith, that decision is not dependent upon a foreknowledge of a future act of faith; God does not foresee a particular man's faith and then decree his salvation. What God foresees of man in faith is what He will make of him by the decree of election to salvation.

From the human angle there is a certain temporal sequence in the movement of faith. Faith is first an adhering to Christ and then a sharing in the benefits of his righteousness. "Those that are not in Christ, or are not united to him, can have no degree of communion with him; for union with Christ, or a being in Christ, is the foundation of all communion with him."[49] This is what we previously found Edwards calling the difference between the "first" and the "second" acts of faith. The first act is the inclination toward the merciful God in Christ presented in the gospel; the second is a trusting in the sufficiency of Christ and his promises and an enjoyment of that sufficiency. Though the second act may follow in a moment, it is to be distinguished from the first act. But the important thing to recall here is that both acts are movements *of faith*. The act of having communion with Christ and receiving his benefits is no less an act of faith than the primary act of uniting with Christ. The reception of Christ's righteousness is no less by faith than the first receiving of union with Christ. Edwards employs some metaphors: being related to Christ in faith is not like being placed as a stone in a building, upon which other stones (Christ's benefits) are stacked and "cemented" together. It is standing in living, continuous relation with Christ and his righteousness, "as subsists between the head and living members, between stock and branches; between which, and the head or stock, there is such a kind of union, that there is an entire, immediate, perpetual dependence for, and derivation of, nourishment, refreshment, beauty, fruitfulness, and all supplies; yea, life and being."[50]

Edwards' approach to the question of justification from the consideration of faith as a "naturally fit" relation or union with Christ decidedly transcends the limitations of the other approach, which defines faith as a divinely bestowed "holy act" or subjective human good that qualifies for justification.

Edwards does not abandon the terminology of the latter approach; it appears in his Puritan doctrine of the covenant (where his reasons for using it emerge more clearly) and is there subject to the same contradictions and shortcomings. But the former approach conforms to the broader range of Edwards' notion of faith: it is consistent with his insistence that it is ungodly man who is justified, with his proviso that the indwelling Spirit not be collapsed into human being, and with his continual battle against an Arminianism that places the origins of salvation in human act. In brief, it accords with a central theme in his major treatise on justification: "Goodness or loveliness of the person in the acceptance of God, in any degree, is not to be considered prior but posterior in the order and method of God's proceeding in this affair" of justification.[51] More importantly, the notion of the naturally fit relation between faith and Christ is an attempt to remain heir to the Protestant Reformation doctrine of imputation while affirming the existential involvement of the human act of faith in salvation. It is Edwards' eighteenth-century effort to hold together and explain what Paul Tillich has deemed two complementary elements in a theory of salvation: the Pauline tenet that justification "is an act of God which is in no way dependent on man, an act in which he accepts him who is unacceptable"; and the conviction that the divine act becomes a concrete reality in human experience, that faith "is the channel through which grace is mediated to man."[52]

CHAPTER VII

COVENANT RELATION

Edwards conceived of man's faith-relation with his saving reality as a "covenant" relation as well as a "fit" relation. The revealed God with whom man stands in faithful relation is a covenanting God; and in this relation man is a covenanting creature. By placing religious faith in the domain of a covenant between God and man, Edwards identified himself with a central, if not *the* central, theme in Puritan thought and experience.

Puritan preachers and theologians had early drawn heavily from the Old Testament view of the God-man relation[1] and had in many cases developed a rather elaborate covenant scheme within which to mark out the divine and human roles in the drama of redemption. Leonard J. Trinterud has pointed out that this scheme so permeated the thinking of the Puritans that in "the first decades of the seventeenth century . . . scarcely a single important figure was not a covenant theologian" among "the Presbyterian and Independent Puritans."[2] It is a matter deserving of some debate whether the covenant was the essential content of Puritan thought or rather functioned as a very useful framework within which various Puritan doctrines and policies could be set and related to one another. But this much is clear: the notion of the covenant was decidedly a pervasive idea in Puritan thought and was believed to be worthy of the most serious attention. Peter Bulkeley, a leading exponent of covenant theology in early New England, stated it candidly: "Among all the parts of Gods heavenly truth, there is none I know of, more worthy of our diligent inquisition, and affectionate acceptation, then [*sic*] is that which concernes the covenant passed betwixt God and us." Attention to the covenant is of extreme importance because God's "goodness towards man, together with man's observance towards him, are therein contained. . . ."[3] The covenant was, above all, a way of viewing the character of both parties: God and man appear in their true natures when they are viewed as standing in covenant-relation. Edwards would adopt this affirmation and with the covenant explicate further, especially in his sermons, the nature of faith.

In its theological essence the Puritan doctrine of the covenant represented a history of the manner in which God dealt with his people. God entered into covenant with man from the beginning. There was first a "covenant of works": here God promised salvation and felicity to man on the condition of man's staying within the boundaries of divine law. Adam's disobedience and fall into sin was a rejection of this first covenant. But rather than giving man up, God instituted a second covenant, a "covenant of grace," which respected man's weakness in sin. The covenant of grace included Israel under the Old Testament as well as the Church under the New. God's grace and promise in Christ were the foundation and possibility of Israel's relation to God in faith, although that grace was hidden under the forms of Israel's historical existence (e.g., certain ceremonies and sacrifices), forms abandoned with the historical coming of Christ. The covenant of grace is similar to the covenant of works in that promises and the performance of conditions are still assumed by both God and man. But the Puritan theologian was quick to point to fundamental differences between the two covenants. William Ames, for example, noted that the covenant of works was "a covenant of friendship between the Creator and the creature" while the covenant of grace "is a covenant of reconciliation between enemies"; the old covenant "was an agreement of two parties, namely God and man," but in the new covenant man "is the party assumed" since he is "dead in sinne" and has "no ability to contract a spirituall covenant with God"; and the condition of the first covenant was man's "perfect obedience of workes" performed of his own strength, while the second covenant requires only faith, which is a gift of God.[4]

The covenant-doctrine had for the Puritan a wider scope than its theological essence. Perry Miller has made abundantly clear how this was especially the case in the Puritan settlement of Massachusetts. "In the migration to Massachusetts all entered into a covenant, among themselves and with the Lord. In the one compact the people were dedicated both to theological and to social duties."[5] John Winthrop's lecture to the passengers aboard the *Arbella* on its voyage to New England is exemplary testimony to the manner in which the covenant was bound up with a Puritan sense of social-political destiny. Winthrop reminded the settlers that "wee must consider that wee shall be as a Citty vpon a Hill, the eies of all people are vppon vs," that "for the worke wee haue in hand, it is by a mutuall consent through a speciall overruleing providence . . . to seeke out a place of Cohabitation and Consorteshipp vnder a due forme of Government both ciuill and ecclesiasticall." And this destiny is one based on covenant: "Thus stands the cause betweene God and vs, wee are entered into Covenant with him for this worke. . . ."[6] The scope of the Puritan covenant-idea was considerably narrowed for Jonathan Edwards: it did not assume for him the same importance for an understanding of the Puritans' social and political life as it had for his forefathers. This is accounted for in large part by the fact that Massachusetts had long since lost her charter (1684) and was forced to accept a royal governor in 1691 along with the granting of freedom of worship to all Christians except Roman Catholics. The link between Church and State was fast dissolving; the covenant of grace and the political-social covenants could no longer be considered strictly commensurate. Edwards did resort to covenant principles in his controversy with the Stoddardeans over the nature of the Church, and, as we shall see, the principles were of utmost significance for Edwards' position in that controversy. Even so, Edwards did not pursue all the intricate ecclesiastical and sociopolitical implications usually involved in the full-blown Puritan covenant theology.

Covenant theology was most valuable to Edwards for a description of the nature of the saints' relation to God in faith, and his church-covenant principles were ramifications of this primary use of the theology. In the development of his doctrine of faith, Edwards' employment of the categories of the covenant scheme comes clearly to light, for there we find him working with two recurrent motifs in the scheme: God's "indebtedness" to man in the covenant of grace; and man's faith as the "condition" of the covenant with God. Edwards' appeal to these two motifs are efforts to clarify the nature of the faith-relation in terms of covenant theology; and an examination of them should reveal the dubiety of Perry Miller's claim that Edwards "threw over the whole covenant scheme" and "declared God unfettered by any agreement or obligation."[7]

God's Indebtedness to Man

Perry Miller cites Edwards' 1731 Boston sermon on man's absolute dependence on God, as a substantiating piece of evidence for the thesis that Edwards abandoned the entire covenant scheme which tied God to an agreement or obligation. In that particular sermon Edwards contends that man's redemption is by the free and sovereign grace of God; hence man may make no claims on, but must simply depend upon, the power of God for salvation. "The Federal [or covenant] Theology is conspicuous in his sermon by its utter absence," says Miller.[8] But in a sermon of 1733, covenant theology is anything but utterly absent from Edwards' thinking. There Edwards not only speaks of salvation within the context of a "Covenant of Grace" which has as its "certain condition" man's believing in "the L.J.X."; he also says, "Salvation is an absolute debt to the believer from God" of which "he may in justice demand delivery."[9] And in another, undated sermon Edwards maintains that men may through Christ demand salvation from God "as a debt."[10]

At first glance this notion of God's indebtedness to man not only appears to contradict the thrust of Edwards' Boston sermon (viz., that man is absolutely dependent for salvation upon the power and grace of a sovereign God); it also seems to be antithetical to other of Edwards' sermons which *explicitly* renounce the position that God is indebted to man. In one such sermon Edwards says:

That which God may not dispose of as he pleases, is not his own; for that which is one's own, is at his own disposal; but if it be not God's own, then he is not capable of making a gift or present of it to any one; it is impossible to give what is a *debt*.—What is it that you would make of God? Must the great God be tied up, that he must not use his own pleasure in bestowing his own gifts . . . ?[11]

In another sermon the same resistance to God's "indebtedness" is expressed:

What kind of thoughts have you of God, that you think he is obliged, as it were, to yield himself up to be abused by men, so that when they have done, his mercy and pardoning grace shall not be in his own power, but he must be obliged to dispense them at their call! . . . Has God no right to his own grace? is it not at his own disposal? and is God incapable of making a gift or present of it to any man? for a person cannot make a present of that which is not his own, or in his own right. It is impossible to *give a debt*.[12]

As unequivocal as these statements are in the disavowal of the presumption that God can be "tied up" by human claims, they by no means spell the abandonment of covenant theology or of the "debt" idea inherent in it. For the notion of God's indebtedness to man for salvation is considered by Edwards in two distinct ways, or on two different levels. In his condemnation of the idea of debt he is rejecting all Pelagian and Arminian claims to salvation on the basis of what man is or does (including the act of belief). Here "debt" is to be understood in a "non-covenantal" way. In his adoption of the debt idea, Edwards is attempting to take seriously the meaning of the Incarnation as God's condescension to man in history. On this level "debt" takes on a very restricted meaning within the context of the Biblical representation of faith as a covenant-relation between God and man and excludes the notion that God is indebted by human performance.

The sermons cited above, where Edwards rejects the idea of God's indebtedness to man for salvation, reveal the first way he conceives of divine indebtedness. It is of no avail for a man to complain that he has done more to deserve salvation than another and that hence God is more obligated to him for salvation than to the other man. God has absolute disposal over the dispensation of salvation. The "great God" cannot "be tied up" by the sinner's claims or high opinions of himself. In the salvation of man, God remains sovereign even as he is merciful. In brief, Edwards' rejection of the debt idea is a rejection of works-righteousness, of the attempt of the sinner to make claims on God on the ground of ostensible human holiness. Edwards stresses here what is central to his treatise on the doctrine of justification by faith alone: God justifies the sinner as a *sinner* who has no case to plead on the basis of his own goodness or righteousness. God is in debt to none. No creature can, on the basis of his own inherent righteousness, "tie up" the bestower of salvation.

Nevertheless, in another sense, God is indebted to man and man may demand his salvation from God as a debt. It is clear that on this level, however, Edwards intends in no way to surrender his position on the debt idea considered on the first level. In the sermon on the sovereignty of God in salvation, immediately prior to his point that the believer may demand salvation from God "as a debt," Edwards avers that "those who are in a state of salvation are to attribute it to sovereign grace alone, and to give all the praise to him, who maketh them to differ from others. Godliness is no cause for glorying, except it be in God."[13] The possibility of the believer's demanding salvation on the basis of his own godliness is precluded. But Edwards proceeds in the same sermon to suggest the manner in which salvation may be demanded as a debt by the believer:

> We learn what cause we have to admire the grace of God, that he should condescend to become bound to us by covenant; that he, who is naturally supreme in his dominion over us, who is our absolute proprietor, and may do with us as he pleases, and is under no obligation to us; that he should, as it were, relinquish his sovereign freedom, and should cease to be merely arbitrary in his dispensations towards believers, when once they have believed in Christ, and should, for their more abundant consolation, become bound. So that they can challenge salvation of this Sovereign; they can demand it through Christ, as a debt.[14]

Man does not "tie up" God, but God ties himself to man in the covenant. This is Edwards' interpretation of the Incarnation: God binds himself in covenant with the sinner, and in so doing God freely limits his freedom for man. The sinner-believer demands salvation through Christ, on the ground of God's binding himself in Christ, and never through or on the basis of his own goodness or obedience. The demand is solely possible through the union a man has with Christ, who is God's covenant-event in history.

The other sermon we cited which openly embraces the debt idea stresses the same fundamental points: the initiative of God in establishing the covenant; and the right of man's claim on salvation through Christ only:

Salvation is an *absolute debt* to the believer *from God*, so that he may, in justice, demand it, on account of what his surety has done. For Christ has satisfied justice fully for his sin; so that it is but a thing that may be challenged, that God should now release the believer from the punishment.[15] [Italics mine]

Again, Edwards presupposes a "limited" or predestinarian doctrine of atonement: the atonement does not open salvation to all but only to those eternally elected to have faith. But for the elect believer God is no longer the distant, arbitrary ruler; he is the God who has "indebted" himself to man through the Christ, and man may now demand his salvation as God's part of the covenant. The notion of God's indebtedness to man borders on blasphemy—in fact it is a kind of "blasphemy of faith." It is the Puritan's attempt to conceive, in view of faith in God's revelation, an alternative to a distant, arbitrary God. For the man of faith, God has drawn near in covenant: that is the meaning of the Christ; and God may be "dealt with" in faith as a covenant partner. Yet it is important to note that for Edwards, as for William Ames, the covenant of grace is one made between the sinful believer and the sovereign God, not one made between equals; hence God must found the covenant. And we must not be too hasty in inferring that the "mystery of God" is destroyed with this covenant notion.

In support of his thesis that Edwards abandoned the motifs of covenant theology, Miller contends that the Puritan covenant theologians broke radically from John Calvin in their belief that the saint may "sue" God for salvation. Conceiving God as bound to conditions of a covenant removes the mystery and inscrutability from "pure Calvinism's Almighty."[16] The imposition of the covenant scheme upon Calvin's doctrines created "in the New England theology an altogether different philosophy from any propounded in Geneva. . . ."[17] The Puritan God is no longer Calvin's God who mysteriously predestines certain men to salvation and certain others to damnation; He is the God who may be dealt with as a covenant partner. "Certainly the implacable mystery celebrated in the *Institutes* has been materially transformed by the time He appears as the God of the covenant. . . . Bound by His own commitment, God must live up to His word. If you do your part, He must, willy-nilly, do His."[18] Thus, according to Miller, Edwards' alleged rejection of covenant theology and of the debt idea was a brushing aside of what was "(by his day)" a "rusty mechanism."[19]

In one very significant respect this interpretation misrepresents Edwards, Calvin, and many of the covenant theologians. Not only did Edwards retain Puritan covenant categories; inscrutability or distant mystery is not of the essence of God's saving operations in Calvin's system. And many of the Puritans did not lose sight of the mystery of salvation but rather accentuated it in the covenant notion. There is no denying that the covenant theologians did not remain within the boundaries of Calvin's system; they availed themselves of other sources (theological and legal) to develop a complex covenant-scheme undisclosed in Calvin himself. Yet on one important point Calvin anticipated them: the God who concerns the believer is not the hidden God but the God who reveals himself in all his mystery in the Christ. According to Calvin, God's eternal decrees are, indeed, inscrutable; but the real divine mystery—that mystery alone into which we are to inquire—is disclosed to the heart of man in the revelation given through God's conjoined Word and Spirit. The mystery is in the revelation. One's attention is to be focused not on the inscrutable decreeing God behind the revealed God in Christ but on the God who mysteriously reflects the saint's election in the "mirror," Christ.[20]

The concept of divine "debt" in the Puritans' covenant theology was one way of accentuating the Calvinist doctrine of Christological revelation by stressing the vital and luminous presence of God in human history. God enters history as the believer's covenant partner. The idea in itself surrenders neither Calvin's warning that man has no claims *of himself* on the Creator nor Calvin's insistence that it is as *sovereign Lord* that God reveals himself and saves man. Certainly one must take account of an important historical point ably discussed by Miller: there was a tendency for New England covenant theologians to lose sight of God's sovereignty and to entrap the Almighty in a legalist framework in their pleas for the necessity of "preparation." The irony is that this tendency manifested itself in some of those covenant theologians who were so opposed to seventeenth-century forms of Arminianism which tied God in dependence to human efforts. Defenders of the preparation scheme actually laid the groundwork for later American Arminianism by obligating God to bestow salvation on those who sufficiently performed their part of the legal bargain by preparing themselves for grace.[21] But that spirit of the Puritan covenant theology which Edwards shared sought not to turn the sovereign God into a powerless business partner bound to a human legal contract, but to account for the Sovereign's abandonment of arbitrariness for the sake of meaningful historical revelation. Indeed, according to this Puritan spirit, the man of faith might demand salvation from God; he might even "sue" God for the salvation promised in Christ. In the words of John Preston, when one is in faith, when he "has Christ" as a gift, he has a "case to plead" with God:

When you have him, you may goe to him for Justification, and say, Lord, give me remission of sinnes, I have Christ, and thou hast promised that all that are in Christ shall have pardon, that they shall have thy Spirit, and be made new creatures; now, Lord, fulfill these promises.[22]

But this demanding from God in faith is what Peter Bulkeley called a "pleading suing." The human soul "lies down at Gods foot-stoole, putting its mouth in the dust, acknowledging Gods righteousnesse if he should condemn and cast off for ever, and yet withall pleads for Grace, that it may be accepted as one of his. . . ."[23] In other words, it is still the *sovereign* God with whom the soul deals in the covenant-relation, but not the *arbitrary* God. God still has the power to withdraw his hand of mercy, but we have his sound testimony in Christ that He wills not to do so. He has the power to withhold salvation from the saints, but on the basis of his promise of salvation in Christ man may "pleadingly sue" him for it with the assurance that he has freely bound himself to give it. In the same breath that the covenant theologian utters his demand to God for salvation, he utters the prayer of thanksgiving that God has come so "neare unto us" in the covenant. "Are we low and despised in the world, yet count this honour enough that God hath lifted us up to this excellency to be one of his people. . . ."[24]

Edwards, then, appeals to a central motif in the Puritan covenant theology. Man sues God in faith for salvation not because he as man deserves it but because God has promised it. It is of the essence of the grace of God, says Edwards, that he "should condescend to become bound to us by covenant," that he "should cease to be merely arbitrary" so that we "can challenge salvation of this Sovereign."[25] But the challenge to the Sovereign *is* a challenge to a *sovereign*. It is hence nothing but a prayer to God to fulfill his promises. Citing a passage from the English divine Thomas Manton, Edwards says that "faith has a double office. It accepts Christ from God, and presents Christ to God. It accepts Christ in the word, and makes use of him in prayer."[26] Along with Manton and Walter Cradock, Edwards finds in Ephesians 3:12 a right for man to have a "holy boldness"[27] before God in faith. "Now when you consent to God's terms, this is to believe in him.—Faith presents Christ to God; Eph. iii, 12, 'In whom we have boldness and access with confidence, by the faith of him.' All religion lieth in coming to God by him."[28]

The demanding of salvation from God as an "absolute debt" is a palatable act for Edwards, therefore, when it is an act of faith. The covenantal description of salvation as a debt to man is, in fact, a further explication of faith as a "fit" relation with Christ. Man may sue God for salvation as His side of the covenant on the ground of no human merit, on the ground of no "moral fitness," but solely because God has initiated a covenant, has sealed it by binding man in faith with the Son, and has promised salvation as He condescended to make covenant. In faith, but only in faith, does man have the "holy boldness" that allows a "prayerful suit."

Faith as "Condition"

As we noticed previously, Edwards expressed a distaste for the word "condition" when applied to saving faith. The word is ambiguous; it hardly clarifies the relation between faith and salvation. If by "condition" one means an "inseparable connection," it may be said that works are conditions of salvation for they also are inseparably connected with it. Above all, if faith is a condition in the sense of being an instrumental cause of salvation which lies outside Christ and salvation and upon which redemption *follows*, the meaning of faith is obscured; for faith is the *actual relation* to or *union with* Christ and his gift of salvation. Nevertheless, Edwards confessed that one is sometimes forced through custom to use this inadequate word "condition" when speaking of faith in order to stress the indispensability of faith for salvation, and we do find Edwards continually referring to faith as the condition of the covenant of grace. In this he supported and propagated another central motif in Puritan covenant theology; but he also posed certain contradictions to his understanding of the nature of faith—contradictions from which he tried to extricate himself—and involved himself in many of the same problems that had faced his Puritan forefathers.

The notion of faith as the condition of the covenant of grace was integrally related to the Puritans' understanding of faith as an "instrument." The covenant of grace was for the Puritans a mutual bond. Faith was the condition on the human side of the bond, salvation the condition on the divine side. But faith, unlike the meritorious work, was a gift of God and was an empty vessel, the instrument, for the reception of God's performance of salvation in Christ. "O, consider," said Thomas Shepard, "the Lord hath overtaken in the covenant of grace to work in all his the condition of the covenant, as well as to convey thee good of it. (Jer. xxxi. 31–34)."[29] And it is of the very nature of faith, proclaimed John Preston, that it "empties a man, it takes a man quite off his owne bottome; faith cometh as an empty hand, and receiveth all from God, and gives all to God."[30] Faith, therefore, does not merit salvation in the covenant; but it is a condition of the covenant in that man is not in saving covenant-relation with God until he believes in Him through Christ—a belief given by God himself.

Faith is a condition given by God himself and one founded on the divine condition, the bestowal of salvation. These two restrictions on faith as a condition of the covenant, however, do not overcome the limitations of so conceiving faith, limitations pointed out by Edwards himself in his criticism of the notion of faith as an "instrument." To understand the human act of faith as the instrumental condition of the covenant is to imply that faith is something performed outside the covenant and its blessings in order to enter the covenant and partake of its blessings. And it is to suggest that faith is not the receiving itself but something *used for* the reception of covenant blessings. In his sermons on justification by faith alone, Edwards rejects the former implication because of its works-righteousness tendency, and he opts for faith as the actual reception of salvation rather than the instrument of the reception.[31] Nevertheless, in the "Qualifications for Communion," a defense of the position that only professing Christians are to be admitted into full communion in the Church, Edwards says that "the grand condition of the covenant of Christ, by which we are in Christ," is "saving faith." "This is what, on our part, brings us *into the Lord*."[32] The same position is assumed in the sermons concerning "A History of the Work of Redemption."[33] And in an observation in his major theological workbook, Edwards notes: "Christ does not promise that he will be the author of our redemption, but upon condition; and we have not performed that condition, until we have believed. Therefore, we have no grounds, until we have once believed, to acquiesce in it that Christ will save us."[34] Here Edwards is, in spite of his avowed dislike for the word "condition," clearly maintaining that faith is the human condition of the covenant of grace; and the covenant is not consummated until man has performed that condition. Edwards places the same restrictions on this concept as did his theological antecedents. Faith as a condition is itself a divine gift; and, unlike the meritorious work, it takes man off his own foundation. God is the efficient cause of faith, of the human condition of the covenant.[35] And faith is the condition of the covenant of grace only to the extent that it is truly faith; that is, to the extent that it allows Christ to perform the ultimate condition of the covenant. The saints' performance of their condition "is consenting to the terms of it; therefore, consenting to the second covenant is with the heart consenting to Christ's working out a perfect righteousness by his obedience and suffering for them; for this is the terms of the second covenant."[36]

This manner of conceiving the role of the human act of faith in the covenant accords with what we called the "first way" Edwards involves faith in justification, and it gets him into the same problems. As in justification, God himself provides faith, the human condition of the covenant; and the human condition points to the covenant partner, not to its own worth. Nevertheless, if the covenant is not consummated *until* a human act of faith is performed—even if performed efficiently by God himself—a human act outside the covenant-relation is made the prius of that covenant. For one thing, this conflicts with Edwards' view that faith is *itself* the saving relation with God rather than the condition upon which a saving-relation waits. For another, it is hardly distinguishable from ascribing a holy goodness to the human act of faith, an ascription involved in the Arminian theologies that called forth Edwards' most vehement opposition during most of his theological career. Far from "throwing over" the covenant-scheme, Edwards at this point had difficulty transcending it, in spite of the problems he saw emerging out of the notion of faith as the "condition" of the covenant.

Edwards attempts to mitigate the problematic character of so conceiving faith by distinguishing between the "covenant of redemption" and the "covenant of grace" and their respective conditions. English and American Puritans in the seventeenth century had proposed a similar distinction;[37] and Edwards, like them, simply skirts the basic issue with the distinction. The covenant of redemption is that covenant which "God made with Christ and with His church or believers in Him"; the covenant of grace is the covenant "between Christ and His church, or between Christ and men."

There is doubtless a difference between the covenant that God makes with Christ and His people, considered as one, and the covenant of Christ and His people between themselves. The covenant that a father makes with his son and his son's wife, considered as one, must be looked upon as different from the marriage covenant, or the covenant which the son and the wife make between themselves. The father is concerned in this covenant only as a parent in a child's marriage, directing, consenting, and ratifying.[38]

Edwards believes that if these covenants are properly distinguished, the problems involved in conceiving faith as the condition of the covenant of grace may possibly be resolved. For the two covenants "differ in their conditions." The condition of the covenant of redemption, that eternal covenant made between the Father and the Son and the believers represented by the Son, is performed by Christ in "*all that Christ has done and suffered to procure redemption.*" The condition of the covenant of grace, that covenant made directly between Christ and believers, "is *that they should close with Him and adhere to Him.*"[39] Neither the two covenants nor their two conditions are to be confused with each other. Above all, man's performance of faith is not to be considered the condition of the covenant-relation between the Father and Christ (Christ as representative of the saints). But how does this distinction resolve the basic issue at stake? That is, how determinative of grace is man's act of faith—the covenant of redemption between Father and Son notwithstanding? Put another way, how are the two distinct conditions—Christ's work and human faith—related? Edwards' answer appears to be that the covenant of grace and its condition are the implementation of the covenant of redemption.[40] Yet this simply puts the problem at one remove; it does not explain to what extent faith is determinative of the efficacy of *either* covenant *for the man of faith*. If the covenant of grace (which has as its condition the act of belief) is the implementation of the covenant of redemption, does this mean, then, that the covenant of redemption is not applicable to a specific saint until the condition of the covenant of grace is performed by the saint? Edwards' distinction between the two covenants leaves this question unanswered and hence does not clear him of the shortcomings, noted above, of viewing faith as the condition of the covenant.

Although Edwards continued to deal with faith as the condition of the covenant of grace in the aforementioned way, there are evidences that he was uneasy about this method of attacking the problem. He confesses that making faith a condition of the covenant "fills the mind with innumerable difficulties about faith and works, and how to distinguish them. It tends to lead men into Neonomianism, and gives the principal force to their arguments."[41] Neonomianism, or the replacing of good morals or works with the act of faith as the human effort which achieves salvation, is implicit in calling faith a condition and is directly contrary to the true nature of the covenant of grace. For "that, which is commonly called the *covenant of grace,* is only *Christ's open and free offer of life,* whereby He holds it out in His hand to sinners, and offers it without any condition."[42] Here Edwards feels that in all propriety he must collapse the two covenants—the covenant of grace and the covenant of redemption—into one. There is one covenant; viz., God's coming to and covenanting with man in the free offer of salvation in Christ—which is not dependent upon any human performance prior to God's consummating the covenant.[43] This is something like what the covenant theologian William Ames had in mind when he said that the new covenant in Christ "requires not any condition properly so called, or going before, but onely following after or comming betweene. . . ."[44] For Edwards, in his critical stance toward faith as a human condition of the covenant, faith is what "comes between" or "follows after." It conforms to the description of faith in the sermons on justification by faith alone: faith is the natural (non-meritorious) relation of man to the covenanting God, man's active reception of salvation in covenant with God, and not a prius to this receptive covenant-relationship.

Understood this way, therefore, faith within the covenant of grace (and within the covenant of redemption, since now the two are no longer distinguished) becomes the reception of the Father's covenanting with the Son and the reception of the benefit of salvation attendant on that covenanting. "Faith cannot be called the *condition* of receiving, for it is *receiving* itself: Christ holds out, and believers receive. There was no covenant made or agreement, upon something that must be done before they might receive."[45] Here lies a major distinction between the "covenant of works" made with Adam and the "covenant of grace" made with the New Adam. In the former something is exacted of man as a condition of the consummation of the covenant; viz., obedience. In the latter man is made an active receiver of what God freely offers in consummating the covenant.

The one is law; the other a testimony and offer. The one is a signification of what God expects that we should do towards him, and what he expects to receive from us; the other a revelation of what he has done for us, and an offer of what we may receive from him. The one is an expression of God's great authority over us, in order to a yielding to the authority; the other is a revelation of God's mysterious and wonderful mercy, and wisdom, and power for us, in order to a reception answerable to such a revelation.[46]

Faith is the covenant-relation with God wherein man receives God's revelation of His mysterious mercy in the Word. Faith, in this context, is a condition of the covenant of grace in only a very restricted sense: not as a human performance outside the covenant-relation on which the consummation of the covenant is dependent, but rather as the saint's being taken up into covenant with God through God's covenanting with him in Christ. And in receiving salvation through the covenant, faith is active dependence in hope and trust upon the God who covenants.

During Edwards' "better moments," then—or during those moments when he conceived the nature of the covenant in the light of the full range of his understanding of faith—he was careful to designate faith as the "condition" of the covenant only in the sense that in faith the covenant and its blessings are concretely *received*. Faith, the reception, is bestowed as God himself consummates the covenant. One suspects that these were the moments, also, when Edwards experienced the greatest need to set himself against the neonomianism of the Arminians, against which he directed repeated attacks for its "conditioning" the freedom of divine grace. Nevertheless, he continued to speak with some abandon of faith as the human condition of the covenant, thereby involving himself in the same problems which had faced his Puritan forefathers. Far from throwing over covenant theology, Edwards was quite dependent upon it; in fact, there is every indication that he had difficulty freeing himself from its categories even at the points where he discerned their shortcomings. In broader perspective, Edwards claimed both Puritan covenant motifs to spell out what he held to be of primary importance in the nature of religious faith: that faith is an active, almost palpable relationship of man with God. Because God has drawn near in covenant, man is taken up through faith into an active, continuous relation of dependence on him. And the God of faith is the God of covenant: a promise-making, promise-keeping God who may be "dealt with" in faith as a covenant partner; not the God of an inscrutable hinterland.

PART THREE:

THE LIFE OF FAITH

CHAPTER VIII

FAITH AND PRACTICE

It is often said, and with a great deal of justification, that the American Puritans were of an overwhelmingly practical bent. These were no speculative theologians engaged in doctrinal study for the sheer delight of spinning out an abstract system. Their theology was intertwined with their concrete task in the New World—the social and political direction of their covenant idea is sufficient testimony to this. Their theology was above all, as Daniel Boorstin has said, "applied theology."

Compared with Americans of the 18th or the 19th century, the Puritans surely were theology-minded. The doctrines of the Fall of Man, of Sin, of Salvation, Predestination, Election, and Conversion were their meat and drink. Yet what really distinguished them in their day was that they were less interested in theology itself, than in the application of theology to everyday life, and especially to society. From the 17th century point of view their interest in theology was practical. They were less concerned with perfecting their formulation of the Truth than with making their society in America embody the Truth they already knew. Puritan New England was a noble experiment in applied theology.[1]

In one sense, virtually every Christian theology worth its salt has been an "applied theology" as it has arisen to meet practical concerns of the Church or of society, or of both, for its period. But the American Puritan sense of social-political destiny lent a peculiarly passionate and vital practicality to Puritan theological formulations. By the same token, the Puritan understanding of religious faith was inextricably bound up with the Puritan understanding of morality. In the words of Perry Miller, ethics was "a corollary of piety"; morality was "the temporal aspect of faith."[2] If theology was no merely speculative matter, faith was similarly no impractical affair. Religious faith was inseparable from one's active, practical life in the world.

As we have already pointed out, for historical reasons

Jonathan Edwards did not work out the practical implications of the Puritan covenant theology in the same way the seventeenth-century Puritans had; but it should become evident in our concluding part that his theological formulations were anything but unrelated to practical issues facing his eighteenth century. And in accordance with his Puritan frame of mind, Edwards never tired of emphasizing the "practical" nature of faith. This should not surprise us in a theologian who stresses the interpenetration of intellect and will in the act of faith. Faith is a hearty, willing, affectionate knowledge. It is a "sense of the heart" that involves a lively movement of will; it "reaches the bottom of the heart" and "gains the heart." "But then only is the heart gained when the will is gained, but when the will is gained the practice is gained; for the will commands the practice."[3] Since faith reaches into man's volitional powers, faith issues in practice; for the will gained in faith is what commands one's active or practical life in the world. Or put in a way that stresses Edwards' "wholistic" view of human nature: *man* is gained or grasped in faith—not a part of man or one of his special functions or powers, but the whole man in his everyday life in the world. The *locus classicus* of this notion is Edwards' statement in his notebook on faith: faith depends upon the Word of God; and "to depend upon the word of another is to believe it, as to dare to act upon it, as if it were really true."[4] Faith or trust in the Word is believing it to the extent that one is ready to risk acting upon it as true. To know the truth of the revealed God in faith means daring to live by it.

It is pertinent to recall here that for Edwards the human act of love involved in faith refers principally to one of two exercises: either to "disinterested" love to God; or to the love to man involved in faith's working in the world. Faithful practice summarily consists in the latter. Edwards did recognize the common reference to "religious practice" as involving specific religious or churchly "duties": "outward acts of worship, such as meeting in religious assemblies, attending sacraments and other institutions, honouring God with gestures, such as bowing, or kneeling before him, or with words, in speaking honourably of him in prayer, praise, or religious conference." But "of vastly the greatest importance in the Christian life" is "our behaviour among men" in obeying God's "moral commands, self-denial, righteousness, meekness, and Christian love."[5] The practice of works of charity toward men grows out of one's love toward God: as for the Apostle Paul in Galatians 5:6, "faith works by love." The love by which faith works, the "how" of faith, is the love to God included in the very essence of the act of faith. "From love to God, springs love to man, as says the apostle, 1 John v. 1."[6] Of even more significance, through the practice of charity toward the neighbor in the Christian life, love to God is most clearly expressed. Apart from a fruitful direction of heart to other men, the propensity of heart directed toward God finds no proper expression. Even the importance of acts of worship pales in comparison with good works toward the fellow man. Charitable behavior toward men is more expressive of the love to God in faith than the performance of such duties as the outward observance of proper worship because "we cannot express our love to God by doing any thing that is profitable to him; God would therefore have us do it in those things that are profitable to our neighbors, whom he has constituted his receivers."[7] Faith, therefore, lovingly directs man to God, but it also inclines him toward his neighbor in love; and charitable practice toward the neighbor is the best expression of faith.

Disposition and Volition in Practice

To provide a philosophical setting in which he may delineate in more detail the relation between faith and practice and the role of religious practice in man's salvation, Edwards invokes two distinctions: the distinction between the "inside" and the "outside" of practice (which proves to be more a manner of speaking than a distinction between two different facts); and the distinction between two internal "acts" of volition, disposition and practice.

The expression of faith in charitable practice consists not simply in what is external, in the outward acts of the body. Good works arising out of faith have both an "inside" and an "outside" which are inseparably joined.[8] Further, there are two kinds of "internal acts" in the volition of the Christian man: the internal act of the will in the love to God involved in the act of faith; and the internal act of volition that is the "inside," so to speak, of the charitable work of obedience or of Christian practice. Edwards summarizes the meaning of the distinctions this way:

Men's actions may be distinguished into two kinds. First, are those acts which consist in the meer immanent exercise of the inclination and spirit of the mind . . . they begin and end in a single exercise of this inclination of the mind. . . . Such are the internal breathings of Love to God and exercises of faith in Christ. . . .

2. Properly voluntary actions, that is, those acts whether internal or external that are immediately caused by [a] preceding act of the inclination and will at whose command it arises, whether this act be in doing some positive thing or in voluntary omitting. . . . Any thing whatsoever is the proper fruit of a man's inclination that is not the immediate first acting of that inclination itself. These are that sort of acts which in Scripture are chiefly meant by works when we are directed to try our sincerity by our works and are told that we shall be judged by them at the Great Day. . . .[9]

It is to be noted, however—and this is not altogether clear in the passage just cited—that though in the "properly voluntary action" one may distinguish between an interior and exterior, this is not a distinction between two different acts but refers to two different aspects of the same act. A major point in Edwards' argument against Arminian free-willism was to be that there is not an internal willing upon which external performance awaits to agree to follow or to decide to reject. Human volition is not to be broken into distinct and possibly contrary internal and external acts. In voluntary actions the "determinations of the will, are indeed *our very actions*, so far as they are properly ours. . . ."[10] The body and the soul are a unity; the outer and the inner are united in the work.[11] As Edwards states in his *Freedom of the Will*, "not only is it true, that it is easy for a man to do the thing if he will, but the very willing is the doing; when once he has willed, the thing is performed; and nothing else remains to be done."[12] The willing in practice is the performance of the act willed. For "'tis known that these commanding acts of the will are not one way, and the actions of the bodily organs another: for the unalterable law of nature is, that they should be united, so long as soul and body are united, and the organs are not so destroyed as to be incapable of those motions that the soul commands."[13]

Edwards' refusal to separate internal volition and external performance of the act is germane to his theory of what constitutes religious practice "godly" or "ungodly": "godliness consists not in an *Heart* to purpose to fulfill God's commandments but in an *Heart* actually to do it."[14] Having a heart or inclination *to purpose* to perform an act, or being at one remove from the actual performance of the act, is not really to incline to perform it at all. When something is willed, there is an inclination *actually to do the act*. And the very willing becomes the doing. It is senseless, therefore, for a man to attempt to excuse his actions by saying that he really willed one thing but did another:

. . . it would be ridiculous for a man to plead, that the commanding act of his will was to go to public worship, while his feet carry him to a tavern or brothel house; or that the commanding act of his will was to give such a piece of money he had in his hand, to a poor beggar, while his hand at the same instant, kept it back, and held it fast.[15]

If the act intended is not performed (and if there are no natural or bodily impediments), the action is not intended by a commanding movement of the will; that is, it is not really willed. In practice or the performance of works, the internal movement of the mind—the exertion of the will in commanding acts—is held in union with the outward actions willed, and this by virtue of "the laws of union between the soul and body, which God, and not the soul has fixed, and does maintain."[16]

As to Edwards' other, more important distinction, although the immanent acts of the will are to be distinguished from those more practical or those directly bent on something to be done outwardly, this is not to say that the immanent acts are "impractical" or *totally unrelated* to practice. The immanent acts "tend to practice," but "more remotely." They remain and terminate in the soul in the sense that they bear no

"*immediate* relation to anything to be done outwardly."[17]
They are definitely indirectly related to works proper, however, in that they constitute the disposition which guides the performance of the commanding-willing in outward action. At this point Edwards' two kinds of human action are connected: the immanent exercises of the will—such as "the internal breathings of Love to God and exercises of faith in Christ"—frame the disposition which guides the "properly voluntary actions" or those acts arising out of the commanding volition and bent on outward action. Not only is it true that when one believes the Word of God, he "dares to act upon it"; his heartily believing the Word in faith guides the direction of the daring action. Two kinds of movements of the will may be distinguished, but they are not to be separated; for it is the same will that wills in both movements—or better, it is the same man who wills in both acts. This means that although the loving inclination toward God in the essence of faith is to be distinguished from the working love directed to the neighbor's good, it is the same will that is inclining, the same man acting, the same willing subject who loves God and who commands his acts of love toward men. As simultaneously faithful and practical, Christian man has a disposition constituted by the immanent acts of the will which guides his doing of works or his "properly voluntary" behavior. The disposition is the "tasting," the "sensing" of divine truth in faith:

. . . there is . . . a divine taste, given and maintained by the Spirit of God, in the hearts of the saints, whereby they are . . . led and guided in discerning and distinguishing the true spiritual and holy beauty of actions; and that more easily, readily and accurately, as they have more or less of the Spirit of God dwelling in them. And thus the sons of God are led by the Spirit of God, in their behavior in the world. . . . So an eminently humble, or meek, or charitable disposition, will direct a person of mean capacity to such a behavior, as is agreeable to Christian rules of humility, meekness and charity, far more readily and precisely, than the most diligent study, and elaborate reasonings, of a man of the strongest faculties, who has not a Christian spirit within him. So also will a spirit of love to God, and holy fear and reverence towards God, and filial confidence in God, and an heavenly disposition, teach and guide a man in his behavior.[18]

This understanding of the relation between immanent acts and working acts of the will is at the heart of Edwards' major treatise on the will. The will is not a self-determining entity but is the human acting which "follows the last dictate of the understanding"—"understanding" being taken here "in a large sense, as including the whole faculty of perception or apprehension," the whole *previous disposition* and *motive* of the mind.[19] So the mind's "filial confidence in God," its "spirit of love to God," the understanding of faith which reaches into the depths of human being, is the disposition that "teaches and guides" the man of faith in his behavior.

In terms of that age-old debate on the will, Edwards is finally a "determinist" rather than a "nondeterminist" or "free-willist" in his exposition of the nature of motivation and volition. Volitions are determined by prior mental events or dispositions such as love to God. There is really no basis for reading Edwards, as Paul Ramsey does, as an eighteenth-century precursor of contemporary phenomenology which "brackets out" questions of antecedents in volition. Ramsey writes: "In defining freedom and analyzing the nature of an act of volition, questions about what *goes before* an act of willing should not be raised. By *placing brackets around* all such questions and removing them from consideration, we can be sure of sticking close to the actual *experience* of freedom and not be tempted to import into the discussion notions of freedom that are the product of confused metaphysical speculation."[20] To be sure, Edwards in his lengthy treatise on the will concentrates on a consideration of the actual experience of freedom and allows, in a sense, a "freedom of the will" (or better, a freedom of the willer). The will is free in that the willing is the doing; actions are the products of man's own volition, including his dispositions and "volitions proper." Yet Edwards does not bracket out of view questions about antecedents to specific volitional acts; consideration of such antecedents is pertinent to his examination of the experience of freedom. The willing that terminates in outward action is determined by the prior disposition of the human spirit—by prior motives, acts or perceptions of the mind. And for the man of faith, the human acts that precede "volitions proper" themselves arise from the prior act of the Spirit. Arthur Murphy is quite correct when he argues that according to Edwards acts of willing "are effects which must have causes. Their causes, the previous mental effects that move the mind to volition, are called motives. These prior events have causes over which the volitions, which are their effects, have no control. For the act of volition does not choose its causes; until they have produced it, it does not exist as a choosing of anything."[21] In terms of the distinctions Edwards draws between human acts, the "immanent exercise of the inclination and spirit of the mind" or the disposition of heart is the determinant of works proper. Although adherence to God in faith is not *in itself* bent on outward action, it nevertheless frames the disposition of heart that motivates the volition involved in charitable works.

Edwards' analysis of the roles of disposition and volition in practice, which amounts to an analysis of the formal relation between faith and practice, provides the context in which he examines two other problems: (1) the role of good works in the order of salvation; and (2) the relation between Christian practice and the assurance of faith. The first problem is the issue presently before us; the second is that of our following chapter.

Practice and Salvation

Faith issues in practice, and acts of Christian practice are the proper evidences of faith. This is a basic premise in Edwards' view of religion. "The act of the man must be the proper Evidence of the act of the Heart. The will must be shown by the voluntary actions."[22] The deed is the best test of religious sincerity. Yet for Edwards practice is evidence of religious faith not only before other men and before oneself but before God as well. Practice is the "grand evidence" before the judgment seat of God: "The Scriptures do abundantly teach us, that the grand evidences which the Judge will make use in the final trial, for these ends, according to which the judgment of every one shall be regulated, and the irreversible sentence passed, will be men's works, or practice, here in this world."[23] In what sense are works evidences before God? What role do good works play in God's salvation of the man of faith? Obviously, if Edwards is not careful on this point, he will deviate from his position that man is "justified by faith alone."

Sometimes in his consideration of the relation between saving faith and good works, Edwards seems to lean rather closely to the medieval doctrine that charity forms faith. But it is only a seeming inclination. Edwards says, for example, that "love belongs to the essence of saving faith," love is "the life and power" of faith.[24] Jan Ridderbos picks up such statements and concludes that Edwards "sometimes takes the doctrine of Rome openly that love is the form and soul of faith."[25] Edwards himself invites this conclusion when he quotes Thomas Goodwin: "Dr. Goodwin, in Vol. I. of his works, p. 286, says, 'The Papists say, wickedly and wretchedly, that love is the form and soul of faith'" and then remarks, "But how does the truth of this charge of wickedness appear?"[26] Despite the fact that Edwards is here apparently questioning the legitimacy of Goodwin's condemnation of the doctrine, it is clear in Edwards' following explication of the way in which love may be said to be the "form" of faith that he does not adhere to the classical notion of charitable *works* being the form of faith. "That true faith, in the Scripture sense of it, implies not only the exercise of the understanding, but of the heart or disposition, is very manifest. . . . It is evident that trust in Christ implies the disposition or will, the receiving and embracing of the heart."[27] The love that is the soul, form, life of faith is nothing other than the inclining, hearty aspect of faithful knowledge. This is not the charitable love, the working love which flows out of faith, but is the love to God that is of the very essence of the faith-act.[28] In the medieval position, where charity brings unformed faith to its true form, love is not the form or life of faith in the sense of being of the very *essence* of faith. Quite the contrary: as St. Thomas explained it, charity does not belong to the essence of faith for "what brings faith to its form, or makes it alive, does not belong to the essence of faith."[29] According to Edwards, faith is not something unformed which is then formed or brought to life by love; rather, faith in its very essence is living, loving, formed. The love which is the life and form of faith is not the love that flows from faith in works but is the love to God which is the act of volition in the essential act of faith itself. Edwards would have received the pronouncement of anathema at the hands of the Council of Trent, which decreed that good works are not "merely the fruits and signs of Justification" but are also the means of "increasing" justification.[30] Edwards says quite explicitly that works of love, charitable acts of Christian practice, remain for him "signs" rather than the "price" of God's favor in justification.[31]

Edwards elaborates upon his meaning when he turns to the Epistle of James on faith and works. Unlike Luther, Edwards will not dispense with the problems posed by James by deeming it an "epistle of straw." Edwards operates with a Calvinist rather than a Lutheran scriptural hermeneutic, and this means that he will attempt to reconcile the statements of James on faith and works with those seemingly contradictory statements in the Pauline epistles. In an effort to take seriously the statement in the second chapter of James about Abraham's faith—"by works was faith made perfect"—Edwards says, "Grace is said to be perfected or finished in holy practice, as therein it is brought to its proper effect, and to that exercise which is the end of the principle; the tendency and design of grace, herein is reached and its operation completed and crowned."[32] Love to God is made perfect in the keeping of God's commandments; a man's faith is finished or brought to fruition in holy practice.[33] We have just seen that for Edwards works of charity cannot bring a supposed dead faith to life. In this sense works cannot "perfect" faith. Yet they may "perfect" faith in this way: they may *exhibit faith's own liveliness and thereby demonstrate the nature of faith.*

To return to earlier categories, immanent acts of the will, such as love to God in faith, though complete in themselves apart from issuance in practice, are not unrelated to practice. The "inward exercises," says Edwards, "are not the less a part of Christian experience, because they have outward behavior immediately connected with them. A strong act of love to God, is not the less a part of spiritual experience, because it is the act that immediately produces and effects some self-denying and expensive outward action, which is much to the honor and glory of God."[34] Though immanent acts of the will may be distinguished from outward volition in act, the two are not to be absolutely divided; for outer-directed volitions issue out of the disposition of mind shaped by the immanent acts. In all propriety one cannot say that the immanent acts are *actualized* by practice; that is, practice does not bring merely potential faith to life. Rather the *acts of Christian practice are instances of living, actual faith expressing itself*.[35] Here lies additional comment on the way in which practice is the "life" and "soul" of faith:

[James 2:26—"For as the body apart from the spirit is dead, even so faith apart from works is dead."] Not that the very works or actions are properly the life of faith, as the spirit in the body; but it is the active, working nature of faith, of which the actions or works done are the signs, that is itself the life and spirit of faith. The sign of a thing is often in Scripture language said to be that thing; as it is in that comparison by which the apostle illustrates it. It is not the actions themselves of the body, that are properly the life or spirit of the body; but it is the active nature, of which these actions or motions are the signs, that is the life of the body.[36]

Faith itself, therefore, is a living, active faith in its own nature. Faith is not to be identified with Christian practice of charity, and practice does not "realize" faith; but practice is connected with faith as the sign of faith's true nature. If faith is genuine, it will manifest itself as a vital, working faith.

Good works "perfect" faith, therefore, by demonstrating its liveliness. Edwards offers this parable as an illustration of what St. James means by works perfecting faith:

If a prince makes suit to a woman in a far country, that she would forsake her own people, and father's house, and come to him, to be his bride; the proper evidence of the compliance of her heart with the king's suit, is her actually forsaking her own people, and father's house, and coming to him. By this, her compliance with the king's suit is made perfect, in the same sense, that the apostle James says, "by works is faith made perfect."[37]

In view of what Edwards has said of faith itself being active and alive, it should be added that the woman's compliance of heart does not come to completion out of incompletion in her forsaking her house and coming to the prince. Rather, if her compliance of heart is genuine it will express itself in her actually coming to the prince. Works perfect faith not in the sense of making perfect something that was imperfect, but perfect it by demonstrating its true character. Practice perfects the *trust* character of faith, for example, by demonstrating that it is really trust, by showing in works that trust is ready to "run a risk":

Practice is the most proper evidence of trusting in Christ for salvation. The proper signification of the word "trust," according to the more ordinary use of it, both in common speech and in the Holy Scriptures, is the emboldening and encouragement of a person's mind, to run some venture in practice, or in something that he does, on the credit of another's sufficiency and faithfulness. And therefore the proper evidence of his trusting, is the venture he runs in what he does.[38]

This recalls Edwards' concise statement about the "practical" or active nature of faith: to depend upon the word of God "is to believe it as to dare to act upon it, as if it were really true." Man's faith is perfected in Christian practice because in practice one has the demonstration of his readiness to dare to act upon the truth to which he adheres in faith.

With the explanation of the manner in which works perfect faith and of how love is the form of faith, Edwards has intimated *how practice may demonstrate one's faith before God*. But now the question is more specifically the role of good works in salvation, and the issue at stake is not simply the way in which St. James should be understood respecting the perfection of faith by works but whether St. James can be reconciled with St. Paul on the meaning of justification, or how perfecting-works of Christian practice fit into the order of salvation. Edwards at this point avails himself of previous Calvinist interpretations of the Epistle of James.

It was part of the Reformed, and especially the Puritan, tradition's concern to link closely faith and morality, piety and practice, which led it to insist that, in a certain sense, one must say with St. James that man is "justified by works." Since faith is practical or active by nature, practice is in some

way involved in salvation or justification itself. The Westminster Confession had formulated it this way: though man
is justified before God by faith alone, he is not justified by
faith which is alone or by a faith which is without works.[39]
The Calvinist theologians sought to reconcile James and Paul
by following Calvin himself who said that James uses the
word "justification" in a different sense than Paul: for James,
works justify "declaratively."[40] Or as Turrettini put it, Paul
speaks "of *justification a priori and constitutively*, James of
the same a posteriori and declaratively."[41] Thomas Manton
elaborated upon the distinction this way:

I conceive, as works are signs *in foro humano*, to men, by which
they may judge of the quality of faith, so *in foro divino*, before God,
God judging "according to our works," as it is distinctly said, Rev.
20. 12. God will evince the faith of his saints to be right by produc-
ing their works, and will discover the ungrounded hopes of others by
their works also, for great and small are all judged according to that
rule. And not only hereafter, but now also doth God judge according
to works; that is, look upon them as testimonies and declarations of
faith.[42]

In agreement with this line of interpretation, Edwards
says that James and Paul use the word "justify" in different
senses; therefore one may say with James (2:21, 24–25) that
man is justified by works and still adhere to the confession
that he is justified by faith alone, or apart from his own
righteousness. For in the second chapter of James, "works are
here spoken of as justifying as evidences." In Romans, justification means not justification by evidences but actually becoming just by the imputation of Christ's righteousness
through faith. In other words, "it is by works that our cause
appears to be good; but by faith our cause not only appears
to be good, but becomes good; because thereby we are united
to Christ."[43] Men are not accepted by God because of the
merits of their works—Edwards has rejected this view in his
doctrine of justification by faith. But God makes use of human works in order to *declare* the acceptance that is actual
only in faith. Edwards insists that, of course, God does not
need the testimonies of works in order to judge of faith's
authenticity. He knows the human heart. But for the sake of

men God chooses to make a declarative judgment with respect to works as well as actually to impute righteousness with respect to faith; and before the judgment throne of God, man both becomes accepted by God through faith and expresses his faith through his deeds.

God himself, when he acts towards men as judge, in order to a declarative judgment, makes use of evidences, and so judges men by their works. And therefore, at the day of judgment, God will judge men according to their works: for though God will stand in no need of evidence to inform him what is right, yet it is to be considered, that he will then sit in judgment, not as earthly judges do, to find out what is right in a cause, but to declare and manifest what is right; and therefore that day is called by the apostle, "the day of the revelation of the righteous judgment of God," Rom. ii. 5.

To be justified, is to be approved and accepted: but a man may be said to be approved and accepted in two respects; the one is to be approved really, and the other to be approved and accepted declaratively.[44]

Faith and works, and actual and declarative justification, are not really of parallel importance. Works are expressions of what is fundamental in salvation (faith); and declarative justice is possible only on the basis of first having Christ's righteousness imputed.[45]

But Edwards carries his argument a step further. Not only do works express faith and hence qualify practice for declarative justification; works are, in a sense, promised the *reward* of salvation. By virtue of the connection between faith and practice, promises of salvation are made to holy practice. Here again Edwards seems in danger of abandoning his position on justification by faith alone; but he hastens to add that the reward of salvation is not made to the human works themselves. And works do not "increase" justification. Any reward to practice is really a reward to Christ's righteousness:

Hence, though it be true that the saints are rewarded for their good works, yet it is for Christ's sake only, and not for the excellency of their works in themselves considered, or beheld separately from Christ; for so they have no excellency in God's sight, or acceptableness to him. . . .[46]

It is only through the mediation of Christ that men's works

are in any sense "good." "By his intercession their good works become acceptable to God and to his praise and glory."[47] Good works are rewardable with salvation only because Christ covers them with his own goodness and loveliness.[48] Thus works of holy practice are concerned in salvation only to the extent that they have the essence of faith in them: that is, to the extent that the practicing Christian continues to receive Christ and be covered by his righteousness.[49] Works do not add anything to the person's own rewardableness; but to the degree that they simultaneously express faith and are covered by Christ's righteousness through faith, they are good and rewardable.

Edwards' attempt, then, is to connect faith and practice as closely as possible in the order of salvation without contending that the human practice of charitable works is, in and of itself, worthy of salvation. If the danger of the attempt is the possible obscuration of his position on justification by faith alone, the strength of the attempt lies in its refusal to turn salvation by faith into an inactive, contemplative withdrawal from the affairs of man. The nature of this close connection between faith and practice is made even more vivid in Edwards' description of acts of holy practice as "new acts" of justifying faith. According to this description, the man of faith believes again and again in practice. Acts of holy practice, which consist essentially in acts of love to the neighbor, may be viewed as new acts of faith in Christ. This portrayal of the relation between faith and works might well imply that works complete faith by adding something which is not available to faith as faith. In a few miscellaneous notes Edwards tends to suggest this. He says, for example: "Our act of closing with and accepting of Christ, is not in all respects completed by our accepting him with our hearts, 'till we have done it practically too, so have accepted him with the whole man, soul, spirit and body."[50] This way of expressing the relation between justifying faith and practice implies that practice, as a "new act," is needed along with the act of faith because the two together involve the whole man in a way in which faith alone does not. This implication is directly contrary to Edwards' insistence that practice perfects faith not by adding anything to an otherwise incomplete faith but by expressing faith's own nature, and to his view of faith as itself a knowledge of heart that involves the whole man. But in his "Justification by Faith Alone," Edwards guards against this implication and amplifies what he intends in this notion of acts of obedience as new acts of faith. There he says, "All evangelical works are works of that faith that worketh by love; and every such act of obedience, wherein it is inward and the act of the soul, is only a new, effective act of reception of Christ, an adherence to the glorious Saviour."[51] Acts of obedience on the part of the Christian are new acts of faith when they are expressions of faith's own nature and tendency. Here acts of obedience are not additions which complete an otherwise incomplete faith. They are, rather, instances of man's receipt of salvation in Christ through faith, occurring again and again in the setting of working love. And the acts of obedience do not of themselves contribute anything to salvation; they are rather the outworkings of the power of Christ received in faith. "Hence that of the apostle, Gal. ii. 20, 'I live; yet not I, but Christ liveth in me; and the life that I now live in the flesh, is by the faith of the Son of God.' And hence we are directed, in whatever we do, whether in word or deed, to do all in the name of the Lord Jesus Christ, Col. iii. 17."[52] The faith which receives Christ within acts of working love constitutes the acts of obedience as new acts of faith. Although acts of working love do not of themselves receive Christ, they are new acts of faith in the sense that faith as the receipt of Christ occurs in and through them. This way of conceiving the close connection between faith and practice stresses the indispensability of a social context for salvation by faith. Saving faith occurs where one is active in the working love directed toward the neighbor. It is a faith that can never amount to a withdrawal from responsible love of the neighbor in order to receive salvation in Christ; it is rather a receipt of salvation and a hearty adherence to the revealed God *within* one's loving the neighbor in practice. Such is the nature of man: he is a creature whose redemption must be a redemption set within the context of his responsibility for his fellow man. And such is the nature of God: his gift of salvation is a gift designed to be received by the man who is responsible toward his neighbor in love.

Works of love can never become adequate substitutes for love to God; practice is not to supplant faith. Yet faith and practice are inseparable, for faith depends upon practice for both its expression and its living milieu.

CHAPTER IX

PRACTICE AND ASSURANCE OF FAITH

Practice, the performance of good works, exhibits the nature of faith before the eyes of the man of faith as well as before God. Edwards claimed Christian practice as the chief means through which one may be assured that he is a man of faith.

The Puritan emphasis upon activity or the practical life as the medium through which the saint may be assured of his election in a predestined world is now fairly commonly known, especially since Max Weber's association of this Puritan emphasis with the "spirit of capitalism." But what is perhaps not so familiar is that in Calvinism, though assurance through practice was not to become complacent self-satisfaction, assurance could be *certain*. Reformed theologians stood firmly with Calvin and against Rome in adhering to the tenet that the saint may be assured of his election to salvation apart from any special or secret revelation from God and with a confidence surpassing mere "conjectural" knowledge. The Westminster Confession stated:

This certainty [of salvation] is not a bare conjectural and probable persuasion, grounded upon a fallible hope; but an infallible assurance of faith, founded upon the divine truth of the promises of salvation, the inward evidence of those graces unto which these promises are made, the testimony of the Spirit of adoption witnessing with our spirits that we are the children of God. . . .[1]

Assurance is not of the essence of faith, for faith may possibly not gain assurance of itself until after a long and arduous battle with doubt—and it remains faith nonetheless.[2] Yet man may find assurance of his saving faith as God's Spirit witnesses with his spirit for that assurance. Most Calvinist theologians were convinced that one had the clearest witness of the Spirit through the performance of good works. There were modifications of, and even exceptions to, this belief in Puritan thought. Solomon Stoddard in one of his treatises found reliable means of assurance in intuition of inner piety or holiness rather than in outward conduct.[3] And in a statement by John Preston good works find limited significance, to say the least, for indicating faith: "Though it be not a good rule to say I have good works, therefore my heart is right, yet it is a good rule to say on the other side, I want good works, therefore my heart is not right."[4] But more often than not, the manifestation of faith in a visibly sanctified life was believed an adequate means of assuring oneself that he was an elected man of faith. Especially in the face of the rise of antinomianism in seventeenth-century New England did right-wing Puritans find it increasingly necessary to insist on the suitableness of the sanctified life as an evidence of justification. Against the antinomian high estimation of the inward testimony of the Spirit to the exclusion of holy works as signs of faith, the orthodox Puritans turned more and more to holy practice as the principal means used by the Holy Spirit to testify to a man of his salvation.[5] Holy practice was man's way of demonstrating to himself, in spite of temptation to the contrary, that he was a man of faith; and this practice was believed a means employed by the Holy Spirit himself.

Edwards also chose works as the chief means employed by God for a man's assurance. He praised his friend David Brainerd for finding assurance of saving faith in its "evidences" in his sanctified life rather than in immediate whisperings of the Holy Spirit.[6] Edwards had no patience with those enthusiasts who limited the testimony of the Spirit to inward, invisible, "impractical" flashes of assurance: such testimony is too ephemeral and too often deluding. Faith gives testimony of its truly vital nature in practice, and the inward testimony of the Holy Spirit to man's spirit that he is chosen for faith is a testimony in and through the acts of man's holy life in the world. Because of the intimate connection between faith and practice, "works are as much the proper evidence of the act of the soul in receiving Christ, as the act of the soul in receiving Christ is the proper evidence of the principle of faith."[7] Furthermore, because of the inseparability of inward volition and outward performance in a work, "the external act is not excluded in that obedience that is in Scripture so much insisted on as a sign of godliness, but the internal exertion of the mind and the external act as connected with it are both included and intended."[8] Edwards does not deny that the Spirit of God works within the heart of a saint for the benefit of that saint's assurance; but he does maintain that when the heart is worked upon, the will is changed. When the will is changed, that change is discernible in practice wherein the willing has both an inside and an outside. Therefore the witness of the Spirit with man's spirit becomes "conspicuous" when man wrestles to perform Christian practice amidst the struggles and trials of life.

The witness or seal of the Spirit that we read of, doubtless consists in the effect of the Spirit of God in the heart, in the implantation and exercises of grace there. . . . But in these exercises of grace in practice, that have been spoken of, God gives witness, and sets to his seal, in the *most conspicuous, eminent* and *evident manner*. . . . So when the Apostle speaks of the "earnest of the Spirit," which God has given to him, in II Cor. 5:5; the context shows plainly that he has respect to what was given to him in his great trials and sufferings.[9] [Italics mine]

Though Edwards consistently maintains that the witness of the Spirit to man of his adoption is made through practice, he nevertheless believes that the "signs of godliness" may be divided into those predominantly inward and those predominantly outward. These two kinds of signs correspond to the two kinds of acts analyzed in our preceding chapter.

First there are those things that are mentioned in Scripture as that wherein godliness doth more primarily and radically consist, such as having and knowing God and spiritually understanding divine things, loving God, fearing God, trusting in God, repentance, believing in Christ, choosing and resting in God and Christ and spiritual and eternal Good as a portion. . . . These . . . signs . . . may be known directly by reflecting upon ourselves and enquiring what we experience within ourselves.

And 2. There are those things that the Scriptures mention as signs of these signs of faith and love, such as bringing forth fruit, doing good works, keeping God's and Christ's commandments universally and perseveringly . . . by which we are to try our sincerity and by which we are to try whether we . . . have those things wherein godliness more radically consists.[10]

According to this distinction, good works are "signs of

signs" inasmuch as faith, of which works are signs, is itself a sign that one is a recipient of grace. However, though there are two basic kinds of signs of grace for Edwards, assurance of grace in one's life is to be gained chiefly in one way: through practice or through the "signs of signs." "These are expressly given in Scripture as signs by which we are to try our sincerity." The distinction between two kinds of signs does not lead Edwards to conclude that there are, correspondingly, two parallel means of assurance: self-examination of inward signs and practice of outward signs. Practice far outweighs self-examination as a means of assurance. Assurance is to be had more readily through the practical act than through contemplative withdrawal; assurance finds its appropriate means in action rather than in self-examination. Self-examination involves the reflective withdrawal from the life of faith in order to examine the nature of the experience. It is reflection upon the experience of faith rather than the *actual experiencing* of faith in its total range of immanent and properly voluntary acts. It is stopping to reflect upon the manner of one's pressing toward the mark rather than actually pressing toward the mark. Clearly, according to Edwards, assurance is gained chiefly through the pressing toward the mark.

Assurance is not to be obtained so much by self-examination, as by action. The apostle Paul sought assurance chiefly this way, even by forgetting the things that were behind, and reaching forth unto those things that were before, pressing toward the mark for the prize. . . . He obtained assurance of winning the prize, more by running, than by considering. The swiftness of his pace, did more towards his assurance of a conquest, than the strictness of his examination.[11]

Assurance of faith, then, involves no excessive searching of one's own experience, no morbid preoccupation with the "status of the soul" that breeds extreme introversion; assurance is gained chiefly as one pushes ahead in Christian practice.

Edwards does believe that a certain amount of self-examination of one's heart and conduct is necessary—but self-examination does not mean introversion, and self-examination has its hazards. When the Psalmist, in Psalm 139, prays that God would search him, to see if there were any wicked way in him, he cannot mean that he should search that he himself might see and be informed, but that the *Psalmist* might see and be informed. He prays that God would search him by his discovering light; that he would lead him thoroughly to discern himself, and see whether there were any wicked way in him.[12]

The saint is conscious that a sinful life is a dishonor and affront to God; hence he is concerned to examine his life through God's help in order to discern, and where possible overcome, particular sinful ways. Yet Edwards can say this and still not counsel men to take their eyes off faith's object. Self-examination is self-reflection, but it is not complete in-turning: it is beholding oneself according to the standard of the Word. It is making "use of the word as a glass, wherein you may behold yourselves."[13] One of the things that sets man apart from the brutes is his capacity for self-reflection, and something he can always do is "join *self-reflection* with reading and hearing the word of God."[14] This self-reflection through the mirror of God's Word, this coming to a knowledge of sin through the Word, is part of that use of the law which the Christian employs in his day-to-day living and working in the world; it is following the law as the "perfect rule by which we ought to walk."[15] It is a self-examination which discovers human sin by allowing the written and spoken Word of God to illuminate one's situation.

Edwards recognizes, however, both the limits and the obstacles resident in self-examination. In the first place, because of the sin within the heart of every man, he must find it extremely difficult to pass any kind of truly accurate judgment on his condition. One is blinded to his true self by his sin;[16] and he is in turn blinded to that sin by the very custom of sin and by the example of others whom he may wrongly judge to be truly godly.[17] But above all, the difficulty of self-examination "is not at all for want of light without us, not at all because the word of God is not plain, or the rules not clear; but it is because of the darkness within us. The light shines clear enough around us, but the fault is in our eyes; they are darkened and blinded by a pernicious distemper."[18]

The major obstacle attending self-examination is that one

may be arrested in his progress in practice by anxiety over sin discovered. Therefore Edwards counsels in a sermon where he stresses the importance of self-examination, "If persons be converted, the most likely way to have the Spirit of God witnessing with our spirits, that we are the children of God, is to walk closely with God."[19] Or as Edwards says in the *Affections*, "Assurance is not to be obtained so much by self-examination, as by action." The Spirit most clearly witnesses with our spirits for our assurance of faith when we are working in love by faith, not when we settle back for reflection on our experiences. Edwards does not suppose, despite Leslie Stephen's opinion, that "dissection of emotion down to its finest and most intricate convolutions" is "of the very essence of religion."[20] On the contrary, "pressing into the Kingdom" through attendance on the means of grace and through practice is vital to the religious life in a way in which concern over one's inward parts is not. Too much stopping by the saints in order to dissect their experiences

tends to *hinder* them in their work . . . they are only working violently to entangle themselves, and lay blocks in their own way; their pressure is not forwards. Instead of getting along, they do but lose their time, and worse than merely lose it; instead of fighting with the giants that stand in the way to keep them out of Canaan, they spend away their time and strength in conflicting with shadows that appear by the way-side.[21]

Much more integral to the life of the man of faith than concern with self-examination is his acting in faith. Assurance of faith comes more readily by working in faith than by self-reflection.

Yet as important as Edwards believed assurance through practice to be, he held with the greater part of his theological tradition that assurance of faith gained through practice is not of the essence of faith. There is a difference between believing and believing you believe. Edwards refuses to involve assurance of faith in the very essence of faith for two fundamental reasons: identifying faith with believing one has faith invites the height of human presumption; and the identification, by refusing to acknowledge priorities, does not allow for the believer's struggle in doubt in his faithful pilgrimage in this world.

In the first place, confusing assurance with faith per se invites men to conclude that if they can simply assure themselves that they are faithful they indeed must be men of faith. "But," Edwards asks, "what Bible do they learn this notion of faith out of, that it is a man's confidently believing that he is in a good estate?"[22] Edwards is well aware that man is prone to convince himself that he is in a state of salvation, for "men do not love to condemn themselves; they are prejudiced in their own favour, and in favour of whatever is found in themselves."[23] If believing one is possessed of saving faith is the same as having faith, "the Pharisees had faith in an eminent degree; some of which, Christ teaches, committed the unpardonable sin against the Holy Ghost."[24] Therefore, though the saint is capable of gaining assurance of faith, the assurance gained is not to be confused with faith itself; for the man of unfaith also is capable of assuring himself, though his assurance be false or one devoid of the witness of the Holy Spirit.

Furthermore, to identify assurance with the essence of faith is to fail to recognize that faith itself must be prior to genuine assurance and that the man of faith may struggle with doubt and still be a man of faith. In his correspondence with Edwards regarding various points of the *Religious Affections*, Thomas Gillespie of Carnock, Scotland, suggested that the believer should never really doubt of his state of salvation since doubting is in direct opposition to believing.[25] Edwards' reply is, "I don't take faith, and a person's believing that they have faith, to be the same thing. Nor do I take unbelief, or being without faith and doubting whether they have it, to be the same thing, but entirely different."[26] The latter distinction rests on the former: the distinction between doubt and unbelief rests on the distinction between faith and assurance. Edwards refers Gillespie to a more careful consideration of what is said in the *Affections* on the matter. There Edwards had stated: "The Scripture represents faith, as that by which men are *brought into* a good estate; and therefore it can't be the same thing, as believing that they are *already in* a good estate."[27] In another letter to

Gillespie, he builds upon this distinction. Since a man may be brought into salvation through faith quite apart from believing that he has been brought there, he—as a man of faith—may at times doubt that the Spirit of God has completed his work in him. "So, if we suppose a very eminent saint is to blame in doubting whether he has so much grace as he really has; he indeed *don't believe the reality of God's work in him, in all its parts, just as it is:* yet he is not therein guilty of the sin of unbelief, against any testimony of God. . . ."[28] One may doubt of his own condition and still adhere in faith to God's testimony in the Word.

Doubt is not, therefore, necessarily the polar opposite of faith; it may, in fact, be the cutting edge of faith that pares away pretentious claims arising out of self-satisfaction. The man of faith, as he believes—and even as he believes he believes—should never give up the struggle against the sin remaining in him. The struggle is the pressing forward in holy practice. "All those who are converted are not sure of it; and those who are sure, do not know that they shall always be so; and still seeking and serving God with the utmost diligence, is the way to have assurance, and to have it maintained."[29] The man of faith may be left with doubt regarding his salvation, for his faith both precedes his assurance and survives his lapses of assurance. And doubting of one's saved condition may very well operate as a necessary component in the struggle or pilgrimage toward the Kingdom through which the Spirit leads a person in this life of imperfection. Through good works, through practice, a man may be assured of faith—but it is truly an assurance through practice: an active, struggling assurance rather than a complacency. Donald Rhoades is quite correct: Edwards had "a distrust of any assurance which should be without concern, if not without trembling. Such assurance might be self-complacency."[30] In sum, man may have more than mere conjectural assurance of faith through the Spirit's witnessing with his spirit in and through his practice, but the assurance is struggling assurance, not self-satisfaction. And since faith is the necessary presupposition of assurance of faith, assurance—genuine assurance—is the "*effect,*" not "a *part, branch, or ingredient* of faith."[31]

As we shall see, this understanding of assurance was pivotal in Edwards' criticism of an attitude gaining wide acceptance in revivalistic America: the attitude that one is not a person of faith unless he "feels" it immediately or is subjectively assured of it. Edwards' reply was that faith is greater than one's subjective feelings; faith precedes assurance, survives its lapses, and invites man to struggle for his assurance. Edwards' Puritan concept of assurance was one that was to manifest itself at another critical moment in American history. Abraham Lincoln scribbled down on a piece of note paper, for his own perusal, a succinct passage from the Puritan Richard Baxter. William Wolf, in his study of Lincoln, sees in the words of the passage a reflection of Lincoln's understanding of his own personal religious situation. And the words pinpoint what Edwards meant by the struggle in practice for assurance:

We have faith given us, principally that we might believe and live by it in daily applications of Christ. You may believe immediately (by God's help), but getting assurance of it may be the work of a great part of your life.[32]

Edwards does grant that doubt may, and often does, arise from unbelief or from the complete absence of faith. Such doubting may be the effect of "want of dependence upon God's almighty power."[33] The doubt arising from unbelief is a doubting of the very ground of faith itself. The doubt which may accompany faith's struggle does not arise directly from unbelief[34] and does not doubt of faith's ground but is simply a doubt about my own condition. This is the difference between doubting that God has pledged himself to save me and doubting that I am already in a saved state. One may doubt his own state of salvation without doubting the ground or the possibility of his salvation, which is another way of saying that one may find a type of assurance that transcends a confidence in his own estate. Edwards is making an important distinction here, but it demands elaboration else he appears to make the absurd suggestion that a person may have certain assurance of faith and doubt it at the same time. Edwards elaborates upon the distinction by treating a doctrine often found in Reformed considerations of the assurance of faith: the doctrine of the *syllogismus practicus*. The practical syllogism is: whoever believes shall be saved; there are practical evidences (viz., my sanctified life) that I believe; therefore I shall be saved. Edwards embraces a form of this "practical reasoning" in his doctrine of assurance, and his interpretation of the syllogism is an important key to a view of assurance which allows for doubt about one's estate by pointing to a higher kind of certainty.

Karl Barth has offered a most enlightening critical analysis of the Calvinist practical syllogism. A short excursus in order to consider this analysis will yield some helpful categories for our consideration of Edwards on the matter. Barth contends that the practical syllogism implicit in Calvin's belief that one may gain assurance of election through good works, contains three points of caution not always observed by his followers. Unlike these later Calvinists, (1) Calvin himself understood that the testimony of works is not a "crown witness" but is subordinate in importance to the testimony God himself makes in the promises of the gospel. (2) Calvin saw that "the testimony of 'works' must not be separated from faith—as if *this* 'fruit' could detach itself from *that* tree and be considered by itself." Practice as a means of assurance is not an evidence detached from faith and its object but is faith itself testifying to the reality of itself and its object. (3) And finally, according to the "caution of Calvin" the practical syllogism "must not be detached from the self-testimony of Christ, from the promise of the forgiveness of sins, or in general from the objective Word of God, as if it had power in itself to penetrate its mystery, or as if there were a kind of pipeline between God's decree on the one hand, and human piety and morals on the other." Barth claims that if these three safeguards are not held within the doctrine of the practical syllogism, assurance through works degenerates into a subjectivistic moralism, into a concentration on human works and experience which turns man hopelessly in upon himself and which loses sight of the primary witness to one's salvation in God's own witness in his Word. But when the cautions are observed, the important *human* aspect of assurance is preserved by the practical syllogism: assurance through God's own testimony in Word and Spirit is real only when man "receives it from himself," when "he himself gives it in his faith and life and 'works.' It is as I live as an elect man that I am and shall be assured of my election."[35] Christian practice, the performance of good works, is inadequate as an independent testimony for assurance; but it is the chief *means* of assurance.

Edwards is as "cautious" as Barth's Calvin in his consideration of the practical syllogism. We noticed in the preceding chapter that though for Edwards faith and works are to be distinguished, they are by no means unrelated: the testimony of works is the active, living nature of faith expressing itself. Edwards would therefore concur with Barth's second point that the testimony of works is not to be separated from faith. Edwards would adhere also to Barth's first and third points: the testimony of works is relative, or dependent on God's own witness in Word and Spirit; and works of themselves do not penetrate the mystery of faith but assure man of faith only on the basis of the Word's witnessing to the forgiveness of sins. Edwards' refusal to make human practice a self-sufficient sign of faith is abundantly clear in an exposition of what we have found him continually emphasizing: the impropriety of taking one's eye off faith's object in order to turn it inward.

Persons can't be said to forsake Christ, and live on their experiences of the exercises of grace, merely because they take them and use them as evidences of grace; for there are no other evidences that they can or ought to take. But then may persons be said to live upon their experiences, when they make a righteousness of them; and instead of keeping their eye on God's glory, and Christ's excellency, they turn their eyes off these objects without them, on to themselves, to entertain their minds, by viewing their own attainments, and high experiences, and the great things they have met with, and are bright and beautiful in their own eyes, and are rich and increased with good, in their own apprehensions, and think that God has as admiring an esteem of them, on the same account, as they have of themselves: this is living on experiences, and not on Christ; and is more abominable in the sight of God, than the gross immoralities of those who make no pretenses to religion.[36]

The experience of Christian practice ceases to be a sign of faith when man attempts to "live upon" it as a kind of independent righteousness or when he beholds it apart from a view of God's glory and Christ's righteousness. The alternative to this abominable trust in one's own experiences is to view practice as an evidence of, a pointer to, grace—an evidence always joined with God's own promise of salvation.

Seen in this light, belief in the minor premise of the practical syllogism—the premise which rests on the consciousness of our own experience—is not of the nature of faith, while belief in the major premise and in the minor premise *joined with the conclusion* is of the nature of faith. That is to say, assent to the premise "whoever believes, shall be saved" is

properly of the nature of faith; because the ground of my assent to that is divine testimony. But my assent to the minor proposition [viz., "I believe" or "there are practical evidences that I believe"], I humbly conceive, is not of the nature of faith, because that is not grounded on divine testimony, but my own consciousness. The testimony that is the proper ground of faith is in the Word of God, "Faith cometh by hearing, and hearing by the word of God" (Rom. 10:17). There is such a testimony given us in the Word of God, that he *that believes shall be saved:* But there is no such testimony in the word of God, as that such an individual person, in such a town in Scotland or New England, believes.[37]

Though assent to the minor premise in itself is not grounded in the divine testimony, belief in the minor premise in conjunction with belief in the conclusion of the syllogism is founded on the Word of God and is properly of the very nature of faith:

. . . if by a man's believing himself to be in a good estate, be understood his believing not only the minor, but the consequence, *therefore I shall be saved, or therefore God will never leave nor forsake me;* then a man's believing his good estate, partakes of the nature of faith; for these consequences depend on divine testimony in the Word of God and gospel of Jesus Christ.[38]

Edwards is here stressing what Barth would call the difference between a moralistic assurance and an assurance through practice that rests upon the "objective" testimony of the Word of God. When human practice is taken *by itself* as an evidence of faith, assurance through practice does not partake of the nature of faith. But when practice serves as a sign of salvation *in conjunction* with God's own promise of salvation, assurance through practice partakes of the nature of faith.

This way of handling the Reformed doctrine of the *syllogismus practicus* harmonizes with Edwards' claim that assurance comes more by action than by self-examination. One is best assured of his faith not by reflective withdrawal from and meditation on his experiences but by actively working in faith in constant dependence upon God's promises. Though assurance is not of the essence of faith—though faith and assurance are not to be confused—assurance does not occur when disjoined from faith; assurance is gained by faith's expressing its active nature of dependence on the Word. Hence assurance through practice is joined with a confidence in the truth of the divine promises of salvation. This type of assurance allows the man of faith to doubt at any time his own "estate" since it joins the medium of human practice with that which transcends the limitations and frustrations of human experience: the certainty of God's own promise in revelation. Edwards is here reaffirming his view that resting in one's own experience or act is the very antithesis of faith. What is decisive for faith is not its own experience in itself, but its source. Correspondingly, what is crucial in assurance of faith is not the medium of assurance—human experience—but the source.

If you would know of what kind your comforts are, follow them up to the fountain, and see what is their source and spring. If you would know of what kind your hope is, examine the bottom of it, and see upon what foundation it stands. . . . What makes you hope that you are in favour with God? Is it because you conceive of God as looking down from heaven upon your heart, on your gracious experiences, and so being as it were, taken with, and receiving you into his favour on account of that? Or is your hope of God's favour built on a sense, which you have of Christ's worthiness, and the saving mercy of God in him, and his faithfulness to the promises, which he has made through him?[39]

Since human practice is the chief sign of faith only as it remains a medium, and not a source, of assurance of salvation, the saint may trust in God and His promises when human experience is dark, when holy practice is not obviously holy. This is not assurance without human experience but assurance in and through a struggling, even dark, practical experience.[40] Or to return again to the categories of the practical syllogism, the strength of belief in the minor premise presupposes belief not only in the major premise but in the conclusion as well. The syllogism is, therefore, a poor one indeed as far as the demands of strictly deductive reasoning are concerned: the conclusion does not presuppose and rest upon the minor premise, but vice versa. Confidence in one's own salvation and practical signs of salvation rests upon the conclusion that God has promised to save me, a sinner. As poor and inconsistent as the logic may be, this understanding of assurance proved to be a sound insight into human nature and into the meaning of faith during Edwards' debates with enthusiasm on the one hand and religious moralism on the other.

Closely related to this understanding of the practical syllogism is another feature of Edwards' doctrine of assurance which was conveniently overlooked by his antagonists in 1750.[41] Men may through the medium of Christian practice be assured of their own, but not of others', faith. Certainly good works are the best available demonstration of our faith not only before our own consciences but before other men as well.[42] The testimony of the Spirit is given clearest expression before men in Christian practice. But a person cannot really know the heart of another man and cannot finally judge of that man's condition.

There is nothing in others, that comes within their view but outward manifestations and appearances; but the Scripture plainly intimates that this way of judging what is in men by outward appearances, is at best uncertain, and liable to deceit; "the Lord seeth not as man seeth; for man looketh on the outward appearance, but the Lord looketh on the heart." (I Sam. 16:7)[43]

Only God, the true searcher of hearts, can finally separate the sheep from the goats, and it is "an indecent, self-exaltation, and arrogance . . . in poor fallible mortals, to pretend that they can determine and know, who are really sincere and upright before God, and who are not!"[44]

A man is always liable to error in judging of his *own* condition: sin blinds him to his own estate and frequently inclines him toward a higher evaluation of himself than is legitimate.[45] Nevertheless, his own judgment regarding his condition of faith or unfaith is more reliable than the judgment of others about him.[46] A man may be assured of his own faith through the medium of practice with a conviction which escapes others, for a man's faith which expresses itself in action is his own faith and not another's; hence he is a better judge of the nature and origin of the practice than another. Or cast in terms of Edwards' understanding of the practical syllogism, only the individual knows in his heart whether his conviction that he is a believer rests upon the conclusion that his sins are forgiven. Put in terms of the "inside" and "outside" of practice, a man is better able than another to judge of his own faith upon the evidence of practice because only the outside is apparent to others but both the inside and outside of practice are visible to the subject of the practice.[47] Of course, since the outward performance of the act is connected with its internal movement, other men through observation of the external can infer the internal. But such inference is made by fallible human judgment coupled with only an indirect knowledge of the internal exercise of the actor's properly voluntary and immanent willing. The judgment of the actor about his own acting, though fallible, has at least the advantage of a "direct and immediate" view of the "exertion and exercise of the soul."[48] Hence he may be assured of his own faith through practice in a way in which he cannot assure another man of that same faith; for his faith itself, as well as the whole of his faithful practice, stands in view of his own consciousness in his action.

To summarize, Edwards could not bring himself to agree with Stoddard that assurance comes principally by intuition of internal grace, but he did join practice with more internal signs of grace. Faith itself is an internal sign of grace, and acts of holy practice are "signs of signs" or signs of an internal act like faith. But practice—including both its inside and its outside, both the commanding acts of will and the outward performance—is the most "conspicuous" sign of grace to a man's own consciousness and is the chief medium through which the Spirit witnesses with the human spirit. Although there is a kind of uncertainty in the saint's assurance, it is an uncertainty deriving from the sinfulness and cloudiness of man's own consciousness. Thus assurance through practice is a struggling assurance, and what is available through the saint's own awareness of himself must be joined with a hope and trust in God's promises of salvation: faith and assurance are distinguishable but not separable. Assurance comes more by acting in faith than by self-examination of an immanent act like faith; but for assurance, the practice of good works must be joined with faith's actual "sensing" of God's promise of love and faithfulness in the "excellency" of the Christ.

Part Four:

CONTROVERSY OVER FAITH

INTRODUCTION

The greater number of Jonathan Edwards' major published treatises were directed toward particular, pressing theological issues of his day. The *Treatise on Religious Affections* spoke to the debate between revivalists and rationalists created by the tides of the Great Awakening, his *Doctrine of Original Sin* was a reply to John Taylor's challenge to that Calvinist doctrine, and the essay *Freedom of the Will* was intended to reduce the arguments of the Arminians to absurdity. Much like Luther in the sixteenth century, Edwards in the eighteenth found his intellectual efforts called forth by specific problems which faced the Church of his period. And instead of developing a systematic scheme within which to set the various aspects of the Christian religion, Edwards theologized as the occasion demanded.[1] Yet, also like Luther, Edwards was not "unsystematic" in the sense of arbitrarily dragging up an idea to meet every occasion; rather, he spoke to each issue from the depth of a developed and largely coherent theological position.

The preceding three parts of this inquiry have attempted to lay out Edwards' doctrine of faith in a systematic form according to its various dimensions and relations. In order to execute this task, however, we found it necessary to turn not only to unpolemical notes, sermons, and tracts, but to the polemical writings as well. This suggests that the doctrine of faith was a factor in Edwards' more controversial writings even when the issue under immediate attention was some other matter. It is the purpose of this our concluding part to show at what points and in what ways Edwards' understanding of the nature of faith was at stake in the leading controversies he faced in his tumultuous eighteenth-century New England.

Edwards' controversies were primarily focused by two polar theological positions: Arminianism and antinomianism. Both positions proved to be equally destructive of the true nature of faith for Edwards, and it was one of his intentions, in doing battle with Arminianism and antinomianism, to transcend their errors by defending and clarifying his own understanding of religious faith. Edwards himself pointed to these positions as the two principal threats to religion looming on the scene. In a letter to a Scottish clergyman in 1749, Edwards endeavors to describe "the present state of religion in these parts of the world."[2] To illuminate the description he quotes at length a statement of a ministerial association "between this [Long Island] and Boston" which declares about the religious condition of America: One must "take heed and beware of the dangerous errors which many have run into; particularly the Arminian and Neonomian on the one hand, and the Antinomian and Enthusiastical on the other."[3] In a letter of the following year, Edwards writes that he lives in a "sorrowful time" when "Arminianism, and Pelagianism, have made a strange progress" and when "many professors are gone off to great lengths in enthusiasms and extravagance, in their notions and practices."[4]

We cannot here occupy ourselves with a historical sketch of either Arminianism or antinomianism. Both traditions do, indeed, have complex histories, and neither is fully specified by its usage as a "brand name" or pejorative type at the hands of the Calvinist. This granted, however, and despite the fact that all parties obviously resented being simply dismissed as "Calvinist," "Arminian," or "Antinomian," the theological labels inevitably did serve in the height of controversy to represent substantial differences regarding the relation between law and gospel—differences which the parties to the controversy understood as the explication of each point of view progressed. The debates between Arminians and Calvinists became centered on such points as freedom of the will and irresistible grace, but "Arminianism" referred essentially to the theology which rested salvation on a man's own act or which at least claimed man's ability to contribute by his act to the divine decision to save, thereby making grace conditional on human endeavor or on the human fulfillment of the law. Hence Edwards and the Calvinist ministerial association believed "Arminianism" to be a form of "neonomianism" or "Pelagianism." "Antinomianism," on the other hand, referred to the theological position which viewed the law as of little or no value for the man of faith. For example, it refused, as we have seen, to accept the sanctified life lived under the law as an authentic evidence of justification. "Calvinist," in this context, meant a strict adherence to salvation by an unearned gift of grace and an adoption of works performed under the law as a manifestation of faith.

In the eighteenth century "Arminianism" was becoming synonymous with a form of "Rationalism," and "antinomianism" with a form of "Enthusiasm." Arminianism represented not simply a "neonomian" understanding of grace but also a rationalistic understanding of religious faith. And antinomianism did not simply stand for a devaluation of law when assessing the nature of the Christian life; it also meant a belief in the secret, emotional revelation of God to the saint through the Holy Spirit. In other words, those Arminians who made the efficacy of divine grace in some way conditional on human belief were also coming increasingly to share the Enlightenment's distrust of all Calvinist positions which could not be adjusted to the priority of dispassionate human reason. And the mid-eighteenth century had not forgotten that the Puritans a century earlier had condemned the antinomianism of Anne Hutchinson because it led to a belief in enthusiastical revelations as well as because it finally disavowed the sanctified life under the law as an evidence of life under grace. Needless to say, those participants in the indecorous acts of extreme revivalistic emotionalism were quickly denominated "Antinomians."

The two basic connotations attached to the terms "Arminianism" and "antinomianism" break this concluding part into its two chapters: "Rationalism and Enthusiasm" and "Neonomianism and Antinomianism." Our concern is not to rehearse all the points of argument between Edwards and these two theological positions; it is rather to highlight main features of the controversy by examining how the nature of religious faith was at stake in the controversy. Our interest in Edwards' debate with the Arminians on the freedom of the will, for instance, is not in the subtle logical and metaphysical arguments themselves, through which Edwards directed his readers—that aspect of the debate has been examined *ad nauseam* since the appearance of Edwards' *Freedom of the Will*. Our interest is rather in what respects the debate was a controversy over faith and how Edwards' view of faith illuminates his stance within the controversy. It will be our contention that Edwards' doctrine of faith substantially informed his position toward two leading theological options of his day and also that his struggle with the options provided him an opportunity to amplify his understanding of the nature of faith.

CHAPTER X

RATIONALISM AND ENTHUSIASM

Chauncy; the Enthusiasts

The symmetry of intellect and feeling in Puritanism had always been a precarious one. As one study has it, there was "a remarkable but ultimately unstable balance in Puritanism between deep religious feeling and rational, even institutional, control."[1] We observed an aspect of this unstable balance in our first chapter: Puritan intentions of preserving the unity of man in faith were often frustrated by the subordination of one human faculty to another. But the tenuous balance maintained between reason and emotion before the eighteenth century was thrown into utter discord by the Great Awakening. New England had witnessed revivalist stirrings before the advent of the Great Awakening of Edwards, Tennent, and Whitefield. In Northampton itself Solomon Stoddard's "powers of persuasion" had earlier effected as many as five "harvests" or periods of conversion.[2] But the early stirrings were preparations for that great flood of revivals which occurred between 1740 and 1742. As a consequence of these great "outpourings of the Spirit" New England was largely split into the rationalist critics of revivalism and the emotional defenders of revivalist religion. The Puritan consciousness became severed into antithetic modes of rational moralism and passionate religiosity—a schizophrenia that still plagues American Protestantism. In the words of Gordon Harland, with the Great Awakening, "despite the tremendous efforts of Edwards, a disastrous cleavage took place between religious feeling and the intellect, a cleavage that has bedevilled our whole religious heritage since."[3] Troubled by the loss of the unity of the life of religious man resulting from this growing division between emotion and intellect, Jonathan Edwards entered the fray between rationalists and enthusiasts in the uncomfortable position of being a defender of the Awakening as a movement but a critic of both rationalism and enthusiasm.

Charles Chauncy, minister at the First Church in Boston, proved to be Edwards' leading antagonist among the rationalist critics of the Awakening. Edwin Gaustad, in his illuminating study of the Great Awakening, has disclosed how Chauncy as well as Edwards realized the complexity of "that cataclysm of human experience in eighteenth-century New England." Fully aware that the situation created by the revivals was a veritable Gordian knot, both Chauncy and Edwards nevertheless sought to appraise as accurately as possible the value of the revivals of religion. The sincerity of each thinker is beyond question, and in the metaphor of Gaustad both "were concerned with separating the wheat from the chaff." The different results sprang from a difference in focus: "the attention of one [Edwards] was fixed on the wheat, the other [Chauncy] on the chaff."[4] But there the parallels of the metaphor terminate. For finally Edwards, not Chauncy, pleaded for the finer sifting. Chauncy concluded that the religious awakening, because of its excesses, could not in any sense be judged a work of the Spirit of God. Edwards argued that more discriminating discernment was called for: the Awakening should be judged not in terms of its excesses and errors alone but also in terms of the *nature* of a true work of God which may appear even in the midst of excesses.

Chauncy meticulously assayed and reported the improprieties of the revival, and abundant improprieties there were: ministers abandoning their own folds for an itinerant ministry, screamings and writhings by the congregations, persons' neglecting their daily vocations to attend to things religious—Chauncy's list was endless.[5] These things in his judgment constituted the very nature of the revival itself; the Awakening was not a work of God's Spirit but a despicable instance of wanton emotionalism. And it was a carefully planned appeal to tradition when Chauncy likened the revivalist preachers and defenders of the revivals (including Edwards, of course) to the antinomians of early New England, whom the established Church had condemned for their enthusiastical errors.[6]

There were undoubtedly several factors which contributed to the opposition between Chauncy and Edwards over the Great Awakening, including differences of temperament and cultural background.[7] But deep theoretical differences between the two New England theologians were no less divisive —differences that would emerge in even clearer detail in Chauncy's later work.[8] Certainly one of the hinges on which the opposition turned was a significant variance in the understanding of the relation between intellect and emotion in religious man.

At the very foundation of Chauncy's condemnation of the revival and his identification of the essence of the revival with its errors is his view of the relationship that should prevail between reason and emotion. In places he sounds very much like Edwards when judging of this relationship. He maintains that when the Spirit of God accomplishes his work, there is not only warmth in the human passions but also an answerable light in the mind.[9] And in his description of faith he says, "It must be remembered, this Faith is not a meer *speculative*, nor yet *unactive* Thing: It will have a powerful Influence both on Men's *Hearts* and *Lives*."[10] Nevertheless, Chauncy's rationalism comes into full play in his insistence that the balance between warmed passions and enlightened reason is to be governed by the authority of enlightened reason. The affective aspect of faith must be subjected to the rule of sober reason:

The plain Truth is, an *enlightened Mind*, and not raised Affections, ought always to be the Guide of those who call themselves Men; and this, in the Affairs of Religion, as well as other Things: And it will be so, where GOD really works on their Hearts, by his Spirit.[11]

Hence regenerate man, the man of faith, is one who keeps his passions under the control of calm reason.

One of the most *essential* Things necessary in the *new-forming* Men, is the Reduction of their *Passions* to a proper Regimen, i.e. The Government of a *sanctified Understanding*: And 'till this is effected, they may be called *New-Creatures*, but they are far from deserving this Character. *Reasonable* Beings are not to be guided by *Passion* or *Affection*, though the Object of it should be GOD, and the Things of another World: They need, even in this Case, to be under the Government of a *well-instructed* Judgment.[12]

When waves of revivals, therefore, create in men high passions or affections that are not closely moderated and governed by what is essential to man's manhood—enlightened, dispassionate reason—they are not the work of God but a work of Satan. Chauncy is a captive of the scholastic psychology which breaks human agency into related but separate faculties; and in deciding what constitutes proper manhood, he subordinates unruly affection to sober reason. Thus religious man—if he is to be *properly* religious *man*—will keep his animal passions under the control of his reason. The influence of God's Spirit is primarily and essentially that of enlightenment of the reason: only thereby does God perform a decorous and authentic work on the heart.

Edwards' view of the nature of man and of the nature of religious faith provides an altogether different definition of an authentic work of God, and an altogether different perspective on the Awakening. Religious man is not one who subjects passions to the rule of reason but one whose reason is passionate and whose affection is intellectual. Edwards, like Chauncy, unhesitatingly declares that "where there is heat without light, there can be nothing divine or heavenly in that heart."[13] But Edwards, unlike Chauncy, has a basis upon which to claim the symmetry of heat and light, reason and emotion in religion: his understanding of the interpenetration of cognition and volition in the act of faith. In religious faith the whole man is engaged. There is a simultaneous and harmonious movement of knowing and affective inclination. The religious affections—for example, the love and joy portrayed in I Peter 1:8—do not constitute a separate domain in man but are, rather, "certain modes of the exercise of the will," "all vigorous lively actings of the will or inclination."[14] The only distinction which Edwards makes within the human subject is that between intellect and will—affections are movements of the will. And since, as we have seen, Edwards views the act of faith as a "sense of the heart" in which intellect and will join in concert, it is for him illegitimate to assign the lively movements of the will a subordinate function in religion. Thus when the Holy Spirit does his work in a revival, there will, indeed, be light in the understanding; but there will also be heat in the will. The recipient of grace from the Spirit is man in his unity—man of intellect and emotion. In terms of the manner of the Spirit's operation, illumination of the mind by the Holy Spirit *is* infusion of a new principle in the will.

Edwards' dissent from Chauncy's rationalistic appraisal of the revivals is dictated to a large extent by his adoption and adaption of the Lockean psychology. Perry Miller has caught the significance of this difference between Chauncy and Edwards:

The irony is that the theological liberal, who in every trait stands for the rational Enlightenment, spoke in the language of outmoded science, and the defender of Calvinism put his case upon a modern, dynamic, analytical psychology in which the human organism was viewed, not as a system of gears, but as a living unit.[15]

Of no less significance is Edwards' view of the internal dynamics and possibility of the faith-act, the correlate of his dynamic psychology. Because the man of faith is willing, affectionate man as well as reasoning man, because the Holy Spirit operates on both human powers when opening the possibility of faith, one cannot judge of the work of the Spirit simply according to whether or not reason prevails over affection. The issue at stake in judging of the revivals is not which prevails, reason or emotion? but do true affections arise as well as false? The question is not whether persons have their affections highly raised, but what are the signs of truly godly affections. This much, Edwards believes, is clear: "True religion, in great part, consists in holy affections."[16] The Scriptures in themselves are evidence enough of that when they speak of "love," "joy," "fear" within the life of religious man. One may not, therefore, rail at either the affectionate preaching or the passionate response to the preaching in the revival by pointing to the inappropriateness of raised affections. Raised affections, even highly raised affections, are a legitimate part of religious experience. Furthermore, things accidental to the work of the Spirit on the heart—such as errors growing out of human weakness or strange bodily effects arising out of raised affections—are not to be confused with the Spirit or with his work on the heart. As Edwards said to his audience at New Haven in 1741, "that the Quakers used to tremble, is no argument that Saul, afterwards Paul, and the

jailer, did not tremble from real convictions of conscience."
And

a thousand imprudences will not prove a work to be not of the
Spirit of God; yea, if there be not only imprudences, but many
things prevailing that are irregular, and really contrary to the rules
of God's holy word. That it should be thus may well be accounted
for from the exceeding weakness of human nature, together with the
remaining darkness and corruption of those that are yet the subjects
of the saving influences of God's Spirit, and have a real zeal for
God.[17]

What one must attempt to do is discover out of Scripture
what are signs of truly gracious affections or of affections
wrought by the Spirit of God. We have already discussed
most all of these signs of godly affections in our preceding
analysis: e.g., divine and supernatural origin, love of God for
himself, tendency toward practice. The point we would make
here is that over against Chauncy, Edwards could not condemn the revivals of his time for their creating highly raised
affections or for their not allowing sober reason to sit as coachman over the emotions. For when the Spirit is at work—when
faith is elicited—affections will be raised, the inclination will
be affectively moved, as well as the reason enlightened. Such
is the nature of faith and the nature of man.

Some of the less formidable "New Lights" (as the New
England revivalists were designated) must have found considerable comfort in the fact that a figure of Edwards' intellectual powers indulged some of the excesses of the revivals
by attributing them to human weakness and by writing many
of them off as accidental to the phenomenon itself. Edwards
did defend the revival as a whole; he even passionately called
upon the uncommitted to support it.[18] Undoubtedly Edwards' endorsement of the revival as a movement is explained
in great part by his chiliastic hope which led him to believe
that it was "not unlikely that this work of God's Spirit [the
Awakening], so extraordinary and wonderful, is the dawning,
or at least a prelude of that glorious work of God, so often
foretold in scripture, which, in the progress and issue of it,
shall renew the world of mankind."[19] Edwards added fuel to
the fire of the "Old Lights" (antagonists of the revival) by

himself being a participant in the revivals of both the 1730s and the 1740s and by welcoming to the Northampton pulpit England's George Whitefield, leading itinerant revivalist in the New England Awakening and critic of the established New England clergy.

Edwards was, despite all this, a critic of the enthusiasm inherent in much of the revival. Though he befriended many a revivalist minister, he certainly did not subscribe to the methods and effects of all the revivalists. Edwards acknowledged that some of the "young instruments" of the revival were given to excessive zeal without the seasoning of age and experience, which led them to errors. He reproved Whitefield for giving too much heed to human "impulses" and for judging too readily other persons to be unconverted.[20] And though he believed that the revival might well be the beginning of the New Age for God's people in America and encouraged them to participate in the inevitable workings of history, Edwards was by no means blinded to the theological errors of enthusiasm which accompanied this work of the Spirit. Edwards not only rejected as evidences of the work of God's Spirit the "accidental" improprieties of the Awakening: bodily effects, errors of imagination, overabundant talking of the things of religion.[21] He also denounced the theological errors of the enthusiasts which perniciously misrepresented the work of God's Spirit. To be sure, the substance of Edwards' argument regarding the Awakening—especially in the *Religious Affections*—was directed against the rationalist rather than the enthusiast position, since he believed the former extreme was the one gaining more apologetic force at the time.[22] But he made quite clear that the enthusiast extreme was for him as equally destructive of the nature of religious faith as the rationalist.

The enthusiasts' exaltation of heat in the heart to the exclusion of light in the understanding is as firmly rejected as the rationalists' subordination of heat to light. And Edwards' understanding of the internal dynamics and possibility of the act of faith again informs the discussion. "Holy affections are not heat without light; but evermore arise from some information of the understanding, some spiritual instruction that the mind receives, some light or actual knowledge."[23] Those enthusiasts who stress the direct, secret breathings of the Spirit of God upon the emotions or will apart from "some instruction or enlightening of the understanding"[24] drive themselves into an irrationalism in which the *understanding* accompanying all gifts of the Spirit is abandoned. They overlook that in religious faith the warmed heart is given simultaneously with a "judging" and "tasting" of the reality of divine things. The

leading of the Spirit is a thing exceeding diverse from that which some call so; which . . . has in it no tasting the true excellency of things, or judging or discerning the nature of things at all. They don't determine what is the will of God by any taste or relish, or any manner of judgment of the nature of things, but by an immediate dictate concerning the thing to be done: there is no such thing as any judgment or wisdom in the case. . . .

What has been said of the nature of spiritual understanding, as consisting most essentially in a divine supernatural sense and relish of the heart, not only shows that there is nothing of it in this falsely supposed leading of the Spirit, which has been now spoken of; but also shows the difference between spiritual understanding, and all kinds and forms of enthusiasm. . . .[25]

That kind of religious enthusiasm which breeds a confidence in secret, emotional actings of the Spirit misrepresents the character of the Spirit's operation. For such is the nature of the faith bestowed by the Spirit: it is an *affective judgment* of the human subject in its unity, in which both basic human powers operate in concert. It is not an irrational, "unenlightened" emotional response to a private revelation.

Extreme revivalistic enthusiasm breeds "unenlightened" religion; but even more damaging to the nature of faith is its tendency toward religious pride through the inordinate amount of attention it gives to human experiences. Spiritual pride is an imminent danger when the Spirit does his work through the proclamation of revivalist ministers. It is a threat for both hearers and proclaimers. The "awakened" who become so wrapped up in their own experience of conversion by the Spirit that the experience itself claims their confidence are guilty of "the first sin that ever entered into the universe, and the last that is rooted out: it is God's most stubborn enemy!"[26] But spiritual pride is a temptation for the minister as well. Edwards is aware of the spiritual pride resident in those revivalists of the Awakening who are more than free with their condemnations of other persons'—especially other ministers'—experiences. So he advises:

The Word of God, which is in itself sharper than any two-edged sword, ought not to be sheathed by its ministers, but so used that its sharp edges may have their full effect, even to the dividing asunder soul and spirit, joints and marrow. Yet they should do it without judging particular persons, leaving it to conscience and the Spirit of God to make the particular application.[27]

The hearers as well as the proclaimers of the Word should "be clothed with humility" (I Pet. 5:5),[28] for pride in one's spiritual experiences is contrary to the posture of faith. Truly converted man is the man of faith who stands in trembling relationship with God; in the presence of God one realizes that his own finite experience is dross in comparison with the loveliness and excellency of the Infinite.

Let no saint, therefore, however eminent, and however near to God, think himself out of danger. He that thinks himself most out of danger, is indeed most in danger. The apostle Paul, who doubtless was as eminent a saint as any now, was not out of danger, even just after he was admitted to see God in the third heaven, 2 Cor. xii.; and yet doubtless, what he saw in heaven of the ineffable glory of the Divine Being, had a direct tendency to make him appear exceeding little and vile in his own eyes.[29]

This abandonment of confidence in one's own experience as part of the reverential, trembling relation with God in faith "is what all the most glorious hypocrites, who make the most splendid show of mortification to the world, and high religious affection, do grossly fail in."[30] The enthusiasm that fosters pride in human conversion-experiences encourages the very opposite of faith's direction, for faith directs man not to himself or to his own experiences but toward God revealed in his Word. And the enthusiast who rests content with his own spiritual experiences can only love God on the basis of those experiences—the antithesis of the love to God included in faith which loves God for himself, on the basis of God's own revealed excellency.

Extreme enthusiasm also leads to the obliteration of the proper relation between Word and Spirit. By finding signs of grace in the height of emotion in spiritual experiences, enthusiasm fails to allow Scripture to judge human experiences; and by encouraging a belief in an immediate whispering and guidance by the Spirit, it subordinates God's Word spoken in Scripture to the Spirit. Edwards does not abandon his claim, over against the rationalist critics of the revival, that affections—and usually highly raised affections—accompany faith. But he refuses to allow the *high degree* of affection *itself* to be a *sign of grace*.

> 'Tis very manifest by the Holy Scripture . . . that there are religious affections which are very high, that are not spiritual and saving. . . . So the Children of Israel were greatly affected with God's mercy to 'em, when they had seen how wonderfully he wrought for them at the Red Sea. . . . But how soon was there an end to all this mighty forwardness and engagedness of affection? How quickly were they turned aside after other gods, rejoicing and shouting around their golden calf?[31]

As we have often had occasion to see, according to Edwards it is not the degree but the source or origin of human affective experience that is crucial for the experience. And one cannot judge of the godliness of a human experience by norms given by that experience itself (such as the degree of the experience). Instead, one must judge of it in light of the standard of Scripture, which may act as the "mirror" to reflect human experience. In other words, in self-examination one ends in either pride or despair if he only turns inward to observe the degree of affection in his experience; God's Word, on the other hand, contains both the norm of human experience and a divine promise that transcends the limitations of that experience. Enthusiasm abandons both values of the Word for the sake of preoccupation with human experience.

Similarly, enthusiastic "discoveries" through strange spiritual "ecstasies and raptures," "immediate revelations from heaven," in short "all enthusiastical impressions and applications of words of Scripture, as though they were words now immediately spoken by God to a particular person, in a new meaning, and carrying something more in them, than the words contain as they lie in the Bible"—all such enthusiasm tears Spirit from Word and turns the work of the Spirit into wizardry. "And in these things seems to lie the religion of the many kinds of enthusiasts of the present day."[32] Edwards feels it is the subtle irony of history that something as glorious as God's renewal of man through the Awakening may become the mask behind which enthusiasm hides in order to wreck the whole movement. Or as Edwards puts it, enthusiasm is the bastard child of authentic religion which diabolically poses as the real thing until it has slain legitimate revivalist forces.

'Tis by such sort of religion as this chiefly, that Satan transforms himself into an angel of light: and it is that which he has ever most successfully made use of to confound hopeful and happy revivals of religion, from the beginning of the Christian church to this day. When the Spirit of God is poured out, to begin a glorious work, then the old serpent, as fast as possible, and by all means introduces this bastard religion, and mingles it with the true; which has from time to time soon brought all things into confusion. The pernicious consequence of it is not easily imagined or conceived of, till we see and are amazed with the awful effects of it, and the dismal desolation it has made. If the revival of true religion be very great in its beginning, yet if this bastard comes in, there is danger of its doing as Gideon's bastard Abimelech did, who never left till he had slain all his threescore and ten true-born sons, excepting one, that was forced to flee.[33]

The "bastard religion" enthusiasm corrupts the essence of religious faith by transforming it into a totally subjective affair, into a matter of "inner experience," through its separation of illumination by the Spirit from the "objective" Word and through its judging human experience by the norm of human experience itself.[34]

Finally, revivalist enthusiasm is destructive of true faith in its identification of assurance with the essence of faith itself. It is noteworthy testimony to the fact that Edwards was closer to a rationalist like Chauncy than he was to the extreme enthusiasts when Chauncy says, in language scarcely to be distinguished from that of Edwards, that the identification of assurance with the essence of faith is not only contrary to Scripture and the Westminster Confession but also offends *against the Generation of God's Children*; many of whom do walk in Darkness, labouring of Doubts and Difficulties, and even go out of the World with prevailing Fears, lest they should not enter into the *Kingdom of Heaven.* ——*The Causes* of these doubts are various. ——Some Times, a *humbling Sense of their own Unworthiness* may be so strong upon their minds as to prevent their taking that Comfort, which really belongs to them; and which others take, who have no better a Right to it than they.[35]

As we saw in our discussion of Edwards on practice, he also resists the identification of faith and assurance. He therefore consciously sets himself against those enthusiasts who, as a consequence of the Awakening, separated themselves from the established congregations and attempted to build their churches only of those who were absolutely assured of their salvation.[36] According to Edwards, the man of faith may have, and should struggle for, assurance; but faith itself, not assurance of one's own estate, is the basis of communion in the church. Judged by Edwards' standards, therefore, when Ebenezer Frothingham, pastor of a "separatist" church, holds that no man who doubts his salvation can perform any proper action toward either God or man—that he cannot even pray in faith,[37] he confuses faith with assurance. The confusion invites the height of human presumption by suggesting that man's ability to convince himself that he has faith is tantamount to his actually being in faith. And it fails to recognize that faith, by virtue of its divine ground, precedes assurance and is rugged enough to survive doubt.

Edwards' controversy in the situation produced by the Great Awakening was a controversy over a number of matters: over marks of the work of the Spirit of God, over eschatology, over the nature of man. But it was also manifestly a controversy over faith. Edwards' views of the dynamics and possibility of the act of faith, of the meaning of grace, and of faith and assurance all appeared as notions vital to his stance within that great stirring of religion in which he was convinced there was "no such thing as being neuter."[38] Under the conviction that neutrality was impossible or at least irresponsible in the midst of the tumult, he supported and encouraged the Awakening as a whole with the hope that it might prove to be the renewal of religion in the colonies.

But his endorsement of the revivals did not blind him to ominous enthusiastical extravagances. Both rationalist and enthusiast extremes were deviations from the nature of religious faith.

Ethics

Edwards' dispute with rationalists and enthusiasts over the nature of faith became also, in certain significant respects, a dispute over ethics. It is only fitting that a thinker who conceived Christian practice as the chief sign of faith should see the closest of relationships obtaining between theological reflection on the nature of faith and theological ethics. Toward the close of his life Edwards composed a treatise on ethics, which was published only posthumously. The treatise is not polemical: like its companion essay, *On the End for Which God Created the World*, it deliberates systematically on certain problems that had been on Edwards' mind for some time, without recourse to the devices of argumentation found in a treatise like *Freedom of the Will*. Nevertheless, in the treatise on ethics Edwards does enter into explicit conversation with the "ethics of feeling" championed by two British rationalists—the third Earl of Shaftesbury and Francis Hutcheson—adopting certain aspects of the ethics and abandoning others. By entering into dialogue with these two, Edwards was also coming to terms with a tradition of ethical reflection that had been spreading in the English-speaking world. R. S. Crane has demonstrated that eighteenth-century ethics tended to identify virtue with "acts of benevolence" and with "feelings of good will" toward men in general. This tendency is clearly discernible in Shaftesbury's *Characteristics of Men, Manners, Opinions, Times*; but behind Shaftesbury lie the "numerous Anglican divines of the Latitudinarian tradition who from the Restoration onward into the eighteenth century had preached to their congregations and, through their books, to the larger public essentially the same ethics of benevolence, 'good nature,' and 'tender sentimental feeling.' . . ."[39] In dialogue with this ethic of feeling, epitomized in Shaftesbury and Hutcheson, Edwards develops his own ethic in *The Nature of True Virtue.*

In one way Edwards' summary definition of virtue accords not only with the thinking of such rationalists as Hutcheson but also, as Edwards says, with that of "the more considerable deists": "it is that consent, propensity, and union of heart to Being in general, that is immediately exercised in a general good will."[40] True virtue is in essence disinterested benevolence or love to Being in general. Hutcheson, who was something of the systematizer of the feeling-ethic,[41] also conceived true human virtue as unselfish benevolence.[42] Virtue is love of an object for its own sake. According to Edwards' distinction, virtue is primarily *love of benevolence* rather than *love of complacence*; that is, true virtue is primarily love of something for its own sake, being, or good rather than for the beauty of the object or for the lover's delight in and gratitude for that beauty.[43] But at two very significant points Edwards sets himself apart from the prevailing ethic of benevolence, and at these two points emerges the substance of Edwards' consideration of the relation between faith and ethics. Clarence Faust has grasped Edwards' departure from the Hutcheson school of thought:

At two points . . . Edwards found objections to Hutcheson's scheme. In the first place, he felt that Hutcheson and others near him in theory were guilty of giving too little place in their systems to man's obligations to the Deity. . . . There was another and much more important point at which Edwards diverged from Hutcheson and his school. This was over the question whether there was in mankind any natural impulse toward virtue. Edwards' answer to this question was an unqualified denial that there was any natural disposition to benevolence in man.[44]

These are points of contention regarding the primary object of and the possibility of human virtue, and both call for a consideration of the nature of faith within the setting of theological ethics.

According to Edwards, "true virtue must chiefly consist in love to God; the Being of Beings, infinitely the greatest and best of Beings."[45] Ethical systems which take only partial account of this chief object of love are suspect, first of all, because of an apparent inconsistency in their arguments.

> There seems to be an inconsistence in some writers on morality, in this respect, that they do not wholly exclude a regard to the *Deity* out of their schemes of morality, but yet mention it so slightly, that they leave me room and reason to suspect they esteem it a less important, subordinate part of true morality; and insist on benevolence to the *created system* in such a manner as would naturally lead one to suppose, they look upon that as by far the most important and essential thing.[46]

Indeed, the "feeling ethicists" claimed God as an object of virtuous benevolence. In the words of Francis Hutcheson, "our *moral faculty* is of the highest use" when human affections are directed "toward the Deity." "The *moral faculty* itself seems that peculiar part of our nature most adapted to promote this correspondence of every rational mind with the great Source of our being and of all perfection, as it immediately approves all moral excellence, and determines the soul to the love of it, and approves this love as the greatest excellence of mind. . . ."[47] Nevertheless, though virtue includes affection to Deity as something of the "highest use" of the "moral faculty," virtue is definable without reference to love to God. Virtue is "universal Benevolence toward all Men," a human affection toward human beings comparable "to that principle of *Gravitation*, which perhaps extends to all Bodies in the *Universe*; but *increases* as the Distance is diminish'd, and is *strongest* when Bodies come to touch each other."[48] Edwards' criticism is that a system of ethics which conceives love to God not as the chief principle of virtue, but as simply one factor in a virtue essentially defined as love "toward all Men," does not take seriously, even according to its own presuppositions, what love to God must mean. For if virtue involves love to God, virtue must—owing to the nature of the object loved—be founded on that love. "If true virtue requires that we should have some regard, some benevolent affection to our Creator, as well as to his creatures, then doubtless it requires the first regard to be paid to him." Since God is both the supreme Good and the supreme plenitude of Being—even for those who allow only a partial regard to love to God in their ethics[49]—He is worthy above all else of benevolent affection.[50] If one is to maintain consistently that God is the supremely perfect Good and has the greatest share of being and that virtue is essentially a propensity of heart toward being, then love to God must be considered not just one factor but the chief object and foundation of that virtuous propensity of heart. The "infinitely greatest and best of beings" demands chief regard from the loving being. In terms of Edwards' distinction between benevolence and complacence, the nature of God qualifies Him for this love on both primary and secondary grounds of virtue.

. . . the *first* objective ground of that love wherein true virtue consists, is BEING simply considered; and, as a necessary consequence of this, that being who has the greatest share of universal existence has proportionably the greatest share of virtuous benevolence, so far as such a being is exhibited to the faculties of our minds, other things being equal. But God has infinitely the greatest share of existence. So that all other being, even the whole universe, is as nothing in comparison of the divine Being.

And if we consider the *secondary* ground of love, or moral excellency, the same thing will appear. For as God is infinitely the greatest Being, so he is allowed to be infinitely the most beautiful and excellent: and all the beauty to be found throughout the whole creation, is but the reflection of the diffused beams of that Being who hath an infinite fulness of brightness and glory. . . . Therefore he that has true virtue, consisting in benevolence to *being* in general, and in benevolence to *virtuous* being, must necessarily have a supreme love to God, both of benevolence and complacence.[51]

Yet virtue must consist chiefly and primarily in love to God not only because otherwise one is inconsistent with a proper notion of God. Above all, when a system of morality does not define virtue as essentially love to God—when it, rather, drags in this aspect of virtue as the factor which "will give a beauty" to virtuous benevolence to mankind[52]—morality verges on idolatry. Loving chiefly the creature rather than the Creator "puts down" God to an "inferior place"; it subordinates the source of all beings to an "infinitely inferior object."[53] Put another way, if virtue does not have its basis in disinterested benevolence to God, one's love is idolatrously selfish and one's morality is shallow. Self-love is quite capable of stimulating man to love a "*particular person, or private* system."[54] Man may, out of self-love or private interest, love any number of particular beings. And the problem of such love is not simply a problem of lack of *breadth*. Edwards does believe that love to God will appropriately *extend* one's love to intelligent existence in general; yet one may extend his affection into the widest possible circles—beyond self, children, and family "to a longer circle," and still his love may be "exclusive of Being in general,"[55] i.e., rooted in love of self rather than in love of Infinite Being. What Edwards sees as the ground of true virtue, what he views as alone transcending selfish love, is the propensity of heart directed toward God, toward the source of all beings, rather than toward either a part of or a collected sum of created beings. Apart from disinterested love toward God, one's love lacks *depth*. For no love limited to individual beings and unfounded on affection toward God—let that restricted love "be more or less extensive, consisting of a greater or smaller number of individuals"—reaches into the reality which comprehends and upholds the totality of particular, finite beings.[56] Only love to God gives depth to one's morality by giving depth to one's love of creation. And only the human love which is basically disinterested love to God overcomes the setting up of the human—human self-interest and the creature loved on the basis of that self-interest—in the place of the Divine. A morality founded on benevolence toward the source of existence is qualitatively, not simply quantitatively, different from a morality founded on the self or the self's love of its particular objects.

In the light of his understanding of the nature of faith, it is clear that Edwards in his treatise on virtue is calling for religious faith as the foundation of morality. Human virtue consists chiefly in the disinterested love to God included in faith. Edwards' first point of disagreement with the tradition of "benevolence ethics" is that it does not properly relate faith and ethics. It does not recognize, to Edwards' satisfaction, that virtuous practice springs from and is an expression of faith, that "properly voluntary acts" of morality issue from the primary act of faith, that love to God is the foundation of unselfish love of man. In the language of *The Nature of True Virtue*, "no affection whatsover to any creature, or any system of created Beings, which is not dependent on, nor subordinate to a propensity or union of the heart to God, the supreme and infinite Being, can be of the nature of true virtue."[57] Apart from this faithful propensity of heart to God as the basis of virtue, morality—regardless of its possible utilitarian intentions—reaches no further than one's confined self-interests in the created world.[58] Needless to say, according to this scheme of things true virtue is no simple possibility, for disinterested love of God is no simple possibility. This leads us to Edwards' second point of disagreement with the rationalist ethic of benevolence.

Truly virtuous morality not only rests on faith by finding its depth and orientation in the love to God included in faith; also its only possibility is the possibility of faith. Francis Hutcheson adopted as one of his premises the proposition that "there is a *universal Determination* to *Benevolence* in Mankind," though the degree of strength of that benevolence will vary from individual to individual.[59] At the roots of human being, said Hutcheson, is a "secret moral sense," analogous to the sense for aesthetic beauty, which is given naturally to man. "It is plain we have some *secret Sense* which determines our Approbation without regard to Self-Interest; otherwise we should always favour the fortunate Side without regard to *Virtue*, and suppose ourselves engaged with that Party."[60] Hutcheson is here voicing what had been a growing opinion among English divines since the latter part of the seventeenth century: the opinion that the heart of man is " 'naturally' good in the sense that when left to its own native impulses it tends invariably to humane and sociable feelings."[61] The natural "moral sense" for unselfish benevolence was an alternative to anything resembling Thomas Hobbes's theory of natural human egoism. Although Hutcheson and the school of thought represented by him overcame in their ethical theory the rationalist subordination of feeling to intellect by construing virtue in terms of moral sense and feeling, they embraced the presupposition, deriving from one side of Locke[62] and from Enlightenment rationalism in general, that the natural powers of the mind are sufficient in morality apart from grace. Natural reason possessed of the moral sense is sufficient for true virtue.

As will emerge in the following chapter, Edwards' view of the natural possibilities of human virtue was anything but so sanguine a view as this. Here it is sufficient to see that for Edwards what every man has by nature is not sufficient for true virtue at all. That moral sense "so much insisted on in the writings of many of late" is essentially only the morally limited operation of natural conscience.[63] The moral sense given naturally to man is the conscience which approves or condemns one's deeds *in light of one's own self-interest* or which gives one a sense of desert in light of that self-interest. For example, a person may naturally approve his treatment of another by recognizing that that is the way he would prefer to be treated; or he may approve or disapprove his treatment of his neighbor out of a sense of reward or punishment for the action. But

thus approving of actions, because we therein act as in agreement with ourselves, or as one with ourselves—and a thus disapproving and being uneasy in the consciousness of disagreeing and being inconsistent with ourselves in what we do—is quite a different thing from approving or disapproving actions because in them we agree and are united with Being in general; which is loving or hating actions from a sense of the primary beauty of true virtue, and odiousness of sin. —The former (i.e., an inclination to agree with ourselves) is a natural principle: but the latter (i.e., an agreement or union of heart to the great system, and to God, the head of it, who is all in all in it) is a divine principle.[64]

Though God may through the self-love and self-interest involved in natural conscience restrain men from many acts of wickedness, still self-love is the ultimate "source of all the wickedness that is in the world."[65] Edwards, unlike the Hutchesonian school, presupposes a radical doctrine of original sin in his ethic; and he, unlike them, believes the reality of faith provides the only possibility of true virtue. True virtue requires that "disposition" or "frame of mind," that spiritual sensing and tasting, characteristic of the nature of faith.[66] Virtue is not a simple possibility available to man for the taking; its possibility is a possibility of faith which, only through the freedom of God's grace, is able to transcend the limitations of a morality based on self-interest by fixing one's propensity of heart on God.

The position that human morality finds its depth and possibility in the act of faith, however, does not preclude but rather supposes the notion that true morality makes its way in the world through active love of the neighbor. Virtue has its basis in the propensity of heart toward Being in general; but from this basis virtuous man is released to love particular beings authentically. Man is free through faith to love the particular created being according to God's intended end for that being in creation.

The most proper *evidence* of love to a created Being, its arising from that temper of mind wherein consists a supreme propensity of heart to God, seems to be the agreeableness of the kind and degree of our love to God's end in our creation and in the creation of all things, and the coincidence of the exercises of our love, in their manner, order, and measure, with the *manner*, in which God himself exercises love to the creature, in the creation and government of the world, and the way in which God, as the first cause and supreme disposer of all things, has respect to the creature's happiness, in subordination to himself as his own supreme end.[67]

Faithful man's love of his particular neighbor, family, or society is given the depth of loving that particular being according to its ultimate end in the created order. Loving the particular within the created order "under the sovereign dominion of *love to God*" is seeking the good of that creature instead of one's own selfish good.

And so far as a virtuous mind exercises true virtue in benevolence to created Beings, it chiefly seeks the good of the creature, consisting in its knowledge or view of God's glory and beauty, its union with God, and conformity to him, love to him, and joy to him.[68]

Edwards' correlation of love to Being in general with love to the particular creature is a further effort to connect as closely as possible faith and practice. In fact, the theory of morality developed in *The Nature of True Virtue* is in great part an ontological-ethical explication of faith and works. True virtue is founded on the essence of the act of faith—the propensity of heart toward, the relishing of, God or Being itself—an act which finds both its most proper expression and its only setting in a practice which consists essentially in active love of the creature or seeking the good of the creature according to his created end. The treatise on virtue, therefore, is not without important implications regarding Edwards' stance toward the enthusiast extremists of the Awakening and, when read in conjunction with his earlier works, illuminates a major criticism of enthusiasm. There was ample testimony in the revivals that when one's heart was supposedly stirred to love God, love of the creature according to that creature's own good did not always follow. And this could only mean to Edwards that the love to God awakened by conversion was not genuine. Those who had become so emotionally caught up in the revivals that they had condemned their neighbors and their ministers for not having experienced conversion according to their understanding of it, or had been more than free with their discerning sin in another's heart, or had divided themselves off from others not so holy as they (the "separatist" impulse)—all such were, according to Edwards, guilty of "bad ethics," of separating faith from practice, of separating love to Being in general from love of the particular being. In terms of one of Edwards' signs of gracious affections, there is in enthusiasm the tendency to neglect godly "symmetry and proportion" in human affections.[69] It does not hold love to God, awakened through conversion, in symmetrical relation with love of man.

Thus as to the affection of love, some make high pretenses, and a great show of love to God and Christ, and it may be have been greatly affected with what they have heard or thought concerning them; but they have not a spirit of love and benevolence towards men, but are disposed to contention, envy, revenge, and evil-speaking . . . and it may be in their dealings with their neighbors, are not very strict and conscientious in observing the rule of doing to others, as they would that they should do to them: 'If a man say, I love God, and hateth his brother, he is a liar: for he that loveth not his brother, whom he hath seen, how can he love God whom he hath not seen?' (I John 4:20)[70]

In short, the cleavage between faithful love to God and working love toward the neighbor—a cleavage opened by the actions and attitudes of many of the enthusiasts and separatists of the revival—was for Edwards a renunciation of Christian ethics. Love of man is shallow, idolatrous morality apart from love to God; but love to God is inactive, complacent love apart from love of man. Edwards' recurring efforts to connect faith and practice, therefore, are at the center of his ethic. The love to God inherent in faith is "perfected" in its expression through good works toward the fellow man. Only in practice, which summarily consists in active love of the neighbor, is "the tendency and design of grace . . . reached, and its operation completed and crowned."[71] Of course, loving man by seeking his good according to God's intention for him in creation, rather than according to one's own self-interest, is no mere simple possibility any more than is disinterested love to God. It also is a possibility only by the grace given through faith. But out of faith, and under the cover of God's forgiveness for his continual failings, Christian man continues to struggle in his practice of love of the neighbor.

Edwards' views on the nature of faith were written into his reflections on the nature of ethics, and ethical considerations proved central in his appraisal of the growing split between rationalists and enthusiasts. Both parties sundered faith and practice: the rationalist in the direction of a morality devoid of sufficient consideration of faith's object and possibility; the enthusiast in the direction of an irresponsible, inactive faith. Practice finds its depth and possibility in faith; faith finds its active, living issuance in practice. Thus faith and ethics are inseparable.

CHAPTER XI

NEONOMIANISM AND ANTINOMIANISM

Anthropology and Soteriology

In his narrative of the "surprising conversions" in Northampton, Edwards writes that about 1734 "began the great noise that was in this part of the country, about Arminianism, which seemed to appear with a very threatening aspect upon the interest of religion here." Edwards goes on to say that some things were then "said publicly" on the doctrine of justification by faith and that though meddling in the problem from the pulpit was ridiculed, "it proved a word spoken in season here."[1] The things "said publicly" were, of course, those sermons on justification which we found in Chapter VI to be directed against the "fashionable new divinity" of Arminianism.

The extent and sources of the fashionable divinity on the American scene of this period are difficult to specify. Francis Christie has submitted that Arminianism had not yet made its way into the standing order of the New England churches. "What Edwards saw and feared was not a spread of Arminianism among the Congregationalists, a desertion of old orthodoxy. It was the rise of Episcopalianism."[2] Certainly Arminian principles were prevalent in the Church of England in the eighteenth century; as Daniel Whitby said in the preface to his Arminian criticism of the Calvinist Synod of Dort's "Five Points," "if any Man say I contradict the Doctrine of the *Church of England* touching these points, he will condemn almost the whole Body of that *Church*, it being certain that, after the Restoration, almost all the *Bishops*, and the great Body of the Clergy, who were eminent for Learning, were of my Opinion concerning these Five Points, and still, I believe, are so."[3] Defections of American clergy and theologians to Episcopalianism in the eighteenth century were viewed by the standing order, therefore, as defections to Arminianism.[4] But the sources of Arminianism in early eighteenth-century America seem to have been more varied

than Christie is inclined to admit. In the 1730s orthodox
Congregationalists were expressing alarm over the propagation
by "some of Our *Young Men*" of the Arminian scheme;[5] and
the writings of such Arminians as John Taylor and Daniel
Whitby were circulated and found some vogue in New
England.[6] It is also instructive that one of the persons who
most opposed Edwards' "meddling in the problem" of justification and Arminianism was Israel Williams, Edwards'
blood cousin and a leader of that Williams clan whose criticism of Edwards' view of Church communion in mid-century
was to assume covert Arminian principles.[7] Also in the
1730s,

Edwards with five other ministers signed a paper advising the church
in Springfield, Massachusetts, to discontinue its efforts to secure as
its pastor the Rev. Robert Breck, who was suspected of holding
Arminian views. The church's disregard of their protest was the signal
for a resounding battle, which was featured by numerous pamphlets,
special meetings of ecclesiastical bodies, and even the arrest and im-
prisonment of Breck himself, the whole matter finally going before
the General Assembly of Massachusetts for review.[8]

At any rate, Edwards believed the Arminian scheme sufficiently widespread and threatening that he preached against
it a series of sermons on justification by faith alone, the
"word spoken in season" in Northampton. Edwards discerned
from the start that his controversy with this "fashionable new
divinity" was a controversy over faith. According to the sermons the essence of Arminianism is its neonomianism. It
conceives faith as a new kind of obedience and the gospel as
a new kind of law. The grace sufficient for salvation is viewed
as conditional on the human performance of faith. This position denies the meaning of the atonement—that is, it denies
that the Christ is given for human imperfection (including
the imperfection of faith) and that through his perfection
alone one is imputed as perfect. As we have seen, Edwards
affirms against the Arminian scheme that faith is not obedience that stands outside justification to be rewarded with
justification but is the human, "natural," non-meritorious
link with Christ and his righteousness. Although imputation
occurs only in and through the human act of faith, faith is

not the cause of the imputation of Christ's righteousness. Faith and imputation are, rather, two indivisible aspects of the same gift of grace.

Though the sermons on justification did, in Edwards' judgment, meet the fashionable new divinity head-on, they were hardly sufficient to stem the flow of Arminianism. In 1750, Edwards said that "Arminianism, and Pelagianism, have made a strange progress within a few years";[9] and in 1757, he wrote the trustees of Nassau Hall that though he had already published against Arminianism he felt it would be necessary eventually to take up publicly all major points in the scheme.[10] Edwards died, however, giving us only two major treatises directed against Arminian principles: *Freedom of the Will* and the *Doctrine of Original Sin*.

A. *The Will.* Edwards leaves us with no doubt that he viewed his dispute with the Arminians on the doctrine of the will as a dispute over their neonomian understanding of faith. In 1757 he wrote to John Erskine concerning the Arminian theory of the "self-determining" will:

The doctrine of a self-determining will, as the ground of all moral good and evil, tends to prevent any proper exercises of faith in God and Christ, in the affair of our salvation, as it tends to prevent all dependence upon them. For, instead of this, it teaches a kind of absolute independence on all those things, that are of chief importance in this affair; our righteousness depending originally on our own acts, as self-determined. Thus our own holiness is from ourselves, as its determining cause, and its original and highest source. And as for imputed righteousness, that should have any merit at all in it, to be sure, there can be no such thing. For self-determination is necessary to praise and merit. But what is imputed from another is not from our self-determination or action. And truly, in this scheme, man is not dependent on God; but God is rather dependent on man in this affair: for he only operates consequentially in acts, in which he depends on what he sees we determine, and do first.

The nature of true faith implies a disposition, to give all the glory of our salvation to God and Christ. But this notion is inconsistent with it, for it in effect gives the glory wholly to man.[11]

The Arminian notion of the will clearly leads, for Edwards, to the reversal of the proper relationship between God and man. In arguing that a self-determining will in faith is the necessary correlate of human *responsibility* (for acceptance or rejection of grace), the Arminians make the bestowal of grace conditional on a human act. This invalidates the Calvinist doctrine of the free imputation of righteousness, which we have repeatedly seen Edwards would maintain at all costs. Underlying Edwards' tireless—for his readers, often tiring— polemic in the *Freedom of the Will* is his conviction that the neonomian understanding of faith and grace is a necessary consequence of the doctrine of the will against which he is contending.

The three figures whom Edwards chooses as representatives of the Arminian position on the will are the Anglican divine Daniel Whitby, the Deist Thomas Chubb, and the Nonconformist Isaac Watts.[12] Edwards grants that these representatives do not equally share in all the Arminian principles. Chubb went beyond Arminianism in his deism, and Watts did not adhere explicitly to all the Arminian tenets though he did adhere to an Arminian notion of the will.[13] Nevertheless, when the Arminian doctrine of the self-determining will is held—as it is in one form or another by all three figures[14]—that doctrine leads, in Edwards' opinion, to other Arminian principles if "pursued in its consequences."[15] Edwards' treatise on the will illuminates our examination of his controversy with the Arminians over the nature of faith when it is seen as a polemical clearing for the Calvinist understanding of grace, and as a further development of Edwards' notion of the kind of volition involved in the act of faith.

Edwards intended his *Freedom of the Will* to silence Arminian objections against the Five Points of the Calvinist Synod of Dort—objections against the total depravity of man, efficacious grace, the sovereign freedom of God's electing certain men to salvation, the limited atonement, and the perseverence of the saints.[16] All five of Dort's points were claimed by Edwards as necessary defenses of God's power and glory in the salvation of man and as necessary means of preventing the ascription of power and glory to man instead. Man is totally corrupt and incapable of extricating himself from sin; the grace which does save him is given freely by the electing God through a "limited" atonement (i.e., limited to elected

saints); and this efficacious grace alone is sufficient for man's
perseverance in faith. Some of Edwards' arguments against
the Arminians were more convincing than others. As Perry
Miller has suitably remarked, in many of his arguments in
the *Freedom of the Will* Edwards was far too satisfied with
mere dialectics. "When, for instance, he came to the stock
Arminian charge that Calvinism makes God the author of
sin, he contented himself by proving that free-will gets no
further from this disturbing reflection than does predestination: it is 'a difficulty wherein the Arminians share with
us.' "[17] The argument which is more to the point and which
recurs in various forms throughout the treatise on the will is
the *reductio ad absurdum* directed against the Arminian view
of "freedom."

The argument takes up the Arminian presupposition that
the will of man is "self-determining" and stays within the
framework set by the presupposition:

Whatsoever the will commands, it commands by an act of the will.
And if it has itself under its command, and determines itself in its
own actions, it doubtless does it the same way that it determines
other things which are under its command. So that if the freedom
of the will consists in this, that it has itself and its own actions
under its command and direction, and its own volitions are determined by itself, it will follow, that every free volition arises from
another antecedent volition, directing and commanding that: and if
that *directing* volition be also free, in that also the will is [self-]
determined; that is to say, that directing volition is determined by
another going before that; and so on, till we come to the first volition in the whole series: and if that first volition be free, and the will
self-determined in it, then that is determined by another volition
preceding that. Which is a contradiction; because by the supposition
it can have none before it, to direct or determine it, being the first in
the train. But if that first volition is not determined by any preceding
act of the will, then that act is not determined by the will, and so
is not free, in the Arminian notion of freedom, which consists in the
will's self-determination.[18]

The Arminian presupposition is that human freedom must
consist in the will's determining itself when man acts. Edwards demonstrates on the Arminians' own ground that this
way of conceiving human liberty contains a logical contradic-

tion. For if the will *freely determines* itself in all its acts, then each act of will must be preceded by another free act. The chain of acts either leads *in infinitum* or stops with a first act which is not self-*determined*. By logically cutting at the ground of their doctrine of free will, Edwards intends to cut away the foundation for the Arminians' attack on the Calvinist understanding of grace.

Within the Arminian scheme, since the self-determining character of the will is constitutive of human freedom, it is destructive of human freedom to say with the Calvinists that grace is irresistible, that the efficacy of the atonement is not contingent upon a free, self-determining act of volition in faith, and that God eternally elects men to salvation irrespective of foreknowledge of future, freely performed faith. By demonstrating that the doctrine of a self-determining will ends in absurdity even on Arminian grounds, Edwards opens the way for his Calvinist alternative of grace as efficacious and faith as divinely determined. But this does not mean that Edwards is prepared to deny human freedom itself. He does reject the Arminian definition of freedom as logically indefensible and as destructive of the meaning of divine grace, but he proposes that freedom can have another meaning—one that conforms to the notion of grace as a determining cause. This leads us to our second consideration: the debate with Arminianism prompted Edwards to develop in further detail the nature of human volition involved in the grace-faith relation.

Edwards shared with Calvinists, Arminians, and the eighteenth century in general the view that human act is either self-caused or caused by a factor transcending human effort, and this meant human act was either self-*determined* or *determined* by a factor other than the act itself. Edwards lays this down as a fundamental principle in his treatise on the will:

I assert, that nothing ever comes to pass without a cause. What is self-existent must be from eternity, and must be unchangeable: but as to all things that *begin to be*, they are not self-existent, and therefore must have some foundation of their existence without themselves. That whatsoever begins to be, which before was not, must have a cause why it then begins to exist, seems to be the first dictate of the common and natural sense which God hath implanted in the minds of all mankind, and the main foundation of all our reasonings about the existence of things, past, present, or to come.[19]

This is the principle Edwards employs in his argument against the Arminian notion of free will: what is in any sense determined must be the effect of something else, and that cause an effect of another cause, etc. Determination of an effect by a cause is not always a "positive influence": the "withdrawment" of the sun is a negative cause of, not a positive influence on, the freezing of water.[20] In sum, "cause" refers for Edwards to that "antecedent, either natural or moral, positive or negative, on which an event, either a thing, or the manner and circumstance of a thing, so depends, that it is the ground and reason, either in whole, or in part, why it is, rather than not; or why it is as it is, rather than otherwise; or, in other words, any antecedent with which a consequent event is so connected, that it truly belongs to the reason why the proposition which affirms that event, is true; whether it has any positive influence, or not."[21]

In our examination of the relation between faith and practice we saw that for Edwards "properly voluntary" acts of the will are determined by the motives or disposition of the mind. "It is that motive, which as it stands in the view of the mind, is the strongest, that determines the will."[22] Similarly, the mind does not give itself its disposition—say the motive or disposition of the "sense of the heart"—but receives it. In neither case, however, does Edwards intend to reduce human act to mere *mechanical response* to an external cause. We have seen that though the properly voluntary acts are dictated by the mind's disposition, they are "free" in the sense that the very willing is the doing. When a man really wills with a commanding act of the will, the thing willed is performed provided there are no natural obstacles that prevent the normal execution of his willing. A man's willing is his own willing and doing, and the disposition which guides such willing is one internal, not external, to his own mind. In much the same way, an immanent act of the mind—such as the act of faith in its essence—is not mechanically moved by an external force. We intimated this in our discussion of the act and possibility of faith: the faculties receive the Light in illumination by the Spirit, but in the very receiving they actively attend to the Light. Edwards amplifies the connection between the gift of grace and the human act which receives it in the doctrine of freedom that he sets against the Arminian doctrine.

Calvin had invoked Augustine to stress that when man is moved by grace he "is not borne along without any motion of the heart, as if by an outside force; rather, he is so affected within that he obeys from the heart."[23] And the Puritan Richard Baxter said:

Doth the Spirit work on a man as on a beast or a stone? and cause you to speak as a clock that striketh it knoweth not what; or play on man's soul, as on an instrument of music that hath neither knowledge of the melody, nor any pleasure in it? No, the Spirit of God supposeth nature, and worketh on man as man; by exciting your own understanding and will to do their parts.[24]

For Edwards, also, the connection between divine grace and the human act of faith is not a connection between an external force and a lifeless object but one between an internal force and a living being. It is those who adopt the Arminian position, says Edwards, who really treat man as a lifeless being. For in contending that the only way to preserve human freedom in salvation is to conceive the human will as "self-determining," they insist that the will must choose out of indifference. Watts says, for example, that the will may be conceived as "indifferent" for it "has power to withhold the assent in many cases"; this "is a very great part of human liberty" which consists essentially in the will's determining itself with regard to its choices.[25] Similarly, Whitby states that when one chooses he chooses between two or more things; and if he is free in the choice, his will cannot be determined to choose any one thing.[26] Edwards replies that it is contrary to common sense and to human nature to view the human self as indifferent; as a willing being, man cannot be indifferent in his choosing but is determined toward a choice. "For how ridiculous would it be for anybody to insist, that the soul chooses one thing before another, when at the very same instant it is perfectly indifferent with respect to each!"[27] In other words, "Choice and preference can no more be in a state of indifference, than motion can be in a state of rest. . . ."[28] And if one could convincingly portray the willing powers of man as ever in a state of indifference, this certainly could not be claimed as anything to the credit of human freedom. For "if there be any acts which are done in a state of equilibrium, or spring immediately from perfect indifference and coldness of heart, they cannot arise from any good principle or disposition in the heart; and consequently, according to common sense, have no sincere goodness in 'em, having no virtue of heart in 'em."[29] When the Arminians attempt to preserve human freedom by postulating that grace must not irresistibly bend the will in faith, that the will must remain indifferent to all its objects before it chooses them, they take the very "heart" out of human volition. The act of faith is in its essence a "sense of the heart," a lively disposition of mind; a state of volitional indifference is its antithesis.

Edwards offers his alternative to the Arminian notion of freedom in the grace–human act relation by keeping faith within the categories of cause and effect but by employing a conventional philosophical distinction between the "natural" and the "moral" necessity of connection between cause and effect. By "moral necessity" Edwards means

that necessity of connection and consequence, which arises from such *moral causes*, as the strength of inclination, or motives, and the connection which there is in many cases between these, and such certain volitions and actions.[30]

By "natural necessity" when applied to human act, Edwards means

such necessity as men are under through the force of natural causes: as distinguished from what are called moral causes, such as habits and dispositions of the heart, and moral motives and inducements. Thus men placed in certain circumstances, are the subjects of particular sensations by necessity: they feel pain when their bodies are wounded; . . . so by a natural necessity men's bodies move downwards, when there is nothing to support them.[31]

The connection of moral necessity is just as certain as the connection of natural necessity. The distinction is not between degrees of certainty but between the nature of the two things connected. In moral necessity,

the cause with which the effect is connected, is of a particular kind: viz. that which is of a moral nature; either some previous habitual disposition, or some motive exhibited to the understanding. And the effect is also of a particular kind; being likewise of a moral nature; consisting in some inclination or volition of the soul, or voluntary action.[32]

When applied to the relation between grace and faith, this distinction denotes that there is a necessary connection between divine grace and human act, but it is a connection of moral, not of natural, necessity. The act of faith still involves an act of the will as grace operates upon the human subject, for grace is the moral, not the natural, cause of the moral, not the natural, effect of faith.[33] Rather than being an external force which moves man's faith as a lifeless object, grace is the divine gift which operates within the living, willing human subject. A miscellaneous note to which we partially referred once before summarizes what Edwards intends here.

In efficacious grace we are not merely passive, nor yet does God do some, and we do the rest. But God does all, and we do all. God produces all, and we act all. For that is what he produces, viz., our own acts. God is the only proper author and fountain; we only are the proper actors. We are, in different respects, wholly passive, and wholly active.

In the Scriptures the same things are represented as from God and from us. God is said to convert, and men are said to convert and turn. God makes a new heart, and we are commanded to make us a new heart. God circumcises the heart, and we are commanded to circumcise our own hearts; not merely because we must use the means in order to the effect, but the effect itself is our act and our duty. These things are agreeable to that text, "God worketh in you both to will and to do."[34]

In the categories of *Freedom of the Will*, "what God does in the affair of man's virtuous volitions" is both "efficacious" and "irresistible"; that is, "God gives virtue, holiness and conversion to sinners, by an influence which determines the effect, in such a manner, that the effect will infallibly follow by a moral necessity." But irresistible grace after the manner of moral necessity does not "at all hinder, but that the state or act of the will may be the virtue of the subject," for it is still the willing, active human subject who is the recipient of irresistible grace.[35] In other words, Edwards adopts that point of view espoused by many a Calvinist before him, including Calvin himself: God's grace is so glorious and so potent that it dissolves the resistance of the mortal recipient; but grace so operates in conformity with human nature that it is received in an active, lively manner.

Against the Arminian notion of liberty of indifference and self-determination, Edwards develops what we have found him repeatedly stressing in his doctrine of faith. In salvation God does not do a "part" with which man co-operates by contributing a "part" through a self-determining will. When saving faith occurs, the will does not of itself determine whether we will co-operate with the motives furnished the mind by the Holy Spirit; rather the will and understanding both are efficaciously moved by God's power in Word and Spirit. "God does all, and we do all. God produces all, and we act all." The human mind cannot give itself the saving illumination of grace, in this sense it is passive; but it receives the Light by actively attending to it. All the human effort that man can muster cannot produce the movement into the faith which comes by the conjoined operation of Word and Spirit; but Word and Spirit work in and through the means of grace and the human effort attendant on the means. Rather than functioning as one cause of justification outside justification itself, faith as the human act of union with God's revelation in Christ is the human act of relation in and through which righteousness is imputed.

B. *Sin.* Clyde Holbrook has remarked that in the English-speaking world of the eighteenth century, "original sin, with its companion problem of theodicy, was to meet an ethos which repudiated its depressing implications and strenuously attempted to show the beneficent rationality of a world in which evil took its proper place."[36] Intellectual life in England was especially of a temper that inclined it away from Calvinism toward an Arminianism that was more confident about man and his uncorrupted potentialities.[37] Jonathan

Edwards' New England was assuming this state of mind, together with its aversion to the Augustinian-Calvinist doctrine of sin. It is extremely difficult to ferret out the factors that led New England in this direction. Arminian encroachments on covenant theology, the spread of Enlightenment confidence in human reason, increasing confidence in all human ability accompanying a preoccupation with business and commerce[38]—all these undoubtedly contributed to the demise of the Calvinist understanding of sin. At any rate, the age was giving its attention to the goodness—the innate moral virtue —of enlightened, enterprising man. Man might indeed sin, but sin was an individual act for which only the individual was "personally" responsible; it was a misuse of innate, innocent principles. Edwards, therefore, was moving against a stream growing in strength when he emerged as an adversary of this confidence in man and as a defender of the doctrine of original sin. It is not, however, altogether appropriate to see the contrast between the Edwardean and the Arminian temper as a simple contrast between "pessimism" and "optimism." To be sure, the Arminians prefigured what R. W. B. Lewis has called the spirit of the "party of Hope"—eulogized by Emerson, Thoreau, Whitman, and other nineteenth-century proponents of American "innocence."[39] Edwards' sense of every man's involvement in the sin of the past, and his sense of human tragedy and fallenness, was, in comparison with the Arminian hope in innocent *man himself*, pessimistic indeed. But like Lewis' nineteenth-century "party of Irony," Edwards' pessimism about human innocence was complemented by a "tragic optimism."[40] His conviction about the human Fall was matched by a buoyant confidence in God's power to deliver man from that Fall. The doctrine of original sin was not for Edwards an end in itself but the supposition— certainly an indispensable supposition—for comprehending the full meaning of man's higher possibilities.

A chief representative of the Arminian spirit and one of the leading foes of traditional Calvinism was the English dissenting divine, John Taylor, whose *Scripture-Doctrine of Original Sin* was read with eagerness in Edwards' New England[41] and was sympathetically received by American

Arminians like Jonathan Mayhew and Samuel Webster.[42] In conformity with the general Arminian temper was Taylor's view of the innocence of human nature: the human faculties are untouched by sin and do not need irresistible grace to move them to faith; rather they themselves freely determine whether grace will "assist" them.

. . . the Aids of the Spirit of God (who can work upon our Minds in Ways and Degrees beyond our knowledge) are perfectly consistent with our Diligence, and are so far from supposing the *previous* Ineptitude of our Minds, or that our Powers are *utterly indisposed, disabled, and made opposite unto all that is spiritually good, and wholly inclined to all evil*, that our *previous* Desire of the Spirit's Assistance, is expressly made the Condition of our receiving that best of spiritual Goods. Luke xi. 9.[43]

The thread of Taylor's argument in his work on sin is that though through the fall of Adam every generation of men is subjected to physical death, labor, and sorrow, Adam's posterity does not inherit eternal death or personal guilt from its human origins. Taylor provides elaborate exegesis of Scripture to substantiate his claim, but at the center of his claim and at the basis of his exegesis lies his conception of the nature of grace and human act in salvation. For Taylor, not only is grace conditional upon the self-determining natural human faculties; when Scripture speaks of the imputation of righteousness, it refers to the person's own act in itself, operating according to the exercises of the natural faculties, as righteous.[44]

To Edwards, Taylor's doctrine smacks of neonomianism and spells the death of the scriptural understanding of justification by grace through faith. Edwards submits that the Calvinist interpretation of original sin is the correlate of the scriptural portrayal of the undeserved imputation of Christ's righteousness. He says in the preface to his reply to Taylor:

I look on the doctrine [of original sin] as of *great importance*, which every body will doubtless own it is, if it be *true*. For if the case be such indeed, that all mankind are by *nature* in a state of *total ruin*, both with respect to the *moral evil* of which they are subjects, and the *afflictive evil* to which they are exposed, the one as the consequence and punishment of the other; then doubtless, the great *salva-*

tion by CHRIST stands in direct relation to this *ruin*, as the remedy to the disease; and the whole Gospel, or doctrine of salvation, must *suppose* it; and all real belief, or true notion of that gospel, must be built upon it.[45]

Edwards sets out to demonstrate the truth of the doctrine by gathering empirical evidences of human sin and divine wrath, by amassing innumerable scriptural texts, and by answering specific Arminian objections to the traditional doctrine. What is of special interest for our purposes here—what focuses his controversy with Taylor over original sin as a controversy over faith—is "The Evidence Given Us Relative to the Doctrine of Original Sin, in What the Scriptures Reveal Concerning the Redemption by Christ."[46]

Since according to Taylor man is either guilty or righteous by his own act of will alone,[47] it follows, says Edwards, that certain persons (e.g., infants) are redeemed by Christ who are innocent or not guilty of sin by their own personal act.[48] But Scripture represents redemption by Christ as a redemption of *sinners*. Hence if redemption is to be sufficient for all men, one must presuppose that all men of all ages and all times since Adam are in such a state of corruption that they demand a deliverer.[49] But of even more consequence, according to Taylor's scheme, redemption becomes quite superfluous for the adult who is capable of fulfilling God's law.

Not only is there no need of Christ's redemption in order to deliverance from any consequences of Adam's sin, but also in order to perfect freedom from *personal* sin, and all its evil consequences. For God has made other sufficient provision for that, viz. *a sufficient power and ability, in all mankind, to do all their duty, and wholly to avoid sin*. Yea, he insists upon it, that "when men have not sufficient *power* to do their duty, they have *no* duty to do. We may safely and assuredly conclude, (says he) that mankind in all parts of the world have *sufficient* power to do the duty which God requires of them; and that he requires of them *no more* than they have *sufficient* powers to do."[50]

Edwards concludes that such confidence in man's power to fulfill the law replaces confidence in God's redemptive power and is, therefore, the inversion of the good news of the New Testament.

If all mankind, in all parts of the world have such sufficient power to do their whole duty, without being sinful *in any degree*, then they have sufficient power to obtain righteousness by the law: and then, according to the apostle Paul, *Christ is dead in vain*, Gal. ii. 21.[51]

Taylor's Arminian scheme further beclouds the redemptive process by, in effect, denying the need for the efficacious work of God's Spirit. "With him [Taylor], *inwrought* virtue, if there were any such thing, would be *no* virtue; not being the effect of our own will, choice, and design, but only of a sovereign act of God's power."[52] And not only is the need of the work of God's sovereign Spirit denied; the nature of the application of redemption is falsified. Scripture represents the application of redemption to man through Word and Spirit as one involving a "new birth," a "repentance," a "circumcision of the heart," a "spiritual resurrection," a "putting off of the old man" and a "putting on of the new."[53] These representations suppose that prior to redemption man is old man, uncircumcised in heart, not yet turned from sin, not yet resurrected—i.e., they presuppose that man is corrupt.[54] The Calvinist doctrine of the corruption of man through the fall of Adam (explained by Edwards as the loss of "supernatural principles" and the selfish use of the natural human principles) is an attempt to take seriously the radical contrast between "old" man and "new"; the doctrine of original sin is the other side of the doctrine of redemption.

By calling attention to Edwards' defense of the Augustinian-Calvinist doctrine of sin as an interpretation of Scripture, especially of the Pauline epistles, we do not intend to suggest that his reply to Taylor was little more than the regurgitation of scriptural passages. One critic has recently charged Edwards with Biblical "fundamentalism"—of citing verses of Scripture in order to defeat Taylor, while ignoring the broader questions about human nature.[55] It is to be recalled that it is in his treatise on sin that Edwards offers his *constructive* thesis on human nature (the differentiation between natural and supernatural human principles, the functions of each, etc.) and his *constructive* metaphysical explanation of the continuity of human being. Scriptural interpretation certainly predominates in the treatise, and Edwards' argument is not without its share of "proof-texting." Yet Edwards turns to this Biblical emphasis not for the sake of ignoring other aspects of the problem under discussion, but for the purpose of putting the question of sin in its proper context (redemption) and in order to meet Taylor *on his own grounds*. The title of Taylor's challenge is important: *The Scripture-Doctrine of Original Sin Proposed to Free and Candid Examination*. Taylor's rejection of Calvinism purported to be a defense of the proper interpretation of Scripture; and Edwards' rejection of Arminianism claimed to be the proper Biblical rendering. Central to Edwards' interpretation is his attempt to show how original sin illuminates the Pauline "justification by faith alone." Salvation by grace through faith means God accomplishes for man what man cannot do for himself; confidence in God's power to deliver has as its correlate a conviction that man needs deliverance by a power not his own. The abandonment of the Calvinist doctrine that all men are totally corrupt *coram deo* has as its counterpart the abandonment of the doctrine of justification by grace through faith. For the depravity of man and the glorious majesty of God's saving grace mutually illuminate each other. That is why Edwards insists that sin is a fall of the race in Adam (the continuity of guilt being maintained by the direct power of God) and not simply a series of separate human acts. It is a corruption of heart that reaches deep into the human subject, a corruption to be estimated primarily by comparing the selfishness of man with the overflowing love of the infinite God.[56] The divine deliverance appears in its true light when one acknowledges that man cannot lift himself out of the mire of his own sin.

Edwards' published writings after 1750 were occupied with the refutation of Arminianism rather than antinomianism. There are no writings of that period directed against antinomianism which parallel his two large treatises aimed against Arminianism. This attention to Arminianism is owing to the fact that Edwards viewed its spread in both England and New England as more prevalent than the other threat.[57] Nevertheless, as late as 1749 Edwards endorsed the judgment of the ministerial association that antinomianism was one of the errors present on the American scene that was to be cautiously avoided. In view of this, Edwards' treatises on will and sin are really best read in conjunction with those earlier works (which we have already looked at in some detail) that address the threat of antinomianism. That is to say, although Edwards directed his last energies against the neonomian inclination to turn gospel into law and faith into obedience, it is well to remember his arguments against antinomianism as well—above all his points that the law still, in a sense, "prepares" man for salvation, and that Christian man's struggle in sanctification through obedience to the law is the chief evidence of his justifying faith. It is no accident that in his treatment of "Christian practice" in the *Religious Affections*, Edwards appeals to the authority of Thomas Shepard's *Parable of the Ten Virgins*, a work growing out of sermons directed against Hutchinsonian antinomianism.[58] Edwards sought to avoid both neonomian and antinomian views of law. Neonomianism through its notions of human freedom and human innocence invites man to achieve his salvation by his own act of obedience. But antinomianism, by stressing the immediacy of assurance and by dwelling on justification apart from sanctified obedience, inclines one toward an impractical faith and a devaluation of God's law. In the former case, gospel becomes law and faith becomes a work. In the latter, faith is transmuted into an impractical matter of the "inner life." In avoiding both extremes, Edwards sought to preserve his understanding of the nature of faith. This was especially true in his controversy with the Stoddardeans over the question of "profession of faith"; for then, in his rebellion against what he believed to be neonomian implications in the Stoddardeans, Edwards had to defend himself against charges of antinomianism.

Profession of Faith

In the late 1740s tension between Edwards and his congregation became pronounced and was climaxed by Edwards' heated controversy with Northampton and with surrounding communities over the qualifications for admission to the Lord's Supper, a controversy which eventuated in the dismissal of Edwards from his pulpit in 1750. The components of the controversy were staggeringly complex. The issue of the requirements for full communion in the Church was obscured by personal conflicts between Edwards and his people. Northampton and nearby villages had long embraced Solomon Stoddard's view of Church and Supper; Edwards' decision finally to reject his grandfather's view could only be taken as an attack on the "venerable Stoddard," especially as the powerful Williams clan (whose conflict with Edwards can be traced back at least as far as the 1734 sermons on justification) came to the defense of Stoddard's principles. Still on the minds of the congregation was their dispute with Edwards over salary. And the "bad book episode"—when Edwards read before the congregation the names of those "naughty" youths who had been secretly enjoying a midwife's book, involving mention of some of the more respectable families in Northampton and not clearly distinguishing between culprits and witnesses—certainly contributed to the way in which Edwards' ideas on Church communion were received.[59] But the controversy was complicated by more theoretical problems as well. New England theology was thrown once again against the perennial question: Just what constitutes the nature of the Christian Church? Is the Church intended to be inclusive or exclusive? What is the place of the sacraments in the life of the Christian community? Are they to be seals of previously given grace, or may they be converting means as well? What is the locus of ecclesiastical authority: in the congregation, in the clergy, or in the church council? The dispute over qualifications for Church communion was a dispute over all these problems.

Yet the problem of religious faith certainly stood for Edwards at the very center of the controversy, and in the defense of his view of faith he found himself having to maintain a position against both neonomianism and antinomianism. We do not mean to suggest that there were avowedly represented in this controversy these two distinct parties. It was Edwards' misfortune that the battle lines were not so clearly drawn. What we find in this fracas is a moralistic view of church membership which could only appear to Edwards as a neonomian misrepresentation of faith. And in defending his own position against this view, Edwards had to distinguish his doctrine of faith from that of antinomianism.

Edwards laid out his position in the sacrament controversy in his lengthy treatise of 1749, *An Humble Inquiry into the Rules of the Word of God, Concerning the Qualifications Requisite to a Complete Standing and Full Communion in the Visible Christian Church*. In brief, Edwards' argument in the treatise was that only those who openly profess faith qualify for full communion in the Church—that is, qualify for celebration of the Eucharist, for adult baptism, and for the baptism of their children. This was a rejection not only of Stoddardism but also of the Puritan "Half-Way Covenant." The Half-Way Covenant, a measure instituted by the Church of the Massachusetts Bay Colony in 1662, sought to check the decline in church membership by allowing the baptism of the children of those second-generation Puritans who were themselves baptized members of the Church but who would not make a public profession of faith. These parents were "half-way" members of the Church in that they could have their children baptized and keep themselves and their children within the Church fold but could not partake of the Lord's Supper.[60] According to Edwards, there could be no "half-way" members of the Church: one is either visibly a member or he is not; and his qualification for membership is profession of faith.

Lest this seem like an unreasonably severe demand, it is worthy of note that Edwards remained consistent in the demand with his doctrine of assurance. When he called for profession of faith as the qualification for Church membership, he by no means required that one be absolutely free from doubt with respect to his own estate. Edwards confessed in the preface to his *Qualifications for Communion* that one of the reasons he approached the subject under consideration "with so much backwardness" was for fear "of a bad improvement, some ill-minded people might be ready, at this day, to make of the doctrine here defended; particularly that wild enthusiastical sort of people, who have of late gone into unjustifiable *separations*, even renouncing the ministers and churches of the land in general, under pretense of setting up a pure church."[61] Edwards insisted that he still rejected the "*spirit of discerning*" and the "*censorious outcries*" of the separatists, as he did in his *Treatise on Religious Affections*.[62]

Edwards feared that his position on profession of faith would be used as an ill-gotten and falsified shield by antinomian separatism; but he soon learned he had more to fear from other antagonists. The "ill-minded" persons who accused Edwards of separatist principles were the followers of the Stoddardean way—in particular, Edwards' published Stoddardean opponent, his cousin Solomon Williams. In a vitriolic reply to Williams' contribution to the controversy, Edwards lists two ways especially in which Williams insinuated that he, Edwards, held antinomian principles.

To make my scheme . . . obnoxious and odious, Mr. W. once and again insinuates, that I insist on an account of such inward FEELINGS, as are by men supposed to be the certain discriminating marks of grace though I never once used the phrase any where in my book. I said not a word about inward feelings, from one end of it to the other. . . . But however, Mr. W. knew that these phrases, experiences and inward feelings, were become odious of late to a great part of the country; and especially the latter of them, since Mr. Whitefield used it so much. . . .

Mr. W. abundantly, in almost all parts of his book, represents my principles to be such as suppose men to be the SEARCHERS of others' hearts. For which I have given no other ground than only supposing that some such qualifications are necessary in order to communion, which have their seat in the heart, and so not to be intuitively seen by others; and that such qualifications must, by profession and practice, be made so visible or credible to others, that others may rationally judge they are there.[63]

Williams' insinuations definitely were attempts to brand Edwards an antinomian separatist. We noted previously that in their attempts to establish churches of the uncorrupt, separatists claimed assurance as the very essence of faith: doubt was faith's opposite. In addition, they frequently came to believe that sanctification could not really be an adequate evidence of justification: the source of assurance was to be sought in the immediacy of subjective states and feelings. They therefore became "searchers of others' hearts," making "the inward actings of their own souls" the models for another Christian man's estate and thereby giving true believers the device for assuring the purity of their church.[64]

In spite of Williams' allegations and insinuations, Edwards maintains that though profession of faith is requisite for full Church communion, it is a profession rooted in hope and trust and not in a confidence in one's own experiences or feelings. And assurance of faith as well as demonstration of faith to others comes through practice; but no man can judge with any finality of another's estate.

Edwards says that when one presents himself for communion he places himself under the "Church's *Christian judgment*" by demonstrating through both his profession and his practice that he is a man of faith; but this is not to say that either the congregation or the minister knows for sure that the professor is a man of faith. Only God knows for sure a man's heart. And though the Church is to be composed only of the "visible saints"—of those who *express* their faith in practice and profession—this is not to say that the Church will be a *pure* one or one unmixed with hypocrites. Edwards adheres to the traditional Calvinist view that the visible Church (the Church visible to the eyes of Christian judgment) is one, but the visible Church is not necessarily identical one-to-one with the invisible Church (the true Church of the saints visible only to the eyes of God). Hence, though the visible Church is to be composed only of those who profess faith and exhibit their faith in practice, one man cannot finally judge of another's estate on the basis of his own "feelings" and thereby secure a "pure" Church.[65]

Edwards further distinguishes his position from antinomian separatism by attaching profession of faith to practice and by acknowledging that the assurance of faith underlying the profession need not be an assurance beyond all doubt. Not simply verbal profession but verbal profession together with a godly life is the visibility of the saint which qualifies him for full communion in the Church. We shall see later that Edwards could not follow the Stoddardeans and endorse a good moral life apart from profession as the qualification. But the other extreme—profession without holy practice—is for him just as unacceptable. In the *Religious Affections* Edwards had maintained that holy practice is the best sign of the professing Christian both before the neighbor and before a man's own conscience.[66] But in the same treatise he had held that practice without profession is not a true sign of faith. "It must be observed, that when Scripture speaks of Christian practice, as the best evidence to others, of sincerity and truth of grace, a profession of Christianity is not excluded, but supposed."[67] Hence in the *Qualifications* Edwards holds together profession and practice as constitutive of the visibility of the Christian.[68] He avoids antinomian separatism by affirming that the sanctified life together with profession of faith, rather than the inward actings of the soul, is the saint's manifestation to himself and to others of his faith.

The assurance underlying profession of faith is not, for Edwards, an immediate revelation from God which removes all doubt for all time but is that noncomplacent assurance which rests on God's promises and which is given through action. Edwards does claim that it is an unacceptable profession for one to say simply that he *will* have faith in the *future*—this is to move totally to the future what one is asked to profess regarding the present. "That outward covenanting which is agreeable to Scripture institution, is not only a promising which is future (though that is not excluded) but a professing what is *present*, as it is in the marriage covenant."[69] Yet this is not to demand that one's confidence be in his own present experience or that his assurance be devoid of all doubt. Solomon Williams said that Edwards could accept as a qualification for communion only "the highest evidence" of a man's faith,[70] implying that assurance must root out all doubt and struggle. We have seen, however, that though practice is for Edwards the best possible evidence before a man's conscience that he has faith, it is by no means infallible evidence. That is to say, assurance gained through practice and underlying profession of faith is not infallible as far as one's own consciousness of his estate is concerned. "Yea," said Edwards in a letter to a friend prior to the appearance of Williams' book, "I should think that such a person, solemnly making such a profession, had a right to be received as the object of a public charity, however he himself might scruple his own conversion, on account of his not remembering the time, not knowing the method of his conversion, or finding so much remaining sin, etc."[71] Edwards sent to the council which examined his case and finally advised the separation between him and his congregation some drafts of profession which he thought appropriate for one seeking communion. The following such proposed profession is typical of Edwards' understanding of what should be involved:

> I hope, I do truly find a heart to give up myself wholly to God, according to the tenor of that covenant of grace which was sealed in my baptism, and to walk in a way of that obedience to all the commandments of God, which the covenant of grace requires, as long as I live.[72]

When one professes, his profession is rooted in hope—not in the hope that God will perform in the future what he has failed to perform in the present, but in the hope that the God to whom one now gives himself provides in power and sufficiency what he as man lacks subjectively. Edwards clearly sets his doctrine of profession of faith apart from the antinomian presumption that since assurance comes by immediate revelation from God one must be so convinced in his profession that all doubt about his estate is lacking. He reasserts the essence of his doctrine of assurance: assurance partakes of the nature of faith not when it springs from a confidence in one's estate but when it is grounded in a trust in God and his promises together with a struggle in practice.

Despite his rejection of antinomian views of profession and assurance, Edwards could not accept the more lax standards of Church membership that were spreading in New England. Over the years Edwards grew more and more dissatisfied with Stoddard's position on Church communion and in his 1749 treatise openly broke with Stoddard's view in order to articulate more fully his own position, which he hoped would stem the tide of what he believed to be a vapid moralism making its way into Puritan attitudes toward the Church. Much has been made of Solomon Stoddard's pragmatic concerns in opening the Supper to those who could not profess saving faith: since Stoddard saw that later generations of American Puritans could no longer "own" the covenant of grace with the same certainty as the first generation, he found the practical answer to the situation in extending full communion as widely as possible, thus assuring the existence of the established Church on American soil. The degree of truth in this judgment, however, need not lead one to conclude that Stoddard was first and last concerned with "numbers" or that he valued a large church more than a church of character. His overarching concern was that the Church's life and work be relevant to its environment; it was to see to it that the Church "watch over" the "lives and manners" of all her Christian people.[73] For the benefit of those people, he surpassed the Half-Way Covenant by opening the Lord's Supper to those "that are Members of the Church and neither ignorant nor scandalous," contending that the Supper "is Instituted for the Conversion of Sinners."[74] The participant need not profess faith; he need only be "morally sincere"—it is the latter that "makes a Man a Visible Saint" and hence qualifies him for the Supper.[75] Stoddard was certainly not the only Puritan clergyman who voiced and practiced such principles in New England around the turn of the eighteenth century; the breakdown of the firm standards of Church membership of the founding fathers had set in with some force, the Half-Way Covenant being the first major break in the chain. But in the Connecticut Valley, Stoddard was a virtual "pope" to the settlers and the "white man's god" to the local Indians.[76] Thus it was with some propriety that the loosening up of the principles of Church communion came to be referred to as "Stoddardism." But the followers of the "venerable Stoddard" were soon to loosen the principles even further.

Though Edwards admitted the Supper may incline toward the conversion of sinners, he held it was not instituted for that purpose. He found the scriptural purpose of the Supper to be the seal of faith rather than the means of initiating faith. Here Edwards consciously set himself against his deceased grandfather and against Stoddard's doctrine of the Church. According to Stoddard, the Church could embrace in its full communion not only those who professed faith but also those who intellectually adhered to the Church's doctrines, led good moral lives, and professed that they were sincere in their struggle through preparation to be men of faith.

Hereby the Church embraced "visible saints" as well as real, "professing" saints.[77] To Edwards this view of qualification for full communion in the Church appeared to overlook that "a visible saint is a visibly *real* saint."[78] Edwards believes Stoddard's distinction between real sainthood (which can be professed) and "visible" sainthood (which is exhibited in "moral sincerity") to be vacuous; a visible saint must be supposed to be a real saint, else the appellation is meaningless. Therefore the saint or the one enjoying full communion in the Church must not only be able to point to his good morals; he must be able to profess *faith* or that which qualifies him as a saint or believer. Scripture knows nothing of the visibility of morals apart from the visibility of faith as a qualification for Church membership. What is required is not the visibility and profession of good moral intentions only, but the profession and visibility of faith as well.

It is evident, that it is not only a visibility of moral sincerity in religion, which is the Scripture qualification of admission into the Christian church, but a visibility of regeneration and renovation of heart, because it was foretold that God's people and the ministers of his house in the days of the Messiah, should not admit into the Christian church any that were not visibly circumcised in heart. Ezek. xliv. 6–9.[79]

Although Edwards was eager to disprove Stoddard's principles of Church communion, he was more concerned to check what his contemporaries were doing on the basis of Stoddard's principles. With Stoddard and those who shared his principles was clearly begun the shift from faith to respectable morals as the determinant of good American churchmanship. Yet the shift from faith to good morals was turned into an *identification* of faith and respectable morals not by Stoddard himself but by Stoddard's devoted disciples in mideighteenth century. It was Edwards' Stoddardean contemporaries, even more than Stoddard, who encouraged the Church to become a "rendezvous for the socially acceptable."[80] The drift from the Stoddardism of Stoddard himself to that of his followers was rather subtle, but Edwards (himself an admirer of other of Stoddard's tenets) was quick to point it out. Edwards put it this way: his contemporary adversaries, in following Stoddard's view of the Supper to its ultimate consequences, were in danger of leading the Church into a moralistic neonomianism that was in direct opposition to Stoddard's sound doctrine of grace. Edwards feared that Solomon Williams in particular, in defending Stoddard's position on the Supper, was proposing things contradictory to a major thrust in Stoddard's thought. After he had been dismissed from his pulpit, Edwards wrote to his Northampton congregation of Williams' book:

What I regard is, not so much the danger you are in of being established by that book in your former principles, concerning the admission of members, (though I think these principles are indeed very opposite to the interest of true piety in churches;) but what I now mean is the danger there is, that while you are making much of that book as a means to maintain Mr. Stoddard's doctrine concerning the terms of communion, you, and especially your children, will by the contents of it be led quite off from other religious principles and doctrines, which Mr. S. brought you up in, and always esteemed as of vastly greater importance than his particular tenet about the Lord's Supper; and be naturally led into notions and principles, which he ever esteemed as of fatal tendency to the souls of men.[81]

One of the things in "that book" by Williams which Edwards finds especially dangerous and opposed to Stoddard's better principles is its neonomianism.

You know it was always a doctrine greatly insisted on by Mr. S. as a thing of the utmost consequence, that sinners who are seeking converting grace, should be thoroughly sensible of God's being under no manner of obligation, from any desires, labours, or endeavors of theirs, to bestow his grace upon them. . . . Whereas, if a sinner seeking salvation believes Mr. W's book, it will naturally lead him to think quite otherwise.[82]

In defending Stoddard's view that good morals and moral sincerity under the law were qualifications for the Supper, Williams made moral sincerity and desire for faith equivalent to faith itself. Moral sincerity was for Williams not simply "as good as" profession of faith when judging who is qualified for full communion in the Church (as it had been for Stoddard). Williams went a step further: profession of moral sincerity and a "Desire of Christ, and the Benefits of the Covenant of Grace" as one seeks to live a good moral life is "for the Matter of it" "true Godliness."[83] In terms of the Puritan morphology of conversion, "belief upon moral evidence" and under "a conviction of the Judgment and Conscience" is equivalent to belief through the saving gift of grace.[84] Therefore, those who cannot profess faith but who prepare themselves for faith through moral endeavor and profess a desire for faith can be counted as believers and be admitted to the Supper. For if one is sincere in his moral life and earnestly desires to be in the covenant of grace, even though he cannot in all honesty say he *is* in that covenant, he is "for the matter of it" a man of faith and a participant in the saving covenant.

Edwards judged Williams' theories to be cancerous neonomian principles spreading into the Puritan view of the Church. Williams was turning gospel into law, faith into works. His position realized a tendency inherent in the earlier Puritan scheme of preparation: it confused conviction of conscience under the law with the gift of grace; it closed the gap between preparation and the covenant of grace with human morality. When Edwards wrote that Williams was abandoning Stoddard's sound principles of grace while defending Stoddard's view of the Supper, this is what he meant; Williams was clearly suggesting that works were acceptable in the place of faith, that God's free gift of redemption in the covenant could be replaced by human moral effort. To Edwards, Williams was proposing principles of Arminian neonomianism "which if they should by degrees generally prevail, will doubtless by degrees put an end to what used to be called saving religion."[85] Indeed, principles like those of Williams would prevail in much American Protestantism, until "by degrees" justification by faith would become a virtually forgotten confession and moral respectability would offer itself as the unquestioned basis of Church membership.

Edwards' own view of the profession of faith accords with his understanding of faith as covenantal. It is of utmost significance that the Puritan notion of covenant, which some suppose Edwards to have abandoned, should be appealed to by Edwards in the controversy that was most consequential for his life. Edwards sees a correlation between faith's covenant relation with God and the visible "owning" of that covenant in profession.[86] Just as good morals do not suffice in one's covenant relation with God for justification, so a mere profession of moral sincerity does not suffice in one's entrance into communion in the Church. When one enters the Church, he enters the public or social aspect of the covenant of grace. And the only profession proper to such entrance is a profession of what is involved on man's part in the covenant. He must "own" the covenant by professing faith—that is, he must "own" it as one really drawn up into covenant with God.

It is not only professing the assent of our understandings, that we understand there is such a covenant, or that we understand we are obliged to comply with it; but it is to profess the consent of our *wills*, it is to manifest *that we do comply with it*. . . . To profess the covenant of grace, is to profess it, not as a spectator, but as one immediately concerned in the affair, as a party in the covenant professed; and this is to profess *that* in the covenant which belongs to us *as a party*, or to profess *our part* in the covenant; and that is the soul's believing acceptance of the Saviour.[87]

Since profession is a publicly owning the covenant, mere "sincere desire" for faith or a moral sincerity not springing from faith itself is no sincerity at all in profession.

To avouch God to be our God, is to profess that he is our God *by our own act*; i.e. that we choose him to be our chief good and last end, the supreme object of our esteem and regard, to whom we devote ourselves. And if we are sensible that we do not do this *sincerely*, we cannot profess that we actually do it: for he that does not do it sincerely, does not do it at all. There is no room for the distinction of a moral sincerity and gracious sincerity in this case. A supreme respect of heart to God, or a supreme love to him, which is real, is but of one sort. Whoever does with any reality at all make God the object of the supreme regard of his heart, is certainly a gracious person. And whoever does not make God the supreme object of his respect with a gracious sincerity, certainly does not do it with any sincerity.[88]

To turn profession into the profession of moral sincerity is to obscure *what* should be professed in entering the Church covenant: one's covenant relation with God in Christ. Since this covenant relation—both in its private and in its communal aspects—is primarily a relation of faith, not primarily a relation of good morals, the sincerity professed must be a sincerity of faith, not a sincerity of morals. In the presence of God one's profession of moral sincerity apart from profession of faith is as legalistic and impotent as one's relying on his own act of obedience for justification. Moral respectability apart from faith is as little a title to communion in the Church as one's acts of obedience to the law are a title to justification. It is to be remembered that Edwards does not require the professor to profess absolute freedom from doubt or to claim complete confidence in his own holiness. But instead of moving from this allowance to the Stoddardean plea that therefore good morals and the profession of moral sincerity be permitted to suffice in the Church covenant, Edwards asks for a profession of hearty trust and confidence in God and his promises which transcend in power the limitations of the human subject. He asks for the profession of *faith*, the human side of the covenant, man's willingness (his "willing") to be taken up into the covenant of grace.

One must be careful not to portray Edwards as too much the innocent martyr, thrown to the jaws of Stoddardean lions, when attempting to make some sense out of the network of events and ideas surrounding 1750. Though Edwards was the victim of those who misrepresented his position, clouded the basic issues with personal animosities, and displayed a kind of hero worship in their submission to some of Stoddard's principles, Edwards himself undoubtedly contributed much to his own fate by his lack of discretion in dealing with his congregation. And though the followers of the Stoddardean way inclined toward a concept of the Church which would identify the Christian community with those persons who are socially and morally respectable, in one respect Edwards' notion of the Church exhibited what C. C. Goen has called "a curious blindness" to the lessons of history. Edwards believed that "if the church insists on experimental religion on the part of the parents as the indispensable prerequisite for having their children baptized all parents will be stirred up to submit themselves to Christ for the sake of their children."[89] The failure of the Puritan Church to attract later generations on this basis should have quashed such a hope.

Nevertheless this complex and contentious slice of American religious history provides a very concrete paradigm of the manner in which Edwards' understanding of faith was vitally at stake in his comportment toward what were becoming two leading theological options for New England. Both the antinomianism of the separatist view of the Church and the neonomianism inherent in the Stoddardean view equally obscured the nature of faith. Edwards' claim was that entrance into full communion requires the profession neither of purity nor of freedom from doubt, but it does require more than the profession of moral sincerity. It demands a visible covenanting with God by professing the faith of the covenant of grace. "For a person explicitly or professedly to enter into union or relation of the covenant of grace with Christ, is the same as professedly to do that which on our part is the uniting act, and that is the act of faith."[90]

CONCLUSION

Jonathan Edwards' New England was the scene of conflicting ideas and movements that increasingly were to shape American religion. The origins of American Unitarianism appeared in Arminianism, a form of pietistic perfectionism in antinomian separatism, the foundation of American deism in rationalism, and the beginnings of anti-intellectual emotional religion with the extreme enthusiasts. Edwards wrestled with powerful religious forces clashing in eighteenth-century America; he is thus a mirror of a momentous epoch in our history.

Yet Edwards' thought was not simply devoted to struggle; it sought to heal. And judged in the light of more than two centuries of history, Edwards failed in his attempt to heal the splits in the American religious consciousness that fostered the forces around him. Speculations on the reasons for Edwards' failure have abounded. It has been suggested that his trumpeting the cause of the Awakening cast him willy-nilly into the role of defending the excesses of revivalism; that Edwards' formulations and solutions were both too abstruse and too encyclopedic to touch the religious life of the everyday; and that his followers, the propounders of the "Edwardean theology," did not adequately preserve the legacy of Edwards but ultimately did the same with their master that the Stoddardeans had done with theirs—employing certain of his principles for their own purposes until they had completely twisted those principles away from the major thrust of his thought. It may also have been that by the time Edwards fully entered the scene the forces he resisted had grown overpowering.

For whatever reasons, Edwards failed. But the effort in which he failed is conceivably all the more illuminating precisely because of his failure. A twentieth-century Protestantism that is aware it has been engulfed by many of those religious currents which Edwards was unable to stem, hears with new attentiveness Edwards' argument that the religious inclinations of his time were destructive of the very nature of religious faith. It was to an age that had begun to confuse man's ability to win a frontier, close a successful business deal, or maintain respectable morals with human ability to rise above the depths of guilt and attain an easy-won righteousness—it was to this age that Edwards delivered his insights into man's profound involvement in the sin and guilt of the race and into the character of the divine gift of forgiveness as transcendent of human effort. In the face of a growing portion of the Church that had relegated religion to the confines of the "inner life," Edwards insisted that religious faith is "practical," active, alive in its works, and that authentic faith directs one away from the security of his "spiritual possessions." And in an America that was responding to revivalism either by becoming drunk on wayward emotions or by growing sober on dispassionate reason, Edwards developed his understanding of faith as an affair of the whole man in which reason and emotion join in concert. Edwards' century does not seem nearly so remote, nor Edwards nearly so quaint, as we might have liked to picture them. And perhaps in the long run what American Protestantism most requires in a figure like Edwards is not a thinker who can successfully manage the forces that shape it, but one who directs it to the significance of those forces and who redirects it to the meaning of its faith. Jonathan Edwards performed the first task by reinterpreting the riches of his Puritan tradition and by bringing them to bear upon his own portentous historical situation. And he performed the second by tapping that same tradition in order to portray religious faith as a vital union of heart with a sovereign, transcendent God who yet covenants in history.

NOTES

INTRODUCTION

1. Joseph H. Crooker, "Jonathan Edwards: A Psychological Study," *New England Magazine*, New Series, II (1890), 165.

2. Charles Angoff, *A Literary History of the American People*, I (New York: Alfred A. Knopf, 1931), 302.

3. Phyllis McGinley, "The Theology of Jonathan Edwards," *Times Three* (New York: Viking Press, 1961), p. 19.

4. Clyde A. Holbrook, "Jonathan Edwards and His Detractors," *Theology Today*, X (October, 1953), 388.

5. Edmund S. Morgan, *The Puritan Dilemma: the Story of John Winthrop* (Boston: Little, Brown, 1958), p. xi.

6. Douglas J. Elwood, *The Philosophical Theology of Jonathan Edwards* (New York: Columbia University Press, 1960), pp. 10–11.

7. Perry Miller, *Jonathan Edwards* (New York: Meridian Books, 1959).

8. Cf. James H. Nichols, Review of Perry Miller's *Jonathan Edwards*, in *Church History*, XX (December, 1951), 79.

9. *Freedom of the Will*, WY, I, 131.

10. "God's Awful Judgment in the Breaking and Withering of the Strong Rods of a Community," WD, VI, 229.

11. Preface to Joseph Bellamy's *True Religion Delineated* (Morris-Town: Henry P. Russell, 1804), p. iv.

12. Letter to Rev. John Erskine, 1748, in Sereno Dwight, *Life of President Edwards*, WD, I, 251.

13. "Catalogue," Yale MSS. This is a list of books, articles, and quotations which Edwards began during his college years and continued throughout his theological career. Although Edwards frequently left no clear indication in this notebook of which sources mentioned he had actually read (though one may check many of the sources against citations in other notes and treatises), it does reveal his reading interests.

14. Edwards is sometimes deemed a "tragic" figure because he abandoned a career of "pure science" or "pure philosophy"—a promising career allegedly foreshadowed in his earliest writings—for the shackling career of theologian-preacher. Clyde Holbrook's comment on this is to the point: "The remarkable fact is that Edwards never seemed to take seriously at any time the possibility of becoming a scientist, a philosopher, or a man of letters. From first to last he was

a theologian in the broadest sense. His early scientific and metaphysical notes were linked to the deeper problem of the nature and the destiny of man in God's world. Nor was he trapped by some system of thought from which he was unable to free himself. Rather he was caught by the vision of a Universe whose every aspect bespoke the handiwork of a righteous, holy, and beauteous God and in which man, fallen though he be, could descry some elements of that justice, power, and glory which bounded his finite existence. Within this wondrous world the rationale of human life at those decisive points where it is judged and redeemed by the divine must be clarified, and to that end science, philosophy, ethics, and the capacities for literary expression must be bent." Holbrook, "Jonathan Edwards and His Detractors," *op. cit.*, p. 392. Cf. Dwight, *Life of President Edwards*, WD, I, 55.

15. Daniel Boorstin, *The Americans: The Colonial Experience* (New York: Vintage Books, 1964), p. 68.

16. Philip S. Watson's definition of motif research in his Introduction to Anders Nygren's *Agape and Eros*, I, ii (London: Society for Promoting Christian Knowledge, 1938), vii.

17. Dwight, *Life of President Edwards*, WD, I, 113.

18. Ola Elizabeth Winslow, *Jonathan Edwards, 1703-1758* (New York: Collier Books, 1961), p. 115.

CHAPTER I

1. Notebook: "Faith," Yale MSS, p. 42. This entry is partially included in "Observations Concerning Faith," WW, II, 623.

2. John Calvin, *Institutes of the Christian Religion*, I, ed. J. T. McNeill, trans. F. L. Battles, Vol. XX of *Library of Christian Classics* (2 vols.; Philadelphia: Westminster Press, 1960), p. 551—Bk. III, Chap. ii, sec. 36.

3. See William Ames, *The Marrow of Sacred Divinity* (London, 1643), pp. 5, 8; William Perkins, *Works*, I (London, 1616), 637; Thomas Manton, *Works*, II (London: James Nisbet & Co., 1871), 145, 147; John Owen, *Works*, V, ed. W. H. Goold (Edinburgh: Johnstone & Hunter, 1851), 71; Thomas Shepard, *Works*, I (Boston: Doctrinal Tract & Book Society, 1853), 8.

4. John Preston, *The Breast-Plate of Faith and Love* (London, 1630), Pt. I, p. 55.

5. William G. Wilcox, "New England Covenant Theology: Its English Precursors and Early American Exponents" (unpublished Ph.D. dissertation, Duke University, 1959), p. 156.

6. *Ibid.*, pp. 157, 160.

7. Shepard, *op. cit.*, p. 205.

8. Thomas Shepard, *The Parable of the Ten Virgins* (Aberdeen, 1838), pp. 176–77. Cf. L. J. Trinterud's comment on this psychology, *The Forming of an American Tradition* (Philadelphia: Westminster Press, 1949), pp. 187–88.

9. Ames, *op. cit.*, p. 5. Ames appears to have also opted at times for the "intellect emphasis." See Perry Miller, *New England Mind: The Seventeenth Century* (Boston: Beacon Press, 1961), pp. 248 f.

10. "Observations Concerning Faith," WW, II, 604, 623, 625.

11. *Ibid.*, p. 606.

12. *"The Mind" of Jonathan Edwards*, text edited and reconstructed by Leon Howard (Berkeley: University of California Press, 1963), p. 113.

13. Solomon Stoddard, *The Nature of Saving Conversion, and The Way Wherein It is Wrought* (Boston, 1770), p. 53.

14. See Miller, *Jonathan Edwards*, pp. 43–68, 186–87 *et passim*. For an instance of disagreement with Miller see Vincent Tomas, "The Modernity of Jonathan Edwards," *New England Quarterly*, XXV (March, 1952), 60–84.

15. Early entries in Edwards' "Catalogue" list writings by Locke, and Edwards' early "The Mind" in part is a dialogue with a number of Locke's theories. See "Catalogue," Yale MSS, inserted front page and pp. 1–4; *"The Mind" of Jonathan Edwards*, pp. 60 ff. Edwards was probably first exposed to Locke through the "Dummer Collection," a collection of books donated to Yale College during Edwards' years there, which included works ranging from Calvin and Owen to Descartes and Locke. See Anne Stokely Pratt, "The Books Sent From England by Jeremiah Dummer to Yale College," *Papers in Honor of Andrew Keogh* (private printing, New Haven: Yale University Press, 1938), pp. 7–44. For references to Locke in Edwards' published writings see *Treatise on Religious Affections*, WY, II, 299; and *Freedom of the Will*, WY, I, 164, 171 *et passim*.

16. Samuel Hopkins, *The Life of President Edwards*, WL, I, 11.

17. *"The Mind" of Jonathan Edwards*, p. 121.

18. *Ibid.*, pp. 27, 60.

19. See John Locke, *An Essay Concerning Human Understanding*, ed. A. C. Fraser, I, (2 vols.; New York: Dover Publications, 1959), 313–15.

20. *Freedom of the Will*, WY, I, 163.

21. *Ibid.*, p. 137; *Affections*, WY, II, 96–97.

22. Manton, *op. cit.*, pp. 154–55.

23. "Observations Concerning Faith," WW, II, 621.

24. *Ibid.*, pp. 621–22.

25. Locke, *Essay*, I, 121–24, 145, 213 ff.

26. *Ibid.*, II, 37.

27. "Faith," Yale MSS, p. 11.

28. *"The Mind" of Jonathan Edwards*, pp. 57, 82.

29. Cf. Perry Miller, "Jonathan Edwards on the Sense of the Heart," *Harvard Theological Review*, XLI (April, 1948), 127.

30. Locke's Chapter on "Enthusiasm" in the *Essay* finally subjects the truth of revelation to the demonstrative powers of natural reason and defines revelation simply as an "enlargement" of natural reason. This would appear repugnant to Edwards not only because, as we shall see, it closes the gap between nature and grace from the side of nature, but also because it exalts and isolates one human power with respect to the truth of revelation, viz., the demonstrative, discursive power of reason exclusive of affective inclination. Locke, *Essay*, II, 431, 438-39.

31. Sermon: "A Divine and Supernatural Light," WW, IV, 443.

32. *Ibid.*, WD, VI, 176-77.

33. *Ibid.*, p. 177.

34. Misc. no. 201, Townsend, p. 247.

35. Sermon: "The Importance and Advantage of a Thorough Knowledge of Divine Truth," WW, IV, 1-15.

36. Misc. no. 212, Yale MSS.

37. *Affections*, WY, II, 272.

38. *Ibid.*, p. 282.

39. "Observations Concerning Faith," WW, II, 601.

40. See Psalms 19:9-10; Calvin, *Institutes*, III, ii, 33; Geoffrey F. Nuttall, *The Holy Spirit in Puritan Faith and Experience* (Oxford: Basil Blackwell, 1947), pp. 38-39; John Smith, *Select Discourses* (3rd ed. rev.; London: Rivingtons and Cochran, 1821), p. 19.

41. *Affections*, WY, II, 272. Cf. Misc. no. 123, Townsend, p. 246.

42. Thomas Aquinas, *Nature and Grace, Selections from the Summa Theologica*, trans. A. M. Fairweather, Vol. XI of *Library of Christian Classics* (Philadelphia: Westminster Press, 1954), pp. 250-51.

43. *Affections*, WY, II, 272.

44. Winslow, *Jonathan Edwards, 1703-1758*, p. 216.

45. Miller, *Jonathan Edwards*, p. 184.

46. Alfred Owen Aldridge, *Jonathan Edwards* (New York: Washington Square Press, 1964), p. 22.

47. "A Divine and Supernatural Light," WD, VI, 186.

48. *Ibid.*, WW, IV, 443.

49. "Observations Concerning Faith," WW, II, 611. Cf. Locke, *Essay*, II, 104 ff.

50. *Ibid.*, 606.

CHAPTER II

1. "This I suppose to be that Blessed Trinity that we read of in the Holy SS. The F. is the Deity subsisting in the Prime, unoriginated & most absolute manner, or the deity in its direct existence. The Son is the deity generated by Gods understanding, or having an Idea of himself & subsisting in that Idea. The Holy Gh. is the deity subsisting in act, or the divine essence flowing out and Breathed forth in Gods Infinite love to & delight in himself. And I believe the whole divine Essence does Truly & distinctly subsist both in the divine Idea & divine Love, and that each of them are Properly distinct Persons." *An Unpublished Essay of Edwards on the Trinity,* ed. G. P. Fisher (New York: Charles Scribner's Sons, 1903), p. 110.

Edwards accounts for the transition from the being and operation of the Persons strictly within the Godhead to their being and operation *ad extra* by an eternal covenant or agreement entered into freely and mutually by the Persons respecting their distinctive roles in redemption. See Edwards' *Observations Concerning the Scripture Oeconomy of the Trinity and Covenant of Redemption,* ed. Egbert C. Smyth (New York: Charles Scribner's Sons, 1880), *passim.*

2. See Augustine's *On The Trinity,* Whitney J. Oates (ed.), *Basic Writings of Saint Augustine,* II (New York: Random House, 1948), 787–88; 792–95. Cf. Cyril C. Richardson, "The Enigma of the Trinity," *A Companion to the Study of St. Augustine,* ed. R. W Battenhouse (New York: Oxford University Press, 1955), pp 240–55.

3. *Unpublished Essay on the Trinity,* pp. 120–21, 123.

4. Ramsey, WY, I, 43.

5. *Ibid.,* n. 5.

6. Edwards, along with most Puritan theologians, distinguished between the extraordinary and the ordinary operation of the Spirit: the former gives extraordinary gifts—visions, private revelations, ability to work miracles, etc.—and works only during special occasions (notably the apostolic period); the latter is the operation of the Spirit wherein are given those gifts to man "such as are continued to the Church of God throughout all ages; such gifts as are granted in conviction and conversion. . . ." The extraordinary operation is subordinate in importance to the ordinary: e.g., "The apostle Paul abounded in visions, revelations, and miraculous gifts, above all the apostles; but yet he esteems all things but loss for the excellency of the spiritual knowledge of Christ." The ordinary operation of the Spirit is further divided into common and saving operations. The

ormer gives gifts common to the godly and the ungodly: e.g., con-
iction of sin; the latter gives gifts to the godly only: e.g., faith. See
'ermon: "The Distinguishing Marks of a Work of the Spirit of
'od," WW, I, 556–57; and *Charity and Its Fruits*, ed. Tryon Ed-
vards (New York: Robert Carter & Brothers, 1852), pp. 41–44.

7. "A Divine and Supernatural Light," WW, IV, 449–50.

8. *Ibid.*, p. 441.

9. *Affections*, WY, II, 200–1. Cf. Misc. no. 408, Townsend, p.
'50.

10. *Ibid.*, 200.

11. *Ibid.*

12. *Ibid.*, p. 201.

13. *Ibid.*, p. 203.

14. *Ibid.*

15. *Ibid.*, p. 205.

16. *Ibid.*, p. 200. "A Divine and Supernatural Light," WD, VI,
74.

17. "A Divine and Supernatural Light," WD, VI, 181.

18. Locke, *Essay*, I, 197.

19. *"The Mind" of Jonathan Edwards*, p. 59.

20. "A Divine and Supernatural Light," WW, IV, 439–40.

21. *Ibid.*, p. 443.

22. *Affections*, WY, II, 203.

23. "A Divine and Supernatural Light, WW, IV, 440–41.

24. *Affections*, WY, II, 210–11.

25. "Distinguishing Marks of a Work of the Spirit of God," WD,
II, 567.

26. "Six Letters of Jonathan Edwards to Joseph Bellamy," ed.
'tanley T. Williams, *New England Quarterly*, I (April, 1928), 230.

27. Peter van Mastricht, *A Treatise on Regeneration*, extracted
nd translated from the *Theologia Theoretico-Practica* (New Haven:
'homas & Samuel Green, n.d.), p. 26. Cf. p. 14.

28. Preston, *Breast-Plate of Faith and Love*, Pt. I, pp. 57–58.

29. Richard Sibbes, "The Bruised Reed and Smoking Flax," *Com-
lete Works of Richard Sibbes*, ed. A. B. Grosart, I (Edinburgh:
ames Nichol, 1862), pp. 81, 83.

30. Stoddard, *The Nature of Saving Conversion*, p. 28.

31. *Ibid.*, p. 53.

32. Thomas Schafer observes this about Stoddard with the com-
nent that the majority of the Reformed divines "along with Dort,
eld that regeneration acts immediately on the will, conferring on it
. new propensity toward spiritual good.' Mastricht preferred the lat-
:r view and Edwards followed him rather than Stoddard at this
oint." Thomas A. Schafer, "Solomon Stoddard and the Theology

of the Revival," A *Miscellany of American Christianity, Essays in Honor of H. Shelton Smith*, ed. S. C. Henry (Durham, N.C.: Duke University Press, 1963), p. 348, n. 88. It should be added, however, that though Edwards did indeed break from Stoddard and join the majority of his tradition by holding that God operates immediately on man's will, he nevertheless overcame that tradition's total separation of the faculties and hence its separation of infusion and illumination.

33. "Observations Concerning Efficacious Grace," WW, II, 566 ff. *et passim.*

34. *Affections*, WY, II, 343.

35. "Treatise on Grace," *Selections from the Unpublished Writings of Jonathan Edwards*, ed. A. B. Grosart (Edinburgh: Ballantyne & Co., for private circulation, 1865), p. 55.

36. "Six Letters of Edwards to Bellamy," *op. cit.*, pp. 229–30.

37. François Turrettini, *Institutio Theologiae Elencticae*, trans. G. M. Giger (unpublished, microfilmed manuscript, Princeton Theological Library, 1954), Topic XV, Question iv, Sec. 13.

38. "Observations Concerning Efficacious Grace," WW, II, 569.

39. *Ibid.*, p. 566.

40. "Treatise on Grace," p. 55.

41. E.g. in his *Charity and Its Fruits*, p. 51.

42. *Affections*, WY, II, 118–19.

43. *Ibid.*, p. 341.

44. "Treatise on Grace," p. 54.

45. "Concerning the Perseverance of Saints," WW, III, 520.

46. "Memoirs of the Rev. David Brainerd," WD, X, 421.

47. *Ibid.*, pp. 415–16.

48. Misc. no. 739, Townsend, p. 207.

49. Thomas Schafer, "Jonathan Edwards and Justification by Faith," *Church History*, XX (December, 1951), 55–67.

50. "An Humble Inquiry into the Qualifications for Full Communion in the Visible Church of Christ," WD, IV, 415. Edwards is here citing the "memorable divine," Solomon Stoddard; the citation is nevertheless taken positively by Edwards and is an effort to make Stoddard speak against the Stoddardean view of Church communion.

51. Misc. no. 567, Yale MSS.

52. See *Charity and Its Fruits*, pp. 22–23.

53. "Treatise on Grace," p. 46.

54. *Ibid.*, p. 44.

55. *Charity and Its Fruits*, pp. 5–6.

56. "A Dissertation Concerning the End for Which God Created the World," WD, III, 82–84.

57. *Ibid.*, pp. 82–83.

58. *Unpublished Essay on the Trinity*, p. 99.

59. Schafer, *op. cit.*, p. 59.

60. *Ibid.*

61. Misc. no. 77, Yale MSS.

62. See Heinrich Heppe, *Reformed Dogmatics*, ed. Ernst Bizer, trans. G. T. Thomson (rev. ed.; London: George Allen & Unwin Ltd., 1950), p. 565. Cf. "Westminster Confession of Faith" in Philip Schaff, *Creeds of Christendom*, III (4th ed. rev.; New York: Harper & Brothers, 1919), 629–30; Sibbes, "Bruised Reed and Smoking Flax," *Works*, I, 78; Ames, *Marrow of Sacred Divinity*, pp. 125 ff.; Calvin, *Institutes*, III, iii, 9; xi, 1.

63. François Wendel, *Calvin, The Origins and Development of His Religious Thought*, trans. Philip Mairet (New York: Harper & Row, 1963), p. 242, n. 31.

64. E.g. in John Owen's *Pneumatology*, *Works*, III, 215 *et passim*.

65. "Some Thoughts on the Revival," WD, IV, 181. Cf. *Affections*, WY, II, 341.

66. Calvin, *Institutes*, III, i, 4. Cf. Owen, *Works*, V, 132; van Mastricht, *Treatise on Regeneration*, p. 28.

CHAPTER III

1. See Regin Prenter, *Spiritus Creator*, trans. John M. Jensen (Philadelphia: Muhlenberg Press, 1953), pp. 247 ff.

2. See H. Shelton Smith, Robert T. Handy, Lefferts H. Loetscher, *American Christianity*, I (New York: Charles Scribner's Sons, 1960), 114 ff.

3. H. Richard Niebuhr, *The Kingdom of God in America* (New York: Harper & Brothers, 1959), p. 63.

4. *Ibid.*, p. 109.

5. Calvin, *Institutes*, II, v, 5.

6. Edward A. Dowey, *The Knowledge of God in Calvin's Theology* (New York: Columbia University Press, 1952), p. 117.

7. *Unpublished Essay on the Trinity*, p. 121.

8. Sermon: "The Wisdom Displayed in Salvation," WW, VII, 70.

9. "Observations Concerning Faith," WW, II, 606.

10. "Covenant of Redemption: 'Excellency of Christ,'" *Jonathan Edwards, Representative Selections*, ed. Clarence H. Faust and Thomas H. Johnson (New York: Hill & Wang, 1962), p. 373.

11. *Images or Shadows of Divine Things*, ed. Perry Miller (New Haven: Yale University Press, 1948), p. 61.

12. Misc. no. 777, Yale MSS.

13. *Images or Shadows of Divine Things, passim.*

14. *Ibid.*, p. 36.

15. "Miscellaneous Observations on Important Theological Subjects," WD, VII, 253 *et passim.*

16. Turrettini, *Institutio*, XV, iv, 23. Cf. Heppe, *Reformed Dogmatics*, p. 521.

17. *Ibid.*, 36.

18. "A Divine and Supernatural Light," WW, IV, 444.

19. *Ibid.*

20. Alexander V. G. Allen, *Jonathan Edwards* (Boston: Houghton, Mifflin & Co., 1891), p. 69.

21. "A History of the Work of Redemption," WD, III, 356.

22. "The Importance and Advantage of a Thorough Knowledge of Divine Truth," WW, IV, 5.

23. Misc. no. 539, Yale MSS.

24. *Ibid.*

25. *Ibid.*

26. "Importance . . . of . . . Knowledge of Divine Truth," WW, IV, 7. Italics mine.

27. Misc. no. 636, Yale MSS.

28. "Importance . . . of . . . Knowledge of Divine Truth," WW, IV, 4–5.

29. *Affections*, WY, II, 225.

30. *Ibid.*

31. *Ibid.*, p. 228.

32. *Ibid.*, p. 225.

33. "Some Thoughts on the Revival," WD, IV, 202 ff. Cf Thomas Shepard: "The Spirit indeed inwardly accompanies the voice of the gospel, but no man's call is by the immediate voice of the Spirit without the gospel, or the immediate testimony of the Spirit breathed out of free grace without the word." *Works*, I, 220.

34. "A History of the Work of Redemption," WD, III, 219.

35. Sermon of 1744, preached at the ordination of the Rev. Mr Robert Abercrombie: "The True Excellency of a Gospel Minister," WD, VIII, 452.

36. "Farewell Sermon," WW, I, 75.

37. "Some Thoughts on the Revival," WD, IV, 159.

38. *Ibid.*, p. 158.

39. *Ibid.*

40. *Ibid.*

41. Perry Miller, *Errand into the Wilderness* (Cambridge: Belknap Press of Harvard University Press, 1956), p. 183.

CHAPTER IV

1. Sermon: "God's Sovereignty in the Salvation of Men," WD, VIII, 119.

2. Quoted in William G. McLoughlin, Jr., *Modern Revivalism: Charles Grandison Finney to Billy Graham* (New York: Ronald Press, 1959), p. 11.

3. *Ibid.*

4. "Miscellaneous Remarks on Important Doctrines," WD, VII, 434.

5. See the elaborate scheme of Calvin's successor in Geneva, Theodore Beza, which is entitled "The Sum of all Christianity, or the Description and Distribution of the Causes of the Salvation of the Elect and of the Destruction of the Reprobate, Collected from the Sacred Writings." Heppe, *Reformed Dogmatics*, pp. 147–48.

6. John Dillenberger and Claude Welch, *Protestant Christianity, Interpreted Through Its Development* (New York: Charles Scribner's Sons, 1954), p. 34.

7. "Treatise on Grace," pp. 25–26.

8. "A History of the Work of Redemption," WD, III, 186.

9. See "Narrative of Surprising Conversions," WW, III, 260 ff.

10. *Affections*, WY, II, 162, 170–71, 329.

11. "Observations Concerning Efficacious Grace," WW, II, 591.

12. Misc. no. 241, Yale MSS.

13. "Observations Concerning Efficacious Grace," WW, II, 590. Cf. Augustine, "On Grace and Free Will," *Basic Writings of Saint Augustine*, ed. W. J. Oates, I, 738, 753–54; and Luther, *On the Bondage of the Will*, trans. J. I. Packer and O. R. Johnston (Westwood, N.J.: Fleming H. Revell Co., 1957), p. 253.

14. A. B. Crabtree, *Jonathan Edwards' View of Man, A Study in Eighteenth Century Calvinism* (Wallington, England: Religious Education Press, 1948), pp. 25–26.

15. "The Great Doctrine of Original Sin Defended," WD, II, 534–37.

16. Aquinas, *Nature and Grace*, pp. 126, 128.

17. Sermon: "Man's Natural Blindness in the Things of Religion," WD, VII, 3–30.

18. Misc. no. 676, Townsend, p. 244.

19. *Images or Shadows of Divine Things*, p. 91.

20. "Original Sin," WD, II, 537.

21. "Man's Natural Blindness in the Things of Religion," WD, VII, 4.

22. "Man's Natural Blindness in the Things of Religion," WD, VII, 5.

23. See B. A. Gerrish, *Grace and Reason, A Study in the Theology of Luther* (Oxford, England: Clarendon Press, 1962), pp. 72–73; and Wendel, *Calvin*, pp. 192 ff.

24. "Original Sin," WD, II, 537.

25. Sermon: "Men Naturally God's Enemies," WW, IV, 42.

26. "A History of the Work of Redemption," WD, III, 333; "An Humble Attempt to Promote Explicit Agreement and Visible Union of God's People in Extraordinary Prayer," WD, III, 450; "God's Sovereignty in the Salvation of Men," WD, VIII, 115. Cf. Thomas A. Schafer, "Jonathan Edwards' Conception of the Church," *Church History*, XXIV (March, 1955), 62.

27. Edwards recognized that the Lord's Supper might indeed *tend* toward conversion, but this was, he felt, no argument that it was instituted for that *purpose* in Scripture. "Qualifications for Communion," WD, IV, 412–13, 423 ff.

28. Sermon: "Pressing into the Kingdom of God," WD, V, 464, 467. J. H. Gerstner believes, on the basis of statements in some of Edwards' sermons which speak of a "possible" and even a "probable" finding in the seeking, that for Edwards "any serious seeking would probably issue in salvation." John H. Gerstner, *Steps to Salvation, The Evangelistic Message of Jonathan Edwards* (Philadelphia: Westminster Press, 1960), pp. 101–2. But for Edwards the possibility or probability of finding does not inhere in the seriousness of the seeking but in the free grace of God. This is especially apparent in Edwards' understanding of "preparation for salvation," considered below.

29. Elwood, *The Philosophical Theology of Jonathan Edwards*, p. 147. For this interpretation of English Puritanism see Nuttall, *The Holy Spirit in Puritan Faith and Experience*, pp. 91–92.

30. "Some Thoughts on the Revival," WD, IV, 216–17. Cf. the agreement of the main-line English Puritans on this point in Miller, *Errand into the Wilderness*, pp. 67–68.

31. Sermon: "The Manner in which the Salvation of the Soul is to be Sought," WW, IV, 370–71.

32. "God's Sovereignty in the Salvation of Men," WD, VIII, 112.

33. "God Glorified in Man's Dependence," WW, IV, 171.

34. Sermon: "The Vain Self-Flatteries of the Sinner," WD, VI, 419.

35. Edmund S. Morgan, *Visible Saints, The History of a Puritan Idea* (New York: New York University Press, 1963), p. 66.

36. Sibbes, *Works*, I, 47; Shepard, *Works*, I, 116–84.

37. Perkins, *Works*, II, 13.

38. Ames, *Marrow of Sacred Divinity*, p. 111.

39. Dwight, *Life of President Edwards*, WD, I, 93.

40. *Ibid.*, pp. 58–60.

41. "Narrative of Surprising Conversions," WW, III, 240 ff. Cf. C. C. Goen, *Revivalism and Separatism in New England, 1740–1800* (New Haven: Yale University Press, 1962), p. 13.

42. See Misc. nos. 1, 116b, 255, 337, 354, 1019, Yale MSS; see also the sermon: "Hope and Comfort Usually Follow Genuine Humiliation and Repentance," WD, VIII, 72, 95.

43. See Perry Miller, "'Preparation for Salvation' in Seventeenth-Century New England," *Journal of the History of Ideas*, IV (June, 1943), 268 ff.

44. *Affections*, WY, II, 161–62.

45. "Narrative of Surprising Conversions," WW, III, 244.

46. Misc. no. 470, Yale MSS.

47. Misc. no. 317, Yale MSS.

48. "Narrative of Surprising Conversions," WD, IV, 35–36.

49. Stoddard, *The Nature of Saving Conversion*, p. 2.

50. Shepard, *Works*, I, 237. It is by no means to be suggested that the Puritans before Edwards were unanimous on this subject. During the seventeenth-century controversy over antinomianism in Massachusetts, Thomas Hooker, who was in agreement with Shepard, found an opponent in John Cotton, who refused to grant that faith can be initiated by preparation in "natural" man. And Giles Firmin attacked Shepard "for demanding too much of natural man before grace." Miller, *Errand into the Wilderness*, p. 87, n. 154.

51. Owen, *Works*, V, 74–75.

52. Misc. no. 732, Townsend, pp. 112–13.

53. Misc. no. 626, Townsend, p. 111.

54. William James's contention that finally Edwards' distinction between converted and unconverted man must fall to the ground is an inevitable ramification of James's position that "the worth of a thing" cannot "be decided by its origin." James believes that in Edwards' *Religious Affections* "one could hardly read a clearer argument than this book unwittingly offers in favor of the thesis that no chasm exists between the orders of human excellence, but that here as elsewhere, nature shows continuous differences, and generation and regeneration are matters of degree." But Edwards, unlike James, presupposes that the value of a thing *is* decided by its origin, a presupposition made quite explicit in the *Affections* and one of the pillars on which the entire treatise rests. In terms of Edwards' "first sign" of gracious affections, the gracious is distinguished from the natural human affection by its *divine* or *supernatural origin*, which precludes Edwards' arguing, even "unwittingly," that the difference between natural generation and saving regeneration is simply a "matter of

degree." In short, Edwards is irredeemably "supernaturalist," if we take this now hackneyed and ambiguous term to mean that whatever human nature is and does from itself is qualitatively different from what it is and does from beyond itself or from the Spirit of God. And the difference is owing to the difference between natural and supernatural origins.

See William James, *The Varieties of Religious Experience* (New York: Collier Books, 1961), pp. 194–96.

55. Misc. no. 1019, Yale MSS.

56. "Hope and Comfort Usually Follow Genuine Humiliation and Repentance," WD, VIII, 96.

57. Misc. no. 669, Yale MSS.

58. *Ibid.*

59. "Justification by Faith Alone," WW, IV, 119.

60. Misc. no. 393, Yale MSS.

61. Trinterud, *The Forming of an American Tradition*, p. 183.

62. Edwin H. Cady, "The Artistry of Jonathan Edwards," *New England Quarterly*, XXII (March, 1949), 69. Cf. "Sinners in the Hands of an Angry God," WW, IV, 313–21.

63. H. Richard Niebuhr, *The Kingdom of God in America*, p. 137.

64. Sermon: "God Makes Men Sensible of Their Misery Before He Reveals His Mercy and Love," WD, VIII, 62.

65. See sermons: "Wicked Men Useful in Their Destruction Only," WW, IV, 300–12; "The Portion of the Wicked," WD, VIII, 195–226.

66. "The True Excellency of a Gospel Minister," WD, VIII, 443.

67. "Sinners in the Hands of an Angry God," WW, IV, 317.

68. Wilbert L. Anderson, "The Preaching Power of Jonathan Edwards," *Congregationalist and the Christian World*, LXXXVII (October 3, 1903), 464.

69. Sermon: "Great Guilt no Obstacle to the Pardon of the Returning Sinner," WW, IV, 422.

70. "Sinners in the Hands of an Angry God," WW, IV, 316.

71. "A History of the Work of Redemption," WD, III, 211.

72. Calvin, *Institutes*, II, vii, 6, 12.

73. "Justification by Faith Alone," WW, IV, 85.

CHAPTER V

1. "Faith," Yale MSS, p. 23.

2. *Affections*, WY, II, 240 ff.

3. *Ibid.*, p. 260.

4. H. Richard Niebuhr, *Radical Monotheism and Western Culture, with Supplementary Essays* (New York: Harper & Brothers, 1960), pp. 46, 123. For suggestions of Edwards' influence on Niebuhr see Sydney Ahlstrom, "H. Richard Niebuhr's Place in American Thought," *Christianity and Crisis*, XXIII (November 25, 1963), 213–17.

5. "Observations Concerning Faith," WD, VII, 556.

6. *Ibid.*, p. 540.

7. Jan Ridderbos, *De Theologie Van Jonathan Edwards* ('s-Gravenhage [The Hague]: Johan A. Nederbragt, 1907), p. 254.

8. Jonathan Edwards, Jr., *Works*, I (Andover: Allen, Morrill & Wardwell, 1842), 490.

9. *Affections*, WY, II, 240.

10. *Ibid.*, pp. 253–54.

11. *Ibid.*, p. 242.

12. *Ibid.*, p. 246.

13. *Ibid.*

14. "Dissertation on the Nature of True Virtue," WW, II, 278.

15. *Ibid.*, p. 279.

16. *Affections*, WY, II, 243–44.

17. *Ibid.*, p. 255.

18. *Ibid.*, pp. 263–65.

19. *Ibid.*, pp. 262–63.

20. Sermon: "The Justice of God in the Damnation of Sinners," WD, V, 519.

21. Joseph G. Haroutunian, "Jonathan Edwards: Theologian of the Great Commandment," *Theology Today*, I (October, 1944), 361–77.

22. See Luther, *Lectures on Romans*, ed. and trans. Wilhelm Pauck, Vol. XV of *Library of Christian Classics* (Philadelphia: Westminster Press, 1961), p. 162; and Calvin, *Institutes*, III, ii, 41.

23. Luther, 1531, *Commentary on Galatians*, ed. P. S. Watson (Westwood, N.J.: Fleming H. Revell Co., 1953), p. 163; Calvin, *Institutes*, III, ii, 41; xviii, 8.

24. See the eighteenth-century English nonconformist, Philip Doddridge, *Practical Discourses on Regeneration in Ten Sermons* (London: M. Fenner & J. Hodges, 1742), p. 66; and the eighteenth-century Bishop of London, Thomas Sherlock, *Works*, I, ed. T. S. Hughes (London: A. J. Valpy, 1830), 239. Doddridge is frequently mentioned and cited in Edwards' "Catalogue" of books (Yale MSS); and Sherlock is quoted at length in the notebook "Faith" (Yale MSS, pp. 48–51).

25. "Original Sin," WD, II, 335.

26. "Distinguishing Marks of a Work of the Spirit of God," WW, I, 536.

27. "Some Thoughts on the Revival," WD, IV, 118.

28. *Ibid.* Edwards is here giving a "particular instance" of a "Work of God" in "a person" (probably his wife). Cf. Miller, *Jonathan Edwards*, pp. 204–6.

29. Calvin, *Institutes*, III, iii, 10. For the retention of this notion in other eighteenth-century revivalists—notably Gilbert Tennent—see Trinterud, *Forming of an American Tradition*, p. 193.

30. "God Glorified in Man's Dependence," WW, IV, 173.

31. "Some Thoughts on the Revival," WD, IV, 96, 183.

32. Sibbes, *Works*, I, 48.

33. William Haller, *The Rise of Puritanism* (New York: Harper & Brothers, Torchbooks, 1957), p. 96.

34. *Ibid.*, p. 38.

35. Dwight, *Life of President Edwards*, WD, I, 81.

36. *Ibid.*, p. 133.

37. "Original Sin," WD, II, 342.

38. "Observations Concerning Faith," WW, II, 607.

39. *Ibid.*, p. 612.

40. *Affections*, WY, II, 377–78.

41. *Ibid.*, pp. 332–33.

42. *Ibid.*, p. 334.

43. *Charity and Its Fruits*, p. 196.

44. "Some Thoughts on the Revival," WD, IV, 123. In view of this balance between awareness of human weakness and awareness of divine glory which is consistently maintained by Edwards, it is indeed strange that A. C. McGiffert could say, "It was not the greatness of God, but the nothingness of man that he [Edwards] was primarily interested to enforce, and all his theology was dominated by this aim." *Protestant Thought Before Kant* (New York: Harper & Brothers, Torchbooks, 1961), pp. 176–77.

45. Sermon: "God the Best Portion of the Christian," WW, IV, 544.

46. "Concerning the Perseverance of Saints," WW, III, 520.

47. *Charity and Its Fruits*, p. 422.

48. "Concerning the Perseverance of Saints," WW, III, 512.

49. *Ibid.*, p. 514.

50. Locke, *Essay*, I, 449.

51. "The Mind" of Jonathan Edwards, p. 28.

52. "Original Sin," WD, II, 555.

53. *Ibid.*, p. 556.

54. *Ibid.*, p. 557.

55. *Ibid.*, WW, II, 491.

56. See I. Woodbridge Riley, *American Philosophy, the Early Schools* (New York: Dodd, Mead & Co., 1907), pp. 127, 155–56; and *American Thought, From Puritanism to Pragmatism and Beyond* (New York: Henry Holt & Co., 1923), p. 31. Frederic I. Carpenter, "The Radicalism of Jonathan Edwards," *New England Quarterly*, IV (April, 1931), 630.

57. Clyde Holbrook, "The Ethics of Jonathan Edwards" (unpublished Ph.D. dissertation, Yale University, 1944), pp. 50–53.

58. Thomas A. Schafer, "The Concept of Being in the Thought of Jonathan Edwards" (unpublished Ph.D. dissertation, Duke University, 1951), p. 37.

59. Dwight, *Life of President Edwards*, WD, I, 60–62.

60. See "Dissertation on the End for Which God Created the World," WD, III, 21 ff.

61. "Some Thoughts on the Revival," WD, IV, 123.

62. Schafer remarks, *op. cit.*, pp. 260–61, that there is in Edwards' thought a discrepancy between viewing man as a sinner and dependent on God and viewing him as excellent, even in his sinful creaturehood, by virtue of his sharing in the very being of God. The discrepancy remains unresolved, Schafer feels, because Edwards does not make a clear distinction "between God as the totality of being and as the highest being."

63. Elwood, *op. cit.*, p. 145.

64. Jerald C. Brauer, "Puritan Mysticism and the Development of Liberalism," *Church History*, XIX (September, 1950), 153.

65. Elwood, *op. cit.*, p. 146.

66. *Ibid.*, p. 143.

CHAPTER VI

1. Luther, *Commentary on Galatians*, p. 227 *et passim*; Calvin, *Institutes*, III, xi, 2, 23.

2. Luther, *op. cit.*, p. 137 *et passim*.

3. Calvin, *Institutes*, III, xi, 2.

4. *Ibid.*, III, xi, 7.

5. Schaff, *Creeds of Christendom*, III, 626.

6. Turrettini, *Institutio*, XVI, vii, 6.

7. Shepard, *Works*, I, 228–29. This way of classifying the causation involved in justification differs from the scholasticism of the Council of Trent, in form of expression, only by the absence of Roman Catholic sacramentalism. For Trent, Christ is the meritorious cause, and the sacrament of baptism which is "the sacrament of faith" is the instrumental cause in one's justification. Trent, how-

ever, opens the way to a human merit scheme by contending that the instrumental cause "co-operates with good works" in increasing justification, while Shepard and the Protestant scholastics hold that faith does not increase justification by co-operating with works but remains a receptive instrument that receives both justification and sanctification of life and works. Schaff, *Creeds of Christendom*, II, 94–95, 99. Shepard, *op. cit.*, pp. 169–70.

8. "Justification by Faith Alone," WW, IV, 77, 89.

9. *Ibid.*, p. 64.

10. *Ibid.*, p. 91.

11. A competent and detailed examination of Edwards on the atonement has been done by Dorus Paul Rudisill, "The Doctrine of the Atonement in Jonathan Edwards and His Successors" (unpublished Ph.D. dissertation, Duke University, 1945). For an older yet fairly reliable treatment see Edwards A. Park, "The Rise of the Edwardean Theory of the Atonement," *The Atonement, Discourses and Treatises* (Boston: Congregational Board of Publication, 1859), pp. ix–lxxx.

12. "Wisdom Displayed in Salvation," WD, VII, 92.

13. "Justification by Faith Alone," WW, IV, 66–67.

14. "Miscellaneous Remarks on Important Doctrines," WD, VII, 506.

15. *Ibid.*, p. 518.

16. *Ibid.*

17. *Ibid.*

18. "Wisdom Displayed in Salvation," WD, VII, 82.

19. *Ibid.*, p. 83. Cf. "God Glorified in Man's Dependence," WW, IV, 174.

20. Schafer, "Jonathan Edwards and Justification by Faith," *op. cit.*, p. 59. Cf. George Nye Boardman, *A History of New England Theology* (New York: A. D. F. Randolph Co., 1899), pp. 155–56.

21. Misc. no. 1070, Yale MSS.

22. *Ibid.*

23. "Justification by Faith Alone," WW, IV, 72–73.

24. *Ibid.*, p. 72.

25. Cf. D. P. Rudisill, "The Doctrine of the Atonement in Jonathan Edwards and His Successors," *op. cit.*, p. 106.

26. Miller, *Jonathan Edwards*, p. 79.

27. *Ibid.*, p. 81.

28. See Thomas H. Johnson, "Jonathan Edwards' Background of Reading," *Publications of the Colonial Society of Massachusetts*, XXVIII (December, 1931), 210.

29. "Justification by Faith Alone," WD, V, 365. Italics mine in last clause.

30. Wendel, *Calvin*, p. 258. Italics mine. Cf. Calvin, *Institutes*, III, ii, 24.

31. "Observations Concerning Efficacious Grace," WW, II, 576.

32. "Justification by Faith Alone," WW, IV, 67.

33. See Misc. nos. 412, 620, 637, *et passim*, Yale MSS. Cf. our discussion of the covenant idea in Chapter VII.

34. "Justification by Faith Alone," WW, IV, 67–68.

35. *Ibid.*, p. 68.

36. *Ibid.*

37. *Ibid.*

38. *Ibid.*, p. 77.

39. *Ibid.*

40. *Ibid.*, p. 96.

41. *Ibid.*, p. 89.

42. *Ibid.*, p. 90.

43. "Observations Concerning Efficacious Grace," WW, II, 580.

44. Sermon: "Safety, Fullness, and Sweet Refreshment, to be Found in Christ," WD, VIII, 361.

45. "Justification by Faith Alone," WW, IV, 71.

46. John Owen perhaps helped Edwards understand that faith cannot precede justification. Owen said that faith is by definition "justifying faith," and justifying faith cannot be considered "to be previous unto justification . . . unless a man may be a true believer with justifying faith, and yet not be justified," which is absurd. Owen, *Works*, V, 112–13. Edwards listed and crossed out "Dr. Owen on Justification" in a very early entry in his catalogue of books. "Catalogue," Yale MSS, page inserted before p. 1. The page is written on the back of an envelope addressed to Edwards "At Yale-Colledge." Cf. Johnson, "Jonathan Edwards' Background of Reading," *op. cit.*, p. 203.

47. "Concerning the Divine Decrees in General, and Election in Particular," WW, II, 545.

48. *Ibid.*

49. "Observations Concerning Efficacious Grace," WW, II, 596.

50. "Observations Concerning Faith," WW, II, 616–17.

51. "Justification by Faith Alone," WW, IV, 76.

52. Paul Tillich, *Systematic Theology*, II (Chicago: University of Chicago Press, 1957), 178–79.

CHAPTER VII

1. H. Richard Niebuhr's description of the importance of the covenant in the life of Israel points to what was operative also in

much Puritan thought: "Man was understood . . . not first of all as rational animal but as promise-making, promise-keeping, promise-breaking being, as man of faith. All life was permeated by the faith in the fundamental covenant between God and man and in every activity some phase of that covenant was re-enacted." Niebuhr, *Radical Monotheism and Western Culture*, p. 41.

2. Leonard J. Trinterud, "The Origins of Puritanism," *Church History*, XX (March, 1951), 50.

3. Peter Bulkeley, *The Gospel-Covenant: or The Covenant of Grace Opened* (London, 1646), p. A2.

4. Ames, *Marrow of Sacred Divinity*, pp. 101–3.

5. Miller, *New England Mind: Seventeenth Century*, p. 415.

6. John Winthrop, "A Modell of Christian Charity," *The Puritans*, I, ed. Miller and Johnson (New York: Harper & Row, 1963), 197–99.

7. Miller, *Errand into the Wilderness*, p. 98.

8. Miller, *Jonathan Edwards*, p. 30.

9. Sermon notebook on Ephesians 3:10, dated March, 1733, Yale MSS. Printed, undated, in WD, VII, under the title "Wisdom Displayed in Salvation," pp. 66–114; and in WW, IV, as "The Wisdom of God, Displayed in Salvation," pp. 133–68.

10. Sermon notebook on Romans 9:18, n.d., Yale MSS. Printed in WW, IV, as "God's Sovereignty," pp. 548–60; and in WD, VIII, as "God's Sovereignty in the Salvation of Men," pp. 105–22.

11. "The Justice of God in the Damnation of Sinners," WD, V, 531.

12. "The Sole Consideration, That God is God, Sufficient to Still All Objections to His Sovereignty," WD, VI, 301–2.

13. "God's Sovereignty," WW, IV, 558.

14. Sermon on Romans 9:18, Yale MSS.

15. "Wisdom Displayed in Salvation," WD, VII, 89.

16. Miller, *Errand into the Wilderness*, pp. 63 ff.

17. Miller, *New England Mind: Seventeenth Century*, p. 367.

18. Miller, *Errand into the Wilderness*, pp. 65, 72.

19. *Ibid.*, p. 50.

20. *Institutes*, II, ii, 20; III, xxiv, 5.

21. See Miller, " 'Preparation for Salvation' in Seventeenth-Century New England," *op. cit.*, pp. 253–86.

22. John Preston, *The Breast-Plate of Faith and Love*, I, 31.

23. Bulkeley, *op. cit.*, p. 306.

24. *Ibid.*, p. 346.

25. Sermon on Romans 9:18, Yale MSS.

26. "Observations Concerning Faith," WW, II, 622.

27. Cradock, *Divine Drops Distilled*, quoted in Nuttall, *The Holy Spirit in Puritan Faith and Experience*, p. 58.

28. "Observations Concerning Faith," WW, II, 622–23.

29. Shepard, *Works*, I, 195. Cf. Bulkeley, *op. cit.*, p. 286.

30. Preston, *op. cit.*, p. 43.

31. "Justification by Faith Alone," WW, IV, 68.

32. "An Humble Inquiry into the Qualifications for Full Communion in the Visible Church of Christ," WD, IV, 321.

33. "A History of the Work of Redemption," WD, III, 198.

34. Misc. no. 329, Yale MSS—printed in "Observations Concerning Faith," WW, II, 628.

35. "Observations Concerning Efficacious Grace," WW, II, 552.

36. Misc. no. 299, Yale MSS.

37. See Perry Miller, *The New England Mind: From Colony to Province* (Cambridge: Harvard University Press, 1953), pp. 220–21.

38. Smyth (ed.), *Edwards' Observations Concerning the Scripture Oeconomy of the Trinity and Covenant of Redemption*, pp. 67–68.

39. *Ibid.*, p. 68.

40. Sermon on John 14:27, cited by Gerstner, *Steps to Salvation: The Evangelistic Message of Jonathan Edwards*, pp. 176–77.

41. Smyth (ed.), *op. cit.*, p. 67.

42. *Ibid.*, p. 66.

43. *Ibid.*, pp. 66–67.

44. Ames, *op. cit.*, p. 102.

45. Smyth (ed.), *op. cit.*, p. 66.

46. "Observations Concerning Faith," WW, II, 614.

CHAPTER VIII

1. Daniel J. Boorstin, *The Americans: The Colonial Experience*, p. 5.

2. Miller, *New England Mind: Seventeenth Century*, p. 49.

3. Misc. no. 868, Townsend, p. 235.

4. "Faith," Yale MSS, p. 4.

5. "Some Thoughts on the Revival," WD, IV, 274–75.

6. *Charity and Its Fruits*, pp. 19–23.

7. "Some Thoughts on the Revival," WD, IV, 275.

8. Notebook: "Signs of Godliness," Yale MSS, p. 12.

9. *Ibid.*, p. 5. Cf. *Affections*, WY, II, 422–23.

10. *Affections*, WY, II, 423. Italics mine.

11. *Ibid.*, p. 425.

12. *Freedom of the Will*, WY, I, 162.

13. *Affections*, WY, II, 425–26.

14. "Signs of Godliness," Yale MSS, p. 12.

15. *Affections*, WY, II, 426.

16. *Ibid.*, p. 423.

17. *Affections*, WY, II, 422. Italics mine.

18. *Ibid.*, pp. 283–84.

19. *Freedom of the Will*, WY, I, 148, 333, *et passim*.

20. Ramsey, WY, I, 11.

21. Arthur E. Murphy, "Jonathan Edwards on Free Will and Moral Agency," *Philosophical Review*, LXVIII (April, 1959), 196–97.

22. "Signs of Godliness," Yale MSS, p. 5.

23. *Affections*, WY, II, 441.

24. "Observations Concerning Faith," WW, II, 625, 619.

25. Ridderbos, *De Theologie Van Jonathan Edwards*, p. 254.

26. "Observations Concerning Faith," WW, II, 625.

27. *Ibid.*

28. *Ibid.*

29. Aquinas, *Nature and Grace*, p. 270.

30. "Canons and Decrees of the Council of Trent," Schaff, *Creeds of Christendom*, II, 115.

31. *Affections*, WY, II, 455.

32. *Ibid.*, p. 435.

33. *Ibid.*, pp. 434–35.

34. *Ibid.*, p. 450.

35. "Justification by Faith Alone," WW, IV, 103 ff.

36. *Ibid.*, p. 126.

37. *Affections*, WY, II, 445.

38. *Ibid.*, p. 446.

39. Schaff, *Creeds of Christendom*, III, 626.

40. Calvin, *Institutes*, III, xvii, 12.

41. Turrettini, *Institutio*, XVI, viii, 22.

42. Manton, *Works*, IV, 245.

43. "Justification by Faith Alone," WW, IV, 125.

44. *Ibid.*

45. *Ibid.*, p. 127.

46. *Ibid.*, p. 111.

47. Misc. no. 41, Yale MSS.

48. Misc. nos. 627, 671, 688, Yale MSS.

49. "Justification by Faith Alone," WW, IV, 107.

50. Misc. no. 996, Yale MSS. Cf. *ibid.*, no. 36.

51. "Justification by Faith Alone," WW, IV, 107.

52. *Ibid.*

CHAPTER IX

1. Schaff, *Creeds of Christendom*, III, 638. Cf. Calvin, *Institutes*, III, xxi, 7; xxiv, 18. Contrast "Canons and Decrees of the Council of Trent," Schaff, *op. cit.*, II, 103, 113–14.

2. Schaff, *op. cit.*, III, 638. Cf. Ames, *Marrow of Sacred Divinity*, p. 8; Turrettini, *Institutio*, XV, viii, 4.

3. Stoddard, *Nature of Saving Conversion*, pp. 79–80. Cf. Schafer, "Solomon Stoddard and the Theology of the Revival," *op. cit.*, p. 355.

4. Preston, *Breast-Plate of Faith and Love*, Pt. III, p. 193.

5. See Shepard, *Works*, I, 258–59.

6. "Memoirs of David Brainerd," WD, X, 418.

7. Misc. no. 859, Yale MSS.

8. Misc. no. 790, Yale MSS. Cf. *Affections*, WY, II, 450.

9. *Affections*, WY, II, 454.

10. "Signs of Godliness," Yale MSS, p. 6.

11. *Affections*, WY, II, 195–96.

12. "Christian Cautions, or the Necessity of Self-Examination," WD, VI, 329.

13. *Ibid.*, p. 340.

14. *Ibid.*

15. *Ibid.*, p. 338.

16. *Ibid.*, p. 336.

17. *Ibid.*, pp. 336–37.

18. *Ibid.*, p. 334.

19. *Ibid.*, p. 363.

20. Leslie Stephen, "Jonathan Edwards," *Littell's Living Age*, 5th series, V (1874), 222.

21. "Pressing into the Kingdom of God," WD, V, 457–58.

22. *Affections*, WY, II, 177.

23. "Christian Cautions," WD, VI, 335.

24. *Affections*, WY, II, 177–78.

25. Letters of Nov. 24, 1746, and Sept. 19, 1748, WY, II, 474, 492.

26. Letter of Sept. 4, 1747, WY, II, 480.

27. *Affections*, WY, II, 178.

28. Letter of Apr. 2, 1750, WY, II, 506.

29. Sermon: "The Christian Pilgrim," WD, VII, 143–44.

30. Donald Hosea Rhoades, "Jonathan Edwards: Experimental Theologian" (unpublished Ph.D. dissertation, Yale University,

1945), p. 206. For a treatment of other Puritans on this noncomplacent aspect of assurance see Morgan, *Visible Saints*, p. 70.

31. Letter to Gillespie of Apr. 2, 1750, WY, II, 505.

32. Quoted in William J. Wolf, *The Religion of Abraham Lincoln* (New York: Seabury Press, 1963), p. 194.

33. *Affections*, WY, II, 178.

34. Edwards says this doubting may be understood as arising indirectly from unbelief in the sense that "if I had had more faith, the actings of it would have been more clear, and so I should have been better satisfied that I had them." But it is not necessarily a direct result of unbelief since my awareness of my own condition of salvation finally depends upon my remembrance and cognizance of the actings of faith "and not on the strength of my reliance on any divine testimony." Letter to Gillespie of Apr. 2, 1750, WY, II, 504.

35. Karl Barth, *Church Dogmatics, The Doctrine of God*, II, 2, ed. and trans. G. W. Bromiley *et al.* (Edinburgh: T. & T. Clark, 1957), 335–36.

36. *Affections*, WY, II, 180–81.

37. Letter to Gillespie of Apr. 2, 1750, WY, II, 502–3.

38. *Ibid.*, p. 503.

39. "Hope and Comfort Usually Follow Genuine Humiliation and Repentance," WD, VIII, 97–98.

40. *Affections*, WY, II, 176–77.

41. See the discussion in our final chapter of the controversy over the "profession of faith."

42. Misc. no. 790, Yale MSS.

43. *Affections*, WY, II, 181.

44. *Ibid.*, pp. 183–84. Cf. "Distinguishing Marks of a Work of the Spirit of God," WW, I, 560–62.

45. "Farewell Sermon," WW, I, 67.

46. "Qualifications for Communion," WD, IV, 401.

47. *Affections*, WY, II, 424. Cf. "Qualifications for Communion," WD, IV, 335.

48. *Affections*, WY, II, 424.

INTRODUCTION TO PART IV

1. Edwards did desire to write something of a *Summa*, which would probably have been patterned after what today would be called a method of *Heilsgeschichte*. Edwards wrote in 1757 to the trustees of the College of New Jersey, who had invited him to become president of the College, "I have had on my mind and heart . . . a great work, which I call a *History of the Work of Redemption*,

a body of divinity in an entire new method, being thrown into the form of a history; considering the affair of Christian Theology, as the whole of it, in each part, stands in reference to the great work of redemption by Jesus Christ; which I suppose to be, of all others, the grand design of God, and the *summum* and *ultimum* of all the divine operations and decrees; particularly considering all parts of the grand scheme, in their historical order." *Jonathan Edwards, Selections,* ed. Faust and Johnson, p. 411. Edwards died the following year, leaving the intended scheme scattered in posthumously published sermons and in notes.

2. Dwight, *Life of President Edwards,* WD, I, 279.

3. *Ibid.,* p. 280.

4. *Ibid.,* p. 413.

CHAPTER X

1. Smith, Handy, and Loetscher, *American Christianity,* I, 310.

2. See Eugene E. White, "Solomon Stoddard's Theories of Persuasion," *Speech Monographs,* XXIX (November, 1962), 235–59.

3. Gordon Harland, "The American Protestant Heritage and the Theological Task," *Drew Gateway,* XXXII (Winter, 1962), 74.

4. Edwin Scott Gaustad, *The Great Awakening in New England* (New York: Harper & Brothers, 1957), pp. 80–81.

5. Charles Chauncy, *Seasonable Thoughts on the State of Religion in New England* (Boston: Rogers & Fowle, 1743), pp. 35 ff.

6. *Ibid.,* pp. iii–xxx.

7. Conrad Wright says, "Between Chauncy and Edwards . . . the dividing line was at least as much one of temperament and diverse traditions as anything. Born to the evangelical tradition of the Connecticut Valley, Edwards was temperamentally inclined to accept revivalism, and regarded the Awakening as a glorious and extraordinary work of the Spirit of God, though unfortunately marred by excesses and extravagances which were no essential part of it. Edwards' mature concern was to distinguish between the work of God in the revival, which he defended; and the excesses, which he deplored. Chauncy, on the other hand, was heir to the sober traditions in religion that had long prevailed in Boston. He was temperamentally predisposed against revivalistic methods, and was not inclined to try to justify the Awakening despite its excesses." Conrad Wright, *The Beginnings of Unitarianism in America* (Boston: Starr King Press, 1955), p. 55. These observations should not—as they incline to do for Wright—obscure or mollify the deep intellectual antagonism between the two theologians. It is also interesting to note that

the Awakening was anything but totally resisted by the "sober traditions of Boston." See Gaustad, *op. cit.*, pp. 43 ff.

8. Chauncy's Arminianism did not fully evolve until after his struggle with Edwards over the Awakening. See Wright, *op. cit.*, pp. 187 ff. Cf. Gaustad, *op. cit.*, p. 101.

9. Chauncy, *op. cit.*, p. 324.

10. *Ibid.*, p. 31.

11. *Ibid.*, pp. 326–27.

12. *Ibid.*, p. 324.

13. *Affections*, WY, II, 120.

14. Edwards prefers to denominate the hearty, emotional, lively, volitional aspect of human being "affection" rather than "passion" because in common parlance the latter is usually taken to refer to those actions that "are more sudden" and that overpower the mind or leave it "less in its own command." *Affections*, WY, II, 98.

15. Miller, *Jonathan Edwards*, p. 178.

16. *Affections*, WY, II, 95.

17. "Distinguishing Marks of a Work of the Spirit of God," WW, I, 529, 534.

18. "Some Thoughts on the Revival," WD, IV, 124 ff.

19. *Ibid.*, p. 128. For an extensive discussion of Edwards' millennialism see C. C. Goen, "Jonathan Edwards: A New Departure in Eschatology," *Church History*, XXVIII (March, 1959), 25–40.

20. "Some Thoughts on the Revival," WD, IV, 100–1; *Life of President Edwards*, WD, I, 147. Gaustad, *op. cit.*, p. 91, also observes that although Edwards was, in his sympathy with the Awakening as a whole, in affinity with "New Lights" like Jonathan Dickinson, Benjamin Colman, and Thomas Prince, he was farther from a revivalist extremist like James Davenport than he was from a rationalist like Chauncy.

21. See Edwards' list of "What are no signs by which we are to judge of a work" in "Distinguishing Marks," WW, I, 526–38; and his list of "What are no certain signs that religious affections are truly gracious, or that they are not" in *Affections*, WY, II, 127–90.

22. *Affections*, WY, II, 119–20.

23. *Ibid.*, p. 266.

24. *Ibid.*, p. 268.

25. *Ibid.*, p. 285.

26. "Some Thoughts on the Revival," WD, IV, 183.

27. *Ibid.*, p. 190.

28. *Ibid.*

29. *Ibid.*, p. 185.

30. *Affections*, WY, II, 315.

31. *Ibid.*, pp. 130–31.

32. *Ibid.*, pp. 287–89.

33. *Ibid.*, p. 287.

34. The other extreme to the enthusiasts' subordination of Scripture to Spirit and spiritual experience, viz., Deistic rationalism's subordination of scriptural revelation to enlightened natural reason, had not in Edwards' day made any prominent headway in America. Although deism was yet to make its impact as a movement on the American scene, a rationalism such as Chauncy's opened the door to it, and the writings of some of the leading English Deists were floating about Edwards' New England. Edwards laid his hands on these Deistic works and studied them with pen in hand. Some of Edwards' notes on the Deist criticism of scriptural revelation are more to the point than others. But one note in particular where Edwards is contending against the English Deist, Matthew Tindal, is a good commentary on Edwards' doctrine of faith. "Tindal's main argument against the need of any revelation, is, that the *law of nature is absolutely perfect*. But how weak and impertinent is this arguing, that because the *law of nature* (which is no other than natural rectitude and obligation) is perfect, therefore the *light of nature* is sufficient. . . . And how far is this from having any reference to that question, whether we have by mere nature, without instruction, all that light and advantage that we need, clearly and fully to know what is right, and all that is needful for us to be and to do, in our circumstances as sinners, etc., in order to the forgiveness of sin, the favour of God, and our own happiness?" "Miscellaneous Observations on Important Theological Subjects," WD, VII, 275. In the realm of salvation, in other words, what is given by God through his grace alone is the only light sufficient to create faith. What the rationalist has from nature is good indeed; but it provides no *sufficient* answer to the question, "What must I do to be saved?"

35. Chauncy, *op. cit.*, p. 271.

36. See Jerald C. Brauer, *Protestantism in America* (Philadelphia: Westminster Press, 1953), p. 55.

37. Goen, *Revivalism and Separatism in New England, 1740–1800*, pp. 44–45.

38. "Some Thoughts on the Revival," WD, IV, 125.

39. R. S. Crane, "Suggestions Toward a Genealogy of the 'Man of Feeling,' " *Journal of English Literary History*, I (December, 1934), 207–8.

40. "Nature of True Virtue," WW, II, 262.

41. Frederick Copleston, *A History of Philosophy*, V (Westminster, Md.: Newman Press, 1961), 178.

42. Francis Hutcheson, *An Inquiry into the Original of Our*

Ideas of Beauty and Virtue, 5th ed. (London, 1753), pp. 168–69, 183–84.

43. "Nature of True Virtue," WW, II, 263. In the treatise on virtue, Edwards makes love of benevolence—which "doth not necessarily presuppose beauty in its object"—of the primary nature of true virtue rather than love of complacence—which "presupposes beauty." *Ibid.* But in the treatise on the affections "a love to divine things for the beauty and sweetness of their moral excellency" is viewed as constitutive of true virtue. *Affections,* WY, II, 253–54. As Thomas Schafer has discerned, sometimes Edwards views love of complacence as primary and sometimes he so views love of benevolence when speaking of virtue: the former view seems to prevail when God, the object of love, is spoken of in terms of his excellency, the latter when He is spoken of within the categories of "Being in general." But in both cases Edwards makes the same point: authentic love to God is not selfish love or love to God for the sake of one's narrow private interests. See Schafer, "The Concept of Being in the Thought of Jonathan Edwards," *op. cit.,* pp. 350 ff.

44. *Jonathan Edwards, Selections,* ed. Faust and Johnson, pp. lxxxiii–lxxxvi.

45. "Nature of True Virtue," WW, II, 266.

46. *Ibid.,* p. 267.

47. Francis Hutcheson, *A System of Moral Philosophy,* I (Glasgow, 1760), 209–10.

48. Hutcheson, *Inquiry,* pp. 225–26.

49. Hutcheson, *System of Moral Philosophy,* pp. 210 ff., 217.

50. "Nature of True Virtue," WW, II, 267–68.

51. *Ibid.,* WD, III, 103.

52. See Hutcheson, *System of Moral Philosophy,* p. 216.

53. "Nature of True Virtue," WW, II, 269. In his treatise on virtue, Edwards appears to conceive God sometimes as a particular Being among beings, but possessed of the greatest amount of being, and sometimes as the ground and structure of all individual entities. *Ibid.,* pp. 266, 276. But when Edwards conceives God in the latter way, he does not intend to *identify* God with the sum of beings: he keeps the distinction between God and creation. *Ibid.,* p. 270. Edwards, in all likelihood, has something like Tillich's "ground of being" in mind: God as Being itself is both the ground and the structure of created being which cannot be identified with the sum of particular entities themselves. Nevertheless, the translation into Tillichian language still inclines toward a monism and leaves us with the question: What is the nature of the distinction between beings and their ground? And as we said earlier, Edwards' Neoplatonism, especially as articulated in *The End of Creation,* never really answers

this question. Yet Edwards' primary concern in the treatise on virtue is not ontological but ethical; ontology is the framework in which the central issue of virtue or morality is discussed. God, whether he be conceived as one Being among others or as the ground and structure of all beings, is the chief object of virtuous benevolence rather than particular created beings.

54. *Ibid.*, p. 268.

55. *Ibid.*

56. *Ibid.*, pp. 269–70.

57. *Ibid.*, p. 270.

58. Copleston, *op. cit.*, p. 182, comments that "we have a clear anticipation of utilitarianism" in Hutcheson's statement that "that action is best which procures the greatest happiness for the greatest numbers, and that worst which in like manner occasions misery." Edwards would hold that a utilitarian love of mankind apart from love of God still contains, at bottom, love for the sake of one's self-interests and is hence selfish love.

59. Hutcheson, *Inquiry*, p. 222.

60. *Ibid.*, p. 116.

61. Crane, *op. cit.*, p. 220.

62. Andrew Brown notes that though Locke in *The Reasonableness of Christianity* maintained that revelation provides men with a "clear knowledge of their duty" that they lack naturally, in the *Essay* he portrayed morality as a possibility open to natural reason itself. Andrew Brown, "John Locke and the Religious 'Aufklärung,' " *Review of Religion*, XIII (January, 1949), 129, 131.

63. "Nature of True Virtue," WW, II, 289.

64. *Ibid.*, p. 286.

65. *Ibid.*, p. 299.

66. *Ibid.*, p. 301.

67. *Ibid.*, p. 270.

68. *Ibid.*, p. 271.

69. *Affections*, WY, II, 365.

70. *Ibid.*, pp. 367–68.

71. *Ibid.*, p. 435.

CHAPTER XI

1. "Narrative of Surprising Conversions," WW, III, 233–34.

2. Francis Albert Christie, "The Beginnings of Arminianism in New England," *Papers of the American Society of Church History*, Ser. 2, III (1912), 169.

3. Daniel Whitby, *A Discourse* (2nd ed.; London, 1735), p. xi.

4. For a record of some of the reactions of the New England clergy who made this identification, see Christie, *op. cit.*, pp. 170–72.

5. Wright, *The Beginnings of Unitarianism in America*, p. 21.

6. Miller, *Jonathan Edwards*, p. 110. Cf. Schafer, "Jonathan Edwards and Justification by Faith," *op. cit.*, p. 55.

7. See Dwight, *Life of President Edwards*, WD, I, 433–34; Winslow, *Jonathan Edwards, 1703–1758*, p. 152; Miller, *op. cit.*, p. 104.

8. *Jonathan Edwards, Selections*, ed. Faust and Johnson, pp. xxxix–xl. Cf. Dwight, *Life of President Edwards*, WD, I, 125–26.

9. Dwight, *Life of President Edwards*, WD, I, 413.

10. *Jonathan Edwards, Selections*, ed. Faust and Johnson, p. 411.

11. WY, I, 468–69.

12. These three figures were all English, but Edwards' choosing them as his foils is not to be taken as an effort to move the problem of Arminianism off American soil. As we have seen, Edwards definitely viewed his battle with the Arminians as a war at home. Exactly why Edwards chose these three figures is an open question, but Claude Newlin's thesis is as plausible as any: Edwards preferred to direct his argument against those writers who had already given freedom of the will a rather weighty defense—they proved to be English. Claude M. Newlin, *Philosophy and Religion in Colonial America* (New York: Philosophical Library, 1962), pp. 144–45. For further discussion of the question see Ramsey, WY, I, 65–66.

13. *Freedom of the Will*, WY, I, 131–32.

14. See Whitby, *op. cit.*, pp. 213–17; Thomas Chubb, *A Collection of Tracts on Various Subjects*, 2nd ed., I (London, 1754), 177, 180–81; Isaac Watts, *Works*, VI (London: T. & T. Longman, 1753), 386, 395.

15. *Freedom of the Will*, WY, I, 132.

16. *Ibid.*, pp. 432–36.

17. Miller, *Jonathan Edwards*, p. 259. Cf. *Freedom of the Will*, WY, I, 398–99.

18. *Freedom of the Will*, WY, I, 173.

19. *Ibid.*, p. 181.

20. *Ibid.*, p. 180.

21. *Ibid.*, pp. 180–81.

22. *Ibid.*, p. 141.

23. Calvin, *Institutes*, II, iii, 14.

24. Quoted by Nuttall, *Holy Spirit in Puritan Faith and Experience*, p. 169.

25. Watts, *op. cit.*, p. 380.

26. Whitby, *op. cit.*, p. 345.

27. *Freedom of the Will*, WY, I, 207.

28. *Ibid.*

29. *Ibid.*, p. 321.

30. *Ibid.*, p. 156.

31. *Ibid.*, pp. 156–57.

32. *Ibid.*, p. 158.

33. *Ibid.*, pp. 433–34.

34. "Observations Concerning Efficacious Grace," WW, II, 580.

35. *Freedom of the Will*, WY, I, 433–34.

36. Clyde A. Holbrook, "Original Sin and the Enlightenment," *The Heritage of Christian Thought, Essays in Honor of Robert Lowry Calhoun*, ed. Cushman and Grislis (New York: Harper & Row, 1965), p. 142.

37. See Roland N. Stromberg, *Religious Liberalism in Eighteenth-Century England* (London: Oxford University Press, 1954), pp. 117–18.

38. Clarence H. Faust, "The Decline of Puritanism," *Transitions in American Literary History*, ed. Harry H. Clark (Durham, N.C.: Duke University Press, 1953), p. 47.

39. R. W. B. Lewis, *The American Adam: Innocence, Tragedy and Tradition in the Nineteenth Century* (Chicago: University of Chicago Press, Phoenix, 1964), p. 7.

40. The term is applied by Lewis to Henry James, *ibid.*, p. 7. See also p. 193.

41. Perry Miller comments that for New Englanders, Daniel Whitby and John Taylor "were the literary spokesmen of the age, and colonial Americans read them as Americans a century later received, let us say, Dickens. When we ask whom Edwards meant by Arminians, we have to consider first of all the steady influx of books from English Nonconformity which were accepted by his countrymen as the latest tidings from the capital, but which he judged little better than unwitting descents into Popery." Miller, *Jonathan Edwards*, p. 110.

42. H. Shelton Smith, *Changing Conceptions of Original Sin* (New York: Charles Scribner's Sons, 1955), p. 37.

43. John Taylor, *The Scripture-Doctrine of Original Sin* (3rd ed.; Belfast, 1746), pp. 254–55.

44. *Ibid.*, "Supplement," pp. 279–80.

45. "The Great Christian Doctrine of Original Sin Defended," WD, II, 307.

46. *Ibid.*, p. 512. Part III of the treatise.

47. Taylor, *op. cit.*, p. 279.

48. "Original Sin," WD, II, 512.

49. *Ibid.*, p. 515.

50. *Ibid.*, pp. 515–16. Cf. Taylor, *op. cit.*, p. 340.

51. "Original Sin," WD, II, 516.

52. "Original Sin," WD, II, 518.

53. *Ibid.*, pp. 519–26.

54. *Ibid.*, p. 527.

55. Alfred Owen Aldridge says, "Edwards ignored the broader aspects of the problem [of sin]—the evidence of observation in the areas of psychology, sociology and economics—and confined himself almost exclusively to proving against Taylor that original sin was indeed taught by Scripture. He was far more anxious to demolish Taylor than to penetrate to the truth concerning human nature." *Jonathan Edwards*, p. 120. Unless Aldridge is absurdly asking that an eighteenth-century American possess nineteenth- or twentieth-century scientific tools, he surely does not take account of the fact that Edwards' point of departure in the treatise on sin is empirical, consisting of "observations" of human corruption in "facts and events." And although Edwards is out to demolish Taylor, he is fighting Taylor on Taylor's own grounds—but without ignoring the general question of human nature, as the theories on human principles and continuity demonstrate.

56. Cf. Holbrook, "Original Sin and the Enlightenment," *op. cit.*, p. 155.

57. "A History of the Work of Redemption," WW, I, 466–67.

58. See Jonathan Mitchell's preface to Shepard's *Parable*, pp. vi–vii; and *Affections*, WY, II, 426, n. 2; 431, n. 4.

59. See Winslow, *op. cit.*, pp. 200–22.

60. On the Halfway Covenant see Smith, Handy, and Loetscher, *American Christianity*, I, 202–4.

61. "Qualifications for Communion," WD, IV, 285–86.

62. *Ibid.*, p. 286.

63. "Misrepresentations Corrected, and Truth Vindicated," WD, IV, 473. Cf. Solomon Williams, *The True State of the Question Concerning the Qualifications Necessary to Lawful Communion in the Christian Sacraments* (Boston, 1751), p. 7.

64. Goen, *Revivalism and Separatism in New England, 1740–1800*, pp. 45–47.

65. "Qualifications for Communion," WD, IV, 293–97, 301. Cf. Letter to Rev. Clark in 1750, "Unpublished Letter of Jonathan Edwards," ed. G. P. Clark, *New England Quarterly*, XXIX (June, 1956), 230.

66. *Affections*, WY, II, 406–26.

67. *Ibid.*, p. 412.

68. "Qualifications for Communion," WD, IV, 304–5.

69. *Ibid.*, p. 324.

70. Williams, *op. cit.*, pp. 7–9.

71. "Misrepresentations Corrected," WD, IV, 465.

72. *Ibid.*, pp. 465–66.

73. Solomon Stoddard, *An Appeal to the Learned* (Boston, 1709), pp. 97–98. When Stoddard advanced his argument that communion could be opened to the unconverted on the basis of the Supper's being a "converting ordinance," he insisted that the Supper was for the conversion *not* of *heathen* but of "professing men," i.e., of those adhering to Christian doctrines yet themselves unconverted at heart to true faith. *Ibid.*, pp. 70–71.

74. *Ibid.*, pp. 65–66, 70–71.

75. From Stoddard's *The Doctrine of Instituted Churches*, cited in Smith, Handy, and Loetscher, *op. cit.*, I, 221.

76. Smith, Handy, and Loetscher, *op. cit.*, p. 220.

77. Stoddard, *Nature of Saving Conversion*, p. 2. Cf. Smith, Handy, and Loetscher, *op. cit.*, pp. 220–29.

78. Schafer, "Jonathan Edwards' Conception of the Church," *op. cit.*, p. 60. Cf. "Qualifications for Communion," WD, IV, 301.

79. "Qualifications for Communion," WD, IV, 311–12.

80. The phrase is Clyde A. Holbrook's, "Jonathan Edwards and His Detractors," *Theology Today*, X (October, 1953), 395.

81. "Letter to the People of Northampton," WD, IV, 597–98.

82. *Ibid.*, pp. 599–600.

83. Williams, *op. cit.*, p. 11.

84. *Ibid.*, p. 10.

85. "Letter to the People of Northampton," WD, IV, 601.

86. As Thomas Schafer has it, "exactly the same relation holds between the eternal church covenant, publicly made at Baptism and Confirmation, and the internal covenant of justification." Schafer, "Jonathan Edwards' Conception of the Church," *op. cit.*, p. 60.

87. "Qualifications for Communion," WD, IV, 320–21.

88. *Ibid.*, pp. 325–26.

89. Goen, *op. cit.*, p. 209. See "Qualifications for Communion," WD, IV, 426–27.

90. "Qualifications for Communion," WD, IV, 321.

WORKS CITED OR REFERRED TO

I. Primary Sources
A. Edwards

COLLECTED WORKS

Works of President Edwards. Edited by Edward Williams
and Edward Parsons. 8 vols. Leeds: 1806–11.

Works of President Edwards. Edited by Sereno E. Dwight.
10 vols. New York: S. Converse, 1829–30.

Works of President Edwards. Reprint of Worcester Edition.
4 vols. New York: Jonathan Leavitt & John F. Trow,
1843–44.

Works of Jonathan Edwards. General editor: Perry Miller.
New Haven: Yale University Press, 1957–   . Vol. I
(ed. Paul Ramsey), 1957; Vol. II (ed. John E. Smith),
1959.

MANUSCRIPTS

"Catalogue" of Books. 43-page booklet. Yale Collection. Yale
Beinecke Rare Book and Manuscript Library.

"Faith." 51-page booklet. Yale Collection. Yale Beinecke
Rare Book and Manuscript Library.

"Miscellanies" Journal. Yale Collection. Yale Beinecke Rare
Book and Manuscript Library.

Sermon Notebooks on Romans 9:18 and Ephesians 3:10.
Yale Collection. Yale Beinecke Rare Book and Manuscript Library.

"Signs of Godliness." 20-page folio. Yale Collection. Yale
Beinecke Rare Book and Manuscript Library.

SELECTIONS AND INDIVIDUAL WORKS

Charity and Its Fruits. Edited by Tryon Edwards. New York: Robert Carter & Bros., 1852.

"Ideas, Sense of the Heart, Spiritual Knowledge or Conviction. Faith." Edited by Perry Miller. *Harvard Theological Review*, XLI (April, 1948), 129–45.

Images or Shadows of Divine Things. Edited by Perry Miller. New Haven: Yale University Press, 1948.

Jonathan Edwards, Representative Selections. Edited by Clarence H. Faust and Thomas H. Johnson. Rev. ed. New York: American Century Series, Hill & Wang, 1962.

"The Mind" of Jonathan Edwards. Text edited and reconstructed by Leon Howard. Berkeley: University of California Press, 1963.

Miscellaneous Observations on Important Theological Subjects. Edited by John Erskine. Edinburgh: M. Gray, 1793.

Observations Concerning the Scripture Oeconomy of the Trinity and Covenant of Redemption. Edited by E. C. Smyth. New York: Charles Scribner's Sons, 1880.

The Philosophy of Jonathan Edwards from His Private Notebooks. Edited by Harvey G. Townsend. Eugene, Oregon: University of Oregon Press, 1955.

Selections from the Unpublished Writings of Jonathan Edwards. Edited by Alexander B. Grosart. Edinburgh: Ballantyne & Co., 1865.

"Six Letters of Jonathan Edwards to Joseph Bellamy." Edited by Stanley T. Williams. *New England Quarterly*, I (April, 1928), 226–42.

An Unpublished Essay of Edwards on the Trinity. Edited by George P. Fisher. New York: Charles Scribner's Sons, 1903.

"Unpublished Letter of Jonathan Edwards." Edited by G. P. Clark. *New England Quarterly*, XXIX (June, 1956) 228–33.

B. Other Primary Sources

Ames, William. *Conscience with the Power and Cases Thereof*. Translated from the Latin. London, 1643.

_____. *The Marrow of Sacred Divinity*. Translated from the Latin. London, 1643.

Aquinas, Thomas. *Nature and Grace: Selections from the Summa Theologica*. Vol. XI of *Library of Christian Classics*. Translated and edited by A. M. Fairweather. Philadelphia: Westminster Press, 1954.

Augustine, Aurelius. *Basic Writings of Saint Augustine*. 2 vols. Edited by Whitney Oates. New York: Random House, 1948.

Barth, Karl. *The Doctrine of God. Church Dogmatics*, II, 2. Translated by G. W. Bromiley *et al*. Edinburgh: T. & T. Clark, 1957.

Bellamy, Joseph. *True Religion Delineated*. (Preface by Edwards.) Morris-Town: Henry P. Russell, 1804.

Bradley, C. (ed.) *Select British Divines*. Vols. VII and VIII of *Flavel's Select Works*. London: L. B. Seeley & Son, 1823.

Bulkeley, Peter. *The Gospel-Covenant; or The Covenant of Grace Opened*. London, 1646.

Calvin, John. *Institutes of the Christian Religion*. 2 vols. Vols. XX and XXI of *Library of Christian Classics*. Edited by J. T. McNeill, translated by F. L. Battles. Philadelphia: Westminster Press, 1960.

Chauncy, Charles. *Seasonable Thoughts on the State of Religion in New England*. Boston: Rogers & Fowle, 1743.

Chubb, Thomas. *A Collection of Tracts on Various Subjects*. 2nd ed. Vol. I. London, 1754.

Doddridge, Philip. *Practical Discourses on Regeneration in Ten Sermons*. London, 1742.

Edwards, Jonathan, Jr. *Works*. Vol. I. Edited by Tryon Edwards. Andover: Allen, Morrill & Wardell, 1842.

Hutcheson, Francis. *An Inquiry Into the Original of Our Ideas of Beauty and Virtue*. 5th ed. London, 1753.

_____. *A System of Moral Philosophy*. Vol. I. Glasgow, 1760.

James, William. *The Varieties of Religious Experience*. New York: Collier Books, 1961.

Locke, John. *An Essay Concerning Human Understanding*. 2 vols. Edited and introduced by A. C. Fraser. New York: Dover Publications, 1959.

Luther, Martin. *The Bondage of the Will*. Translated by J. I. Packer and O. R. Johnston. Westwood, New Jersey: Fleming H. Revell Co., 1957.

———. *A Commentary on St. Paul's Epistle to the Galatians*. A revised and completed translation based on the 'Middleton' edition of the English version of 1575. Edited by Philip S. Watson. Westwood, New Jersey: Fleming H. Revell Co., 1953.

———. *Lectures on Romans*. Vol. XV of *Library of Christian Classics*. Edited and translated by Wilhelm Pauck. Philadelphia: Westminster Press, 1961.

Manton, Thomas. *Works*. Vols. II and IV. London: James Nisbet & Co., 1871.

Mastricht, Peter van. *A Treatise on Regeneration*. Extracted and translated from the *Theologia Theoretico-Practica*. New Haven: Thomas & Samuel Green, n.d.

Miller, Perry, and Johnson, Thomas H. *The Puritans*. 2 vols. New York: Harper Torchbooks, 1963.

Niebuhr, H. Richard. *Radical Monotheism and Western Culture, with Supplementary Essays*. New York: Harper & Bros., 1960.

Owen, John. *Works*. Vols. III and V. Edited by W. H. Goold. Edinburgh: Johnstone & Hunter, 1851–52.

Perkins, William. *Works*. Vols. I and II. London, 1616 and 1613.

Preston, John. *The Breast-Plate of Faith and Love*. London, 1630.

———. *The New Covenant or the Saints Portion*. London, 1630.

Shepard, Thomas. *The Parable of the Ten Virgins*. Aberdeen, 1838.

———. *Works*. Vol. I. Boston: Doctrinal Tract & Book Society, 1853.

Sherlock, Thomas. *Works*. Vol. I. Edited by T. S. Hughes. London: A. J. Valpy, 1830.

Sibbes, Richard. *Works*. Vols. I and IV. Edited by A. B. Grosart. Edinburgh: James Nichol, 1862–63.

Smith, John. *Select Discourses*. Reprint of the 1673 edition. London: Rivingtons & Cochran, 1821.

Stoddard, Solomon. *An Appeal to the Learned*. Boston, 1709.

_____. *A Guide to Christ*. Boston, 1735.

_____. *The Nature of Saving Conversion, and The Way Wherein It is Wrought*. Boston, 1770.

Taylor, John. *The Scripture-Doctrine of Original Sin*. 3rd ed. Belfast, 1746.

Turrettini, François. *Institutio Theologiae Elencticae*. Topics 3–6, 9–10, 12, 14–17. Translated into English from the Latin by George M. Giger. Microfilmed by the University of Chicago by permission of Princeton Theological Library, 1954.

Watts, Isaac. *Works*. Vol. VI. London: T. & T. Longman, 1753.

Whitby, Daniel. *A Discourse*. 2nd ed. corrected. London, 1735.

Williams, Solomon. *The True State of the Question Concerning the Qualifications Necessary to Lawful Communion in the Christian Sacraments*. Boston, 1751.

II. Secondary Works

Ahlstrom, Sydney E. "H. Richard Niebuhr's Place in American Thought." *Christianity and Crisis*, XXIII (November 25, 1963), 213–17.

Aldridge, Alfred Owen. *Jonathan Edwards*. New York: Washington Square Press, 1964.

Allen, Alexander V. G. *Jonathan Edwards*. Boston: Houghton, Mifflin & Co., 1889.

Anderson, Wilbert L. "The Preaching Power of Jonathan Edwards." *Congregationalist and the Christian World*, LXXXVIII (October 3, 1903), 463–66.

Angoff, Charles. *A Literary History of the American People*. Vol. I. New York: Alfred A. Knopf, 1931.

Battenhouse, Roy W. (ed.). *A Companion to the Study of*

St. Augustine. New York: Oxford University Press, 1955.

Boardman, George Nye. *A History of New England Theology.* New York: A. D. F. Randolph Co., 1899.

Boorstin, Daniel J. *The Americans: The Colonial Experience.* New York: Vintage Books, 1964.

Brauer, Jerald C. *Protestantism in America.* Philadelphia: Westminster Press, 1953.

————. "Puritan Mysticism and the Development of Liberalism." *Church History,* XIX (September, 1950), 151–70.

Brown, Andrew. "John Locke and the Religious *Aufklärung.*" *Review of Religion,* XIII (January, 1949), 126–54.

Cady, Edwin H. "The Artistry of Jonathan Edwards." *New England Quarterly,* XXII (March, 1949), 61–72.

Carpenter, Frederic I. "The Radicalism of Jonathan Edwards." *New England Quarterly,* IV (October, 1931), 629–44.

Christie, Francis Albert. "The Beginnings of Arminianism in New England." *Papers of the American Society of Church History,* Series 2, III (1912), 153–72.

Copleston, Frederick. *A History of Philosophy.* Vol. V: *Hobbes to Hume.* Westminster, Maryland: Newman Press, 1961.

Crabtree, A. B. *Jonathan Edwards' View of Man, A Study in Eighteenth Century Calvinism.* Wallington, England: Religious Education Press, 1948.

Crane, R. S. "Suggestions Toward a Genealogy of the 'Man of Feeling.'" *Journal of English Literary History,* I (December, 1934), 205–30.

Crooker, Joseph H. "Jonathan Edwards: A Psychological Study." *New England Magazine,* New Series, II (1890), 159–72.

De Jong, Peter Y. *The Covenant Idea in New England Theology, 1620–1847.* Grand Rapids, Michigan: Wm. B. Eerdmans Publishing Co., 1945.

Dexter, Franklin B. "The Manuscripts of Jonathan Edwards." *Proceedings of the Massachusetts Historical Society,* 2nd series, XV (1902), 2–16.

Dowey, Edward A. *The Knowledge of God in Calvin's Theology.* New York: Columbia University Press, 1952.

Dwight, Sereno E. *Life of President Edwards.* Vol. I of *Works* (Dwight). New York: S. Converse, 1829.

Elwood, Douglas J. *The Philosophical Theology of Jonathan Edwards.* New York: Columbia University Press, 1960.

Faust, Clarence H. "The Decline of Puritanism." *Transitions in American Literary History.* Edited by Harry H. Clark. Durham, North Carolina: Duke University Press, 1953, pp. 3–47.

Faust, Clarence H., and Johnson, Thomas H. (eds.) *Jonathan Edwards, Representative Selections.* Rev. ed. New York: American Century Series, Hill & Wang, 1962.

Fisher, George Park (ed.). *An Unpublished Essay of Edwards on the Trinity.* New York: Charles Scribner's Sons, 1903.

Foster, Frank Hugh. *A Genetic History of the New England Theology.* Chicago: University of Chicago Press, 1907.

Gaustad, Edwin Scott. *The Great Awakening in New England.* New York: Harper & Bros., 1957.

Gerrish, B. A. *Grace and Reason: A Study in the Theology of Luther.* Oxford, England: Clarendon Press, 1962.

Gerstner, John H. *Steps to Salvation: The Evangelistic Message of Jonathan Edwards.* Philadelphia: Westminster Press, 1960.

Goen, C. C. "Jonathan Edwards: A New Departure in Eschatology." *Church History,* XXVIII (March, 1959), 25–40.

———. *Revivalism and Separatism in New England, 1740–1800.* New Haven: Yale University Press, 1962.

Haller, William. *The Rise of Puritanism.* New York: Harper Torchbooks, 1957.

Harland, Gordon. "The American Protestant Heritage and the Theological Task." *Drew Gateway,* XXXII (Winter, 1962), 71–93.

Haroutunian, Joseph G. "Jonathan Edwards: A Study in Godliness." *Journal of Religion,* XI (July, 1931), 400–19.

———. "Jonathan Edwards: Theologian of the Great Commandment." *Theology Today,* I (October, 1944), 361–77.

———. *Piety Versus Moralism.* New York: Henry Holt & Co., 1932.

Heppe, Heinrich. *Reformed Dogmatics.* Edited by E. Bizer.

Translated by G. T. Thomson. London: Allen & Unwin Ltd., 1950.

Holbrook, Clyde Amos. "The Ethics of Jonathan Edwards." Unpublished Ph.D. dissertation, Yale University, 1944.

———. "Jonathan Edwards and His Detractors." *Theology Today*, X (October, 1953), 384–96.

———. "Original Sin and the Enlightenment." *The Heritage of Christian Thought; Essays in Honor of Robert Lowry Calhoun.* Edited by R. E. Cushman and E. Grislis. New York: Harper & Row, 1965, pp. 142–65.

Hopkins, Samuel. *Life of President Edwards.* Vol. I of *Works* (Leeds). Leeds, England: 1806.

Howard, Leon (ed.). *"The Mind" of Jonathan Edwards, A Reconstructed Text.* Berkeley: University of California Press, 1963.

Johnson, Thomas H. "Jonathan Edwards' Background of Reading." *Publications of the Colonial Society of Massachusetts*, XXVIII (December, 1931), 193–222.

———. *The Printed Writings of Jonathan Edwards, 1703–1758.* Princeton: Princeton University Press, 1940.

Lewis, R. W. B. *The American Adam: Innocence, Tragedy and Tradition in the Nineteenth Century.* Chicago: Phoenix Books, 1964.

"The List of Books Sent by Jeremiah Dummer." Prepared by Louise May Bryant and Mary Patterson. *Papers in Honor of Andrew Keogh.* New Haven: private printing, Yale University Press, 1938, pp. 423–92.

McGiffert, A. C. *Protestant Thought Before Kant.* New York: Harper Torchbooks, 1962.

McLoughlin, William G. *Modern Revivalism: Charles Grandison Finney to Billy Graham.* New York: Ronald Press Co., 1959.

Miller, Perry. *Errand into the Wilderness.* Cambridge: Belknap Press of Harvard University Press, 1956.

———. "The Half-Way Covenant." *New England Quarterly*, VI (December, 1933), 676–715.

——— (ed.). *Images or Shadows of Divine Things.* New Haven: Yale University Press, 1948.

———. *Jonathan Edwards.* New York: Meridian Books, 1959.

Miller, Perry. "Jonathan Edwards on the Sense of the Heart." *Harvard Theological Review*, XLI (April, 1948), 123–29.

———. *The New England Mind: From Colony to Province.* Cambridge: Harvard University Press, 1953.

———. *The New England Mind: The Seventeenth Century.* Boston: Beacon Press, 1961.

———. "'Preparation for Salvation' in Seventeenth-Century New England." *Journal of the History of Ideas*, IV (June, 1943), 253–86.

———. "Solomon Stoddard, 1643–1729." *Harvard Theological Review*, XXXIV (October, 1941), 277–320.

More, Paul Elmer. "Edwards." *Cambridge History of American Literature*, I. New York: G. P. Putnam's Sons, 1917, 57–71.

Morgan, Edmund. *The Puritan Dilemma, The Story of John Winthrop.* Boston: Little, Brown, 1958.

———. *Visible Saints: The History of a Puritan Idea.* New York: New York University Press, 1963.

Murphy, Arthur E. "Jonathan Edwards on Free Will and Moral Agency." *Philosophical Review*, LXVIII (April, 1959), 181–202.

Newlin, Claude M. *Philosophy and Religion in Colonial America.* New York: Philosophical Library, 1962.

Nichols, James H. Review of *Jonathan Edwards* by Perry Miller. *Church History*, XX (December, 1951), 75–82.

Niebuhr, H. Richard. *The Kingdom of God in America.* Chicago: Willett, Clark, & Co., 1937.

Nuttall, Geoffrey F. *The Holy Spirit in Puritan Faith and Experience.* Oxford, England: Basil Blackwell, 1947.

Park, Edwards A. "The Rise of the Edwardean Theory of the Atonement." *The Atonement, Discourses and Treatises.* Boston: Congregational Board of Publication, 1859.

Parrington, Vernon Louis. *Main Currents in American Thought.* New York: Harcourt, Brace & Co., 1927.

Pratt, Anne Stokely. "The Books Sent From England by Jeremiah Dummer to Yale College." *Papers in Honor of Andrew Keogh.* New Haven: private printing, Yale University Press, 1938, pp. 7–44.

Rhoades, Donald Hosea. "Jonathan Edwards: Experimental Theologian." Unpublished Ph.D. dissertation, Yale University, 1945.

Rice, Howard C., Jr. "Jonathan Edwards at Princeton: With a Survey of Edwards Material in the Princeton University Library." *Princeton University Library Chronicle*, XV (Winter, 1954), 69–89.

Ridderbos, Jan. *De Theologie Van Jonathan Edwards*. 's-Gravenhage [The Hague]: Johan A. Nederbragt, 1907.

Riley, I. Woodbridge. *American Philosophy, the Early Schools*. New York: Dodd, Mead & Co., 1907.

————. *American Thought from Puritanism to Pragmatism and Beyond*. New York: Henry Holt & Co., 1923.

Rudisill, Dorus Paul. "The Doctrine of the Atonement in Jonathan Edwards and His Successors." Unpublished Ph.D. dissertation, Duke University, 1945.

Schafer, Thomas Anton. "The Concept of Being in the Thought of Jonathan Edwards." Unpublished Ph.D. dissertation, Duke University, 1951.

————. "Jonathan Edwards' Conception of the Church." *Church History*, XXIV (March, 1955), 51–66.

————. "Jonathan Edwards and Justification by Faith." *Church History*, XX (December, 1951), 55–67.

————. "Solomon Stoddard and the Theology of the Revival." *A Miscellany of American Christianity: Essays in Honor of H. Shelton Smith*. Edited by S. C. Henry. Durham, North Carolina: Duke University Press, 1963, pp. 328–61.

Schaff, Philip. *The Creeds of Christendom*. 3 vols. 6th ed. New York: Harper & Bros., 1919.

Smith, H. Shelton. *Changing Conceptions of Original Sin*. New York: Charles Scribner's Sons, 1955.

Smith, H. Shelton; Handy, Robert T.; and Loetscher, Lefferts A. *American Christianity: An Historical Interpretation with Representative Documents*. Vol. I. New York: Charles Scribner's Sons, 1960.

Smyth, Egbert C. (ed.) *Observations Concerning the Scripture Oeconomy of the Trinity and Covenant of Redemption*. New York: Charles Scribner's Sons, 1880.

Stephen, Leslie. "Jonathan Edwards." *Littell's Living Age,* 5th series, V (1874), 219–36.

Stromberg, Roland N. *Religious Liberalism in Eighteenth-Century England.* London: Oxford University Press, 1954.

Trinterud, Leonard J. *The Forming of an American Tradition.* Philadelphia: Westminster Press, 1949.

_____. "The Origins of Puritanism." *Church History,* XX (March, 1951), 37–57.

Walker, Williston. *The Creeds and Platforms of Congregationalism.* Boston: Pilgrim Press, 1960.

Wendel, François. *Calvin: Origins and Development of His Religious Thought.* Translated by Philip Mairet. New York: Harper & Row, 1963.

White, Eugene E. "Solomon Stoddard's Theories of Persuasion." *Speech Monographs,* XXIX (November, 1962), 235–59.

Wilcox, William G. "New England Covenant Theology: Its English Precursors and Early American Exponents." Unpublished Ph.D. dissertation, Duke University, 1959.

Winslow, Ola Elizabeth. *Jonathan Edwards, 1703–1758.* New York: Collier Books, 1961.

Wolf, William J. *The Religion of Abraham Lincoln.* New York: Seabury Press, 1963.

Wright, Conrad. *The Beginnings of Unitarianism in America.* Boston: Starr King Press, 1955.

_____. "Edwards and the Arminians on the Freedom of the Will." *Harvard Theological Review,* XXXV (October, 1942), 241–61.

INDEX

Adam, 1, 58, 60, 82, 83, 84, 101, 108, 122, 198, 199, 200, 201; covenant of works, 83, 108; second, 83, 122

Affections, 13, 17, 166, 167, 178, 180, 184; degree of exercise, 80; intellectual, 167; raised, 173

Allen, A. V. G., 48

Alpha and omega, 26. *See also* Beginning and end

America, 101, 216, 217; new age, 170; religious condition of, 161; revivalistic, 151

American, 209, 210; innocence, 197; Protestantism, 12, 164, 212, 216, 217; religious conscience, 216; Unitarianism, 216

Ames, William, 13, 108, 113, 121; quote, 63

Anderson, W. L., 69

Anselm, St., 93

Anthropology, 186–202; Catholic, 58; theological, 58

Anti-intellectual: emotional religion, 216; tradition, 22

Antinomianism, 8, 144, 160, 161, 162, 201, 202, 203, 215; and Enthusiasm, 162; Hutchinsonian, 202; and neonomianism, 186–215

Arbella, 109

Arminian, 58, 122, 160, 161, 162, 187, 188, 190, 192, 193, 196, 197, 198, 199; American, 197–98; controversy on freedom of will, 162; doctrine of the self-determining will, 95, 189, 190, 191; free-willism, 129; neonomianism, 212; principles, 186, 187, 189; and synod of Dort, 189

Arminianism, 92, 95, 101, 102, 106, 111, 119, 160, 161, 162, 186–89, 191, 196, 201, 216; American, 115; controversy, 186–91; and rationalism, 162;

seventeenth-century forms of, 115; two basic points, 162

Assurance, 143–58, 174, 175, 205, 206, 207; doctrine of, 152–56, 204, 208

Atonement, 95, 101, 187, 191; doctrine of, 93, 113; theory of, 93

Augustine, St., 25, 58, 78, 192

Augustinian: doctrine of illumination, 26; doctrine of perseverance, 82; theory of identity, 82; tradition, 19

Authoritarianism, 44

Augustinian-Calvinist doctrine of sin, 197; defense of, 200

Awakening, 8, 9, 24, 33, 165, 167, 169, 170, 171, 174, 175, 184, 216. *See also* Great Awakening

Balaam, 52

Barth, Karl, 6, 152, 153, 154

Baxter, Richard, 151; quote, 192

Beginning and end, 25, 31. *See also* Alpha and omega

Bellamy, Joseph, 4, 34

Benevolence, 176–81, 183, 184; acts of, 176; and complacence, 179; disinterested, 177, 179; ethics of, 176, 177, 180, disagreement with, 180, 181; love of, 177

Boorstin, Daniel, 5; quote, 126

Boston, Massachusetts, 165

Brainerd, David, 38–39, 144

Brauer, Jerald, 87

Breck, Robert, 187

Bulkeley, Peter, 107, 115

Cady, E. H., 68

Calvin, John, 3, 12, 21, 45, 56, 57, 60, 70, 77, 78, 91, 99, 113, 114–24, 138, 143, 152, 192, 195; covenant scheme and doctrines, 113, 114; first and third functions of law, 70; practical syl-

Calvin, John (cont'd)
logism, 152; predestination, 57; quotes, 43, 45; statement on faith, 91–92

Calvinism, 2, 5, 6, 12, 85, 87, 99, 113, 143, 168, 190, 196, 197, 201; objectivism, 85; Puritan, 2–3; theory of predestination, 56

Calvinist, 3, 162, 191, 195; association, 161; categories, 6; confession, 62; doctrines, 1, 160, 189, of Christological revelation, 114, of the corruption of man, 200, 201; interpretation of Epistle of James, 197; interpretation of original sin, 198; orthodoxy, 5; scheme of election, 95; scriptural hermeneutic, 135; Synod of Dort's Five Points, 186, 189; theologians, theology, 3, 6, 56, 138, 143; thought, 3, 78; tradition, 6, 41; understanding: of grace, 191, of sin, 197; view, 56, 206

Cambridge Platonists, 4, 21

Causes and effects, 132, 192, 194; categories of, 194

Chauncy, Charles, 164, 165–69; First Church in Boston, 165; in opposition to Edwards, 165–66; quotes, 166, 175

Choice. See Volition

Christ, 45, 46, 49, 52, 54, 57, 65, 68, 69, 70, 72, 73, 74, 77, 80, 81, 83, 91, 92, 93, 94, 95, 99, 102, 103, 114, 115, 118, 119, 120, 122, 134, 139, 140, 141, 145, 149, 151, 152, 153, 154, 155, 157, 196, 199, 213; and covenant of grace, 83, 108, 113, 121; and faith, 97, 98; historical coming of, 108; righteousness of, 91, 92, 93, 97, 99, 100, 103, 104, 105, 138, 139, 140, 153, 187, 188, 198; and soul, 100–1; union with, 105, 113, 117

Christian: church, 174, 203, 210; community, 203, 214; ethics, 184; experience, 135; grace, 87 (see also Grace); humility, 81; life, 162; man, 185, 202; mysticism, 85; practice, 136, 137, 140, 143, 145, 146, 153, 156, 176, 202, 207; theology, 126; thought, 44; trinitarian principles, 25

Christie, Francis, 186

Christological revelation, Calvinist doctrine of, 46, 114

Cognition and volition, 12–24, 25, 41, 49, 72, 77, 167

College of New Jersey, 9

Complacence, 179; benevolence and, 179; love of, 177

Congregationalists, 186, 187

Connecticut, 8, 209

Conscience, 32, 66, 69, 156, 169, 181, 207, 212; Saul, 168; and self-love, 182; terrors of, 70

Continuity, 82–84

Controversy over faith, 186–215; treatise, An Humble Inquiry . . . , 204

Conversion, 38, 39, 41, 56–69, 85, 172, 184, 209; and change, 38, 39; experiences, 172; instantaneous, 57, 58; narrative on, 186; regenerative, by grace, 57; steps in, 64

Corruption of heart, 200, 201; doctrine of the corruption of man, Calvinist, 200, 201

Covenant, 59, 212, 213; and Christ, 112; church, 213; doctrine of the, 106, 108; of grace, 83, 108, 109, 110, 113, 117, 118, 119, 120, 121, 208, 212, 213, 214, 215, distinction between redemption and, 119, 120, 121; Half-Way, 204, 209; marriage, 120; political-social, 109, 126; Puritan categories, 114; of redemption, 119, 120–21; relation, 107–23, 213; scheme, abandonment of, 110, 111, 119, 123; theology, 114, 115, 116, 123, 197 (see also Puritan); of works, 83, 108, 122, differences between grace and, 108

Crabtree, A. B., 58

Crane, R. S., 176

Davenport, James, 54

Debt idea, 110–14, 116, 123

Deistic rationalism, 5

Despair, holy, 79–80

Devil, 32, 33

Diary, use of, 79; Edwards, 79–80; Puritan, 79

Dillenberger, 56

Divine habit, 34–35

Divine Light as new principle, 30–31, 42

Doctrine of: assurance, 152–56, 204, 208; atonement, 93, 113; charity, 134; Christological revelation, 114; Church of England, 186; conversion, 126; corruption of man, 200, 201; covenant, 106, 108, 109; election, 104, 126; faith, 109, 160, 163, 196; Fall, 58, 126; grace, 6, 211; Holy Spirit, 35; illumination, 30, 37; imputation, 92, 95–96, 106; infusion, 26, 35, 36, 37, 38; innate ideas, 18; justification, 7, 90, 112, 141, 186, 201; original sin, 6, 9, 126, 160, 182, 188, 197, 198, 200; predestination, 6, 56, 113, 126; profession of faith, 208; redemption, 200; Rome, 134; salvation, 62–63, 64, 73, 126; self-determining will, 188–94; *syllogismus practicus*, 151–57; Trinity, 25, 26; virtue, 177, 180. *See also* Treatise

Dort's Five Points, 186, 189

Doubt, 204, 207, 208, 214; freedom from, 215; and unbelief, distinction between, 149, 150, 151

Dowey, Edward A., 45

East Windsor, Connecticut, 8

Edwards, Jonathan, Jr., 73

Effects. *See* Causes

Effort, human, 91, 92, 121

Elwood, Douglas J., 61, 87

Emerson, Ralph Waldo, 197

Emotionalism, 165

Emotion and intellect, 164, 166, 167. *See also* Intellect

End for Which God Created the World, The, essay, 9

Enfield sermon, 1, 68

England, 101, 196, 201

Enthusiasm, 162, 164–76, 184; criticism of, 184; extreme, 171, 173, 176, 184; theological errors of, 170

Enthusiasts, 164, 170, 171, 172, 174, 175, 184, 185; faith and practice, 185

Episcopalianism, 186

Erasmus, 91

Erskine, John, 188

Ethical systems, 177–78; considerations of, 185

Ethics: of benevolence, 176, 180; dispute over, 176; of feeling, 176, 177; relation between faith and, 177; treatise on, 176

Evidence, 139, 154; of faith, 154; of grace, 153; grand, 133–34; of justification, 138, 144, 162, 205, 207; of practice, 157

Faculties, human: description of, 16; and Divine Light, 29; division of, 14, 35; interpretation of, 18; mental, 29, 30; moral, 178; natural, 19, 30, 31, 60; new principle, 29–30; new simple idea, 25; Puritan proponents of, 16; separate, 167; subordination of one to other, 16, 22; of will, 15–16, 36, 75

Faculty psychology, 13, 14, 16, 17

Faith: and assurance, 143–58, 175; and Christ, 97, 98, 102–3, as condition, 100, 101, 109, 117–23; controversy over, 175–76, 186–215; description of, 21, 22; doctrine of, 109, 160, 163, 196; essence of, 20, 73, 80, 134, 140, 155; ethics of, 180, 185; exercises of, 30, 32; fitness relation, and three major problems, 97, 98, 99–106; justification by, 7, 90–106, 119, 138, 140; and love, 39 ff.; and practice, 126–42, 143–58, 183, 184, 185, 192; and its reality, 90, 91, 99; understanding, 7, 14, 132; and works, 103, 138, 139, 140, 153, 183

Fall, 59, 60, 83, 93, 108, 197, 200, 201; doctrine of the, 58; quote, 59

Faust, Clarence, 177; quote, 177

Federal Theology, 110

Feeling. *See* Emotion

Feeling-ethic, ethicists, 176–78

Finney, Charles Grandison, 56

Fit, fitness, 99, 107, 116; moral, 97, 102, 116; natural, 97, 99, 101; three problems of, 99–106

Flacius, 59

Freedom of the Will, treatise, 9, 129, 132, 160, 163, 176, 188, 189, 190, 191, 192, 202; cate-

Freedom of the Will (*cont'd*)
gories of, 195; quotes, 129–30, 191–92, 194, 195

Friendship, analogy, 94

Gaustad, Edwin, 165; metaphor of, 165; study of Great Awakening, 165

Gideon's bastard Abimelech, 174

Gillespie, Thomas, 149; letter to, 149–50, 154

God's indebtedness to man, 109–16; debt idea, 110–14, 116, 123

Goen, C. C., 214

Goodwin, Thomas, 134

Gospel, 48, 51, 53, 64, 67, 68, 70, 80, 95, 101, 102, 105, 152, 154, 187, 198, 202, 212; law of, 69; relation of law and, 161

Grace: common, 66; covenant of, 83, 108; doctrine of, 6, 35, 38, 211; exercises of, 145; gift of, 30, 33, 50, 58, 97, 162, 192, 212; as habit, 37; in history, 60, 61; and human nature, 37; interpretation of, 34; Jesuit position, 36; means of, 60, 61, 62, 87, 88, 148, 196; nature and chasm of, 58; outward and internal, 61–62, 63, 87; signs of, 145, 146 (*see also* Signs); and sin, 78, 79, 80, 82; special, 66; Thomist view, 36

Grand evidence, 133–34

Gravitation, principle of, comparison, 178

Great Awakening, 9, 12, 31, 52, 160, 164, 165; and controversy, 175; study of, by Gaustad, 165. *See also* Awakening

Guilt, 32, 66, 84, 93, 94, 150, 198, 201, 217

Habit, 36, 37, 42; abiding, 38; infused, 34–35, 37, 39

Half-Way Covenant, 204, 209

Haller, William, 79

Harland, Gordon, 164

Haroutunian, Joseph G., 77

Heart, hearts: consent, 177; depravity of, 78; propensity of, 71, 72, 74, 77, 128, 177, 179, 180, 181, 182, 183; union of, 177, 181, 182. *See also* Sense of the heart

Hell-fire sermon, 68, 69

Hobbes, Thomas, 181, 182; school of thought, 181, 182; theory of natural human egoism, 181

Holbrook, Clyde, 1, 85, 196

Holy principle. *See* Simple idea, new

Holy Spirit: and Divine Love, 41; and human faculties, 29 ff.; new principle, 29–30, 37, 42

Howard, Leon, 15

Human powers. *See* Faculties, human

Hutcheson, Francis, 4, 176, 177, 178, 181

Hutchinson, Anne, 162; antinomianism, 64, 162

Ideas: complex, 18; innate, 18; new, 25, 26, 29, 30, 42, 49, 50, 51, 54; simple, 15, 18, 19, 20, 21, 23

Identity. *See* Selfhood

Illumination, 26, 27–33, 34, 35, 36, 37, 49, 50, 78, 192, 196; divine, 32; and human faculties, 29–30, 37; imaginative, 32; sense of the heart, 30; and spirit, 28, 29, 30

Imaginations and visions, 33

Immediacy, 48, 57, 60

Imputation, doctrine of: 188; righteousness, 100, 103, 138, 139, 198

Inclination. *See* Will

Infusion, 26, 27, 33, 34–39, 49, 57; of divine habit, 34–35; of grace, 35, 37; language of, 35

Intellect, 12, 13, 16, 17; balance of, in Puritanism, 164; and emotion, 164, 166, 167; and emotional approach, 12; and will, 13, 16, 19, 21, 24, 28, 29, 127, 167; will, affections and, breakdown of, 14

Internal acts, two kinds, 129

James, Epistle on faith and works, 135; Calvinist interpretation, 137

James: parable on, 136; and St. Paul, 137, 138; second chapter, 135

Jesuit position, 36

Jesus the Christ, 46, 80, 83, 95, 154. *See also* Christ

Johannine illuminism, 26

Judgment: act of, 12; inclination and relation of, 24

Justification by faith, 90–106, 119, 138, 140, 187, 201; and act of faith, 97 ff.; cause of, 196; doctrine, 7, 90, 112, 141, 186, 201; sermons on, 203

Kierkegaard, Søren, 54
Kingdom of Earth, 60
Kingdom of Heaven, 60, 175
Knowledge: of faith, 49; speculative and practical, 50

Latitudinarian tradition, 176
Law, 5, 66, 67, 68, 70, 161, 162; devaluation of, 162; first and third function of, Calvin, 70; gospel, relation between, 161; terrors of, 68
Legalism, 44, 63, 67, 69, 101
Letter: to a friend, 207–8; to Gillespie, 149–50, 154; to a Scottish clergyman, 161
Lincoln, Abraham, 151
Locke, John, 4, 15–16, 18, 21, 23, 26, 30, 83, 181; concerning human understanding, 15–16; empiricism, 15; philosophy, 15; principle of personal identity, 83; quote, 18
Lockean psychology, 168
Logos, 45, 46
Love, disinterested, 71, 73–74, 126, 180, 181
Luther, Martin, 44, 56, 58, 60, 77, 91, 135, 160; statement on faith, 91
Lutheran scriptural hermeneutic, 135

McGinley, Phyllis, 1
McLoughlin, William, 56
Man: elect, 153; of faith, 78, 80, 81, 82, 84, 113, 120, 132, 140, 143, 144, 148, 150, 153, 155, 162, 168, 172, 175, 206, 212; old and new, 78, 79, 82, 200; regenerate, 78; tension between, 79; unfaithful, 75, 149; ungodly, 92, 93, 96, 97, 106; whole, 13, 33, 127, 140, 141, 167
Manton, Thomas, 16–17, 116; quote, 17, 138
Massachusetts: General Assembly of, 187; Northampton (see Northampton); settlement of, 108–9, and covenant, 108–9, loss of charter, 109; Stockbridge, 9
Massachusetts Bay Colony, Church of the, 204
Mastricht, Peter van, 34; quote, 34; system of divinity, 34
Mayhew, Jonathan, 198
Means. See Grace, means of
Mediator, 45, 46, 67, 83, 94
Merit, two degrees, 98, 99
Meritum de condigno, 98
Meritum de congruo, 98
Miller, Perry, 3, 15, 22, 46, 54, 98, 108, 110, 113–14, 115, 126, 168, 190; quote, 22, 168
Miscellaneous notes, 140; quote, 195
"Miscellanies," 6, 41; quote, 42, 66, 67
Mnemonic powers of mind, 30
Monism, 86
Moralism, rational, 164
Morality, 126, 178, 179, 180, 181, 182, 183, 184, 185; and benevolence, 180; foundation of, 180; and grace, 181; and idolatry, 179; and self-love, 180; theory of, 183, true, 183
Moral sense, 181, 182
Morgan, Edmund S., 2, 63
Motivation and volition, 132
Murphy, Arthur, 133
Mysticism, 85–88; Christian, 85; Edwards, 85–88; Western, 85

Nassau Hall, trustees of, 188
Natural fitness. See Fitness
Nature of ethics, 185
Nature of faith, 8, 23, 72, 100, 108, 117, 126, 143, 154, 161, 167, 169, 177, 180, 182, 189, 208; difficulty of defining, 23; dispute of, 176; quote, 23; views of, 185
Nature and grace, chasm of, 58
Nature and man, 167, 169, 175
Nature of Saving Conversion, 14
Nature of True Virtue, The, 9, 177, 180, 183
Neonomian, 161, 162, 188, 202, 203
Neonomianism, 8, 120, 122, 162, 211, 215; and antinomianism, 186–215; Arminian, 212

Neoplatonic, 86
Neoplatonist metaphysic, 87
New birth, 57, 58, 200; time of, 57–58
New England, 3, 4, 9, 13, 32, 44, 51, 63, 66, 107, 109, 113, 115, 144, 154, 164, 165, 170, 187, 197, 201, 208, 209, 215, 216; churches, 186; eighteenth century, 160; New Lights, 169; Puritans, 2; theologians, theology, 113, 166, 203. *See also* Revivals
New Haven, Connecticut, 168, 174
New Jersey, 9
New Testament, 108, 198
Newton, Isaac, 98
Niebuhr, H. Richard, 68, 72
Niebuhr, Reinhold, 6
Northampton, Massachusetts, 7, 8, 9, 14, 20, 53, 56, 63, 65, 164, 170, 187, 203, 211; pulpit, dismissal from, 61
Notebook on faith, 12–14, 18; quotes, 18–19, 127
Notebook, "The Mind", 30

Obedience, 101, 102, 112, 119, 129, 141, 144, 187, 202, 207, 214; acts of, 141; and faith, 101–2
Observations concerning faith, Edwards, 12
Old Testament, 107, 108
On the End for Which God Created the World, Edwards, 176
Original sin, doctrine of, 6, 9, 126, 160, 188, 197, 200
Owen, John, 66

Participation, 29, 32
Party of Hope, 197
Party of Irony, 197
Paul, St., 29, 38, 86, 92, 116, 137, 138, 146, 172, 200; Saul, 168
Pauline confession, 90; epistles, 135, 200; justification by faith alone, 201, tenet, 106
Pelagian, 58; semi-, 59
Pelagianism, 59, 91, 111, 161, 188
Perception and speculation. *See* Intellect
Perkins, William, 63
Personal Narrative, 86
Peter, St., 83; quotes, 83, 167, 172
Piety, 137

Plato, 30
Platonic: illuminism, 26; scheme, 46
Post-Puritan era, 2
Posture of faith, 71–88
Powers, human. *See* Faculties
Practical syllogism. *See* Doctrine of *syllogismus practicus*
Practice, 135, 148, 150, 175, 180, 184, 185, 206, 207; and assurance of faith, 143–58; faith and, 126–42, inside and outside acts, 128–29, 157; interpretation of practical syllogism, 152; as means of, 152; moralistic, 154; performance of, 129–30; and piety, 137; Puritan concept of, 151; and salvation, 133–42
Prayer of thanksgiving, 116
Predestinarians, 56, 97
Predestination, 57; doctrine of, 6, 56
Preparation, 70, 115; doctrine of, 62–63; legal, 65, 66, 67, 68, 69, 70; manner and nature of, 64; Puritan, 63, 64; steps in, 63–65, three, 64
Preston, John, 13, 34, 115, 117, 144; quote, 34, 115
Pride, religious, 79, 81, 171–72
Princeton, New Jersey, 9
Principles: metaphysical, 84; natural, 59, 60, 66; new, 30–31, 42; supernatural, 59, 60, 66
Priorities, 99
Private interest. *See* Self-interest
Profession of faith, 202–15; doctrine of, 208
Protestant: churches, history of, 90; doctrine of imputation, 106; Reformation, 41, 77, 90, 91, 94; reformers, 3, 77, scholasticism, 35, 36, 92; thought, 44, 77
Protestantism, American, 212, 216, 217
Psalms, 32, 139, 146–47
Puritanism, 2, 44, 87, 164; intellect-feeling, 164; left-wing, 87; right-wing, 144
Puritan, Puritans, 2, 3, 5, 12, 13, 16, 19, 21, 44, 62, 63, 79, 87, 107, 113, 114, 115, 162, 164, 204; American, 64, 126, 208, Protestantism, 164, of seventeenth century, 119; ancestors,

Puritan, Puritans (cont'd)
4–5, 79, 117; church, 214; covenant: categories, 114, 123, idea, 109, 114, theology, 109, 110, 113, 114, 115, 116, 117, 123, 127, 212; diary, 79; doctrines, 106, 107, 108; English, 119; morphology of conversion, 63, 212; orthodox, 87, 144; settlement of Massachusetts, 108–9, and covenant, 108–9; studies, 2; theologians, theology, 3, 61, 62, 63, 65, 68, 107, 108, 126; thinkers, 12; thought, 13, 87, 107, 143; tradition, 3, 4, 12, 87, 137, 143, 217

Quakerism, 44
Quakers, 44, 168; attitude as compared to Puritans, 5
Qualifications for Communion, 39, 204, 207, 210, 213

Ramsey, Paul, 26; quote, 132
Rationalism, 162, 164 ff.; Chauncy's appraisal, 165–68; Enlightenment, 168, 181
Rationalist ethic of benevolence, 181
Rationalists, 160, 164, 170, 173, 174, 176, 177, 181, 185; critics of, 164, 165; debate between revivalists and, 160; faith and practice, 185
Reason, 164, 166, 167; and emotion, 164, 166, 167; human, 162; rule of, 166, 167
Redemption, 26, 27, 31, 45, 118, 141, 199, 200, 212; trinitarian explication of, 26
Reformation, 41, 77, 90, 91, 94. See also Protestant Reformation
Reformed, 60, 137; heritage, 92; scholastics, 35–36, theologians, 42, 143; thesis, 47; tradition, 43, 92
Reformers, 77, 78; Rhineland, 3; sixteenth-century, 90
Regeneration, 37, 42–43, 57, 58, 62
Relation: Israel's to God, 108; man's with Christ, 97, 98, 99, 100–1; natural and moral fit, 97
Relation between faith: and grace, 195; and salvation, 117

Relation between practice and the assurance of faith, 143–58
Religious Affections, Treatise on, 9, 35, 74, 148, 149, 160, 170, 172, 202, 205, 206–7
Religious experiences, emotional, 173; faith, 170, 180
Religious faith, 5, 19, 23, 24, 44, 123, 133, 161, 162, 217; center of controversy, 203; objective and subjective aspects, 44 ff.; understanding of, 16. See also Faith
Religious man, 167, 168; affections, 167; faith, 167, 171, 174; pride, 171–72
Repentance, 62, 67, 70; evangelical, 67
Restoration, 176, 186
Revelation, 138, 171; and unsaved man, 52
Revivalism, 13, 216, 217; American, 56; critics of, 13; emotional defenders of, 164; examination of, 9; old tradition, 56; rationalist critics of, 164
Revivalistic emotionalism, 162, 174
Revivalists, 56, 57, 160, 171; debate between rationalists and, 160
Revivals, 32, 51, 66, 164, 165, 167, 168, 169, 170, 173, 174, 176, 184; antagonists of, 169–70; excesses of, 52; of the 1730s, 7; 1740 and 1742, 164
Rhineland reformers, 3
Rhoades, Donald, 150
Ridderbos, Jan, 134
Romans, 138; fourth chapter, 92; quotes, 40, 154; sermon on, 111
Rome, 143

Saint, saints, 28, 29, 30, 31, 37, 38, 39, 40, 43, 45, 51, 74, 78, 79, 80, 81, 82, 87, 95, 109, 113, 114, 116, 120, 122, 131, 138, 143, 145, 147, 148, 149, 150, 155, 157, 162, 172, 206, 207, 209, 210; affections of, 74; and condition, 119, 120; and covenant, 109
Salvation, 56, 58, 61, 62, 64, 65, 67, 68, 73, 77, 79, 80, 81, 87,

Salvation *(cont'd)*
90, 91, 92, 94, 95, 96, 97, 98, 99, 102, 103, 104, 105, 106, 108, 110, 111, 112, 113, 114, 116, 118, 121, 133, 137, 138, 139, 140, 141, 143, 144, 149, 150, 151, 154, 155, 156, 157, 161, 162, 175, 187, 188, 189, 191, 198, 201, 202; Arminian doctrine, 95; indispensability of faith, 100; relation between faith and, 117; and role of religious practice, 128

Sanctification, 41–43

Satan, 4, 38, 53, 79, 167, 174

Schafer, Thomas, 39, 41, 86

Scholasticism: medieval, 36; Protestant, 35, 36

Scholastic psychology, 167

Scotland, 149, 154

Scriptures, 14, 21, 28, 29, 32, 38, 40, 46, 47, 50, 51, 52, 53, 55, 57, 64, 71–72, 74, 78, 83, 86, 90, 92, 116, 117, 128, 129, 133, 134, 136, 137, 138, 139, 141, 145, 146, 149, 154, 156, 167, 168, 169, 173, 174, 184, 195, 198, 199, 200, 201, 207, 210; and conversion, 65; and preaching, 48, 49, 61; and Spirited Word, 50; and uninterrupted phrases, 53

Self-determination, 188–90, 191; Arminian doctrine, 188, 191, 192

Self-examination, 146–48, 155, 157, 173; *Religious Affections*, 148; sermon on, 148

Selfhood, 80–84, 88; loss of, 82

Self-interest, 180, 181, 182, 185

Self-love, 59, 60, 74, 75, 179, 180, 182

Self-reflection, 147, 148

Self-satisfaction, 81, 150

Semi-Pelagian, 59

Sense of the heart, 14, 19, 20, 21, 22, 23, 28, 30, 51, 127, 167, 192, 194; conviction of, 23; and reasoning faculty, 20; quote, 22; and simple idea, 19, 20. *See also* Heart

Separatists, 184

Sermons, 1, 7, 8, 50–51, 53, 54, 68, 69, 108, 110, 111, 112, 118: Boston, 110; on divine illumination, 27–28, quote, 27, 28; Enfield, 1, 68, farewell, 9, 53, quote, 53; hell-fire, 68, 69; "A History of the Work of Redemption," 118; Hutchinsonian antinomianism, 202; on justification, 118, 186, 187, 188, 203; "Qualifications for Communion," 118; quotes, 19, 51, 61, 62, 110, 113; on Romans, 111; on self-examination, 148; undated, 110; "Wisdom Displayed in Salvation," 45

Shaftesbury, third Earl of, 176, 177; *Characteristics of Men, Manners, Opinions, Times,* 176

Shepard, Thomas, 13, 63, 65, 117; *Parable of the Ten Virgins,* 202; quote, 13

Sibbes, Richard, 63, 79; quote, 34

Signs: of affection, 74, 75, 184, second, 74, third, 75; of faith, 153, 155, 176; of godliness, 144, 145; of grace, 157, 173, two kinds of, 145, 146; of salvation, 154, 156; of signs, 145, 146

Simple idea, 15, 18, 19, 20, 21, 33; Edwards, 18–19, 20; and faith, 18, 19, 21, 23; Locke, 18–19, 26

Simple idea, new, 25, 26, 29, 30, 42, 49, 50, 51, 54

Sin, 93, 94, 102, 147, 150, 156, 171, 182, 184, 196–202; Calvinist understanding of, 197; and forgiveness, 152, 153, 156, 157; and grace *(see* Grace); and guilt, 84

Soteriology, 73, 186–202

Spirit: natural, 31; and new simple idea, 29; supernatural, 31, 32

Spirited Word, 45 ff.

Spiritual. *See* Religious

Stephen, Leslie, 148

Stockbridge, Massachusetts, 9

Stoddard, John, 3

Stoddard, Solomon, 8, 14, 34–35, 61, 65, 143, 157, 164, 203, 208, 209, 210, 211, 212, 214; *The Nature of Saving Conversion,* 35; quotes, 14–15, 34; treatises of, 143, 209, 210

Stoddardeans, 202, 205, 214, 215, 216

Stoddardism, 209, 210

Subjectivism, 44; spiritualist, 44

Supernatural, 36, 37; and natural principles, 59
Supralapsarian, 104
System of coherence, 99

Taste, tasting, 28, 51, 53, 131, 171, 182; metaphor of, 21, 22; sensation of, 21, 22
Taylor, John, 160
Tennent, Edwards, 164
Theological: history, 90; tradition, 148
Theology: applied, 126; late medieval, 91
Theory of: atonement, 93; conversion, 63; faith, 6; imputation of righteousness, 91; relation between faith and salvation, 98, 99; salvation, 106; simple idea, 15, Trinity, 25. See also Doctrine, Treatise
Thomas, St., 134
Thomistic distinction of faith, 21–22
Thomist notion, 36
Thoreau, Henry David, 197
Tillich, Paul, 30, 106; theory of salvation, 106
Treatise on: ethics, 176; Freedom of the Will, 9, 129, 132, 160, 163, 176, 188, 189, 190, 191, 192, 202; grace, 35, quote, 38; Humble Inquiry into the Rules . . . , 204; original sin, 84 (see also doctrine of original sin); Religious Affections, 9, 35, 74, 160, 205, 206–7; sin, 202; virtue, 184. See also Doctrines
Trinitarian: Christian principles, 25; explication of redemption, 26, 30–31; God, 38; scheme, 45
Trinity, 25, 26
Trinterud, Leonard, 68, 107
Trust and humility, 78–82
Turrettini, François, 36, 37, 92, 138; quote, 47; reformed thesis, 47

Unbelief. See Doubt
Understanding, 20, 35, 134, 196; faculty of, 15–16; of the nature of faith, 7, 14; sense of, 132, sin, Calvinist, 197; speculative theological, 20; unity of man, 164;

unpublished essay on Trinity, 25, 39; and will, 14, 21, 35

Virtue, 177, 178, 179, 181, 182; natural possibilities, 181–82; nature of, 177; primary and secondary grounds of, 179, 180. See also Doctrine, Treatise
Vision, 33; Edwards', 86
Volition, 16, 21, 23, 35, 39, 132, 190, 194, 195; emphasis, 13; internal acts, two kinds of, 129–30, 136, 144; and motivation, 132; and perception, 16; powers of, 127; and religious practice, 127–30

Watts, 193
Weber, Max, 143
Webster, Samuel, 198
Welch, 56
Wendel, François, 99
Wesley, John, 44, 78
Westminster Confession, 92, 138, 143, 174
Whitby, Daniel, 186, 187, 193
Whitefield, George, 9, 164, 170
Whitman, Walt, 197
Whole man, 13, 33, 127, 140, 141, 167
Will, 13, 14, 15, 16, 17, 20, 24, 27, 35, 39, 129, 132, 134, 145, 188–96; act of, 12, 13, 129–31, 195, 199; affection, 17, 167; Arminian doctrine of self-determining, 188–96; and change, 145; commanding, 130–31, 157, 192; exercise of, 16, 167; faculty of, 15–16, 36, 75; freedom of, controversy with Arminians, 162, 188–96; immanent, 130–31, 135, 136, 146, 157, and working, relation between, 132; power of, 27; subordination of, 13; treatise: freedom of the, 9, 129, 132, 160, 163, 176
Williams, Israel, 187
Williams, Solomon, 205, 206, 207, 211, 212
Williams clan, 203
Willing, 27, 195, 214; act of, 35
Winslow, Ola, 2, 22; quote, 22
Winthrop, John, 109
Wolf, William, 151; quote on Lincoln, 151

Word and Spirit, 44–55, 56, 96, 114, 152, 153, 173, 196; God's, 48 ff., 131; man's, 48

Workbook, major theological, quote, 118

Workbook on the subject of faith, 7

Works, 135, 138, 139, 162, 168; charitable, 134; as compared to faith, 102–3; covenant of, 83, 108; and faith, 100, 138, 139, 153; good, 140, 143, 144, 145, 150, 157, role of, 133, 137, 153; of love, 142; testimony of, 152